OXFORD STUDIES IN

Series editor: Laurence Whitehead

• • • • • • • • • • • • • • • •

DEMOCRACY AND DIVERSITY: POLITICAL
ENGINEERING IN THE ASIA-PACIFIC

OXFORD STUDIES IN DEMOCRATIZATION

Series editor: Laurence Whitehead

. . . .

Oxford Studies in Democratization is a series for scholars and students of comparative politics and related disciplines. Volumes will concentrate on the comparative study of the democratization processes that accompanied the decline and termination of the cold war. The geographical focus of the series will primarily be Latin America, the Caribbean, Southern and Eastern Europe, and relevant experiences in Africa and Asia.

OTHER BOOKS IN THE SERIES

The New Politics of Inequality in Latin America:
Rethinking Participation and Representation
Douglas A. Chalmers, Carlos M. Vilas,
Katherine Roberts Hite,
Scott B. Martin, Kerianne Piester,
and Monique Segarra

Human Rights and Democratization in Latin America:
Uruguay and Chile
Alexandra Barahona de Brito

Regimes, Politics, and Markets: Democratization and
Economic Change in Southern and Eastern Europe
José María Maravall

Democracy Between Consolidation and
Crisis in Southern Europe
Leonardo Morlino

The Bases of Party Competition in Eastern Europe:
Social and Ideological Cleavages in Post Communist States
Geoffrey Evans and Stephen Whitefield

The International Dimensions of Democratization:
Europe and the Americas
Laurence Whitehead

Citizenship Rights and Social Movements:
A Comparative and Statistical Analysis
Joe Foweraker and Todd Landman

Democracy and Diversity: Political Engineering in the Asia-Pacific

BENJAMIN REILLY

OXFORD

UNIVERSITY PRESS

OXFORD

UNIVERSITY PRESS

Great Clarendon Street, Oxford OX2 6DP

Oxford University Press is a department of the University of Oxford.
It furthers the University's objective of excellence in research, scholarship,
and education by publishing worldwide in

Oxford New York

Auckland Cape Town Dar es Salaam Hong Kong Karachi
Kuala Lumpur Madrid Melbourne Mexico City Nairobi
New Delhi Shanghai Taipei Toronto

With offices in

Argentina Austria Brazil Chile Czech Republic France Greece
Guatemala Hungary Italy Japan Poland Portugal Singapore
South Korea Switzerland Thailand Turkey Ukraine Vietnam

Oxford is a registered trade mark of Oxford University Press
in the UK and in certain other countries

Published in the United States
by Oxford University Press Inc., New York

British Library Cataloguing in Publication Data
Data available

Library of Congress Cataloging in Publication Data
Data available

Typeset by SPI Publisher Services, Pondicherry, India

Printed in Great Britain
on acid-free paper by
Biddles Ltd., King's Lynn, Norfolk

ISBN 978–0–19–928687–4 (Hbk.)
978–0–19–923870–5 (Pbk.)

1 3 5 7 9 10 8 6 4 2

....
Foreword
....

Is there an Asia-Pacific model of democracy? Over the past two decades, more than a dozen Asian and Pacific states have undergone transitions to democracy based on fundamental political liberties and freely contested elections. But many of these states are also extremely diverse in social terms, divided along ethnic, linguistic, religious, and regional lines. The interplay of these cultural cleavages with competitive electoral politics can create real challenges for democratic consolidation and effective government.

This book shows how political reformers across the Asia-Pacific region have responded to the reality of their internal diversity by deliberate, innovative, and often highly ambitious forms of political engineering. Harking back to the success of the East Asian 'Tigers' and their unorthodox but successful interventions in the economic arena, democratizing Northeast Asian, Southeast Asian, and Pacific Island states are now seeking to manage political change by far-reaching reforms to their electoral, parliamentary, and party systems.

The result of these reforms has been the evolution of a distinctive Asia-Pacific model of political engineering aimed at fostering aggregative political parties, centripetal electoral competition, and stable executive governments. This book analyses the causes of this new approach to the design of democratic institutions, and its consequences for broader issues of governance and development across the Asia-Pacific and other world regions.

·············
Preface
·············

In August 1998 I received an unexpected phone call from Indonesia. The collapse of the long-ruling Suharto regime three
months earlier had stimulated a flurry of political reforms, and
an interim government was busy preparing for Indonesia's first
democratic elections since the 1950s. I had written on how the
choice of electoral systems might help or hinder democratic transitions. Could I offer some advice?

Ten days later, in the sultry heat of a tropical afternoon, I stood
outside Indonesia's Home Affairs Ministry, a nondescript con-
crete office block in suburban Jakarta. What was going on inside,
however, was truly extraordinary. A small group of government
officials and academics known as *Tim Tujuh*—'the team of
seven'—were refashioning the architecture of the Indonesian
state. The basic political institutions of what is today the world's
third-largest democracy—its electoral system, political party
regulations, division of powers, and laws on decentralization
and autonomy—were being redesigned from the ground up.

Over successive long evenings, the deeper objectives driving
this process became clear. The reform team sought nothing
less than a fundamental reorientation of Indonesian politics.
After thirty years of authoritarian rule, this was their chance
to build a genuine democracy in which politicians could be
held directly accountable to voters via open and competitive
elections. It was also an opportunity to shape the development
of the party system by promoting broad-based political parties
which could represent national goals rather than regional or
sectarian interests. Most of all, the reform team wanted to lay
the foundations for stable and effective government that could
produce credible public policy and advance ordinary people's
lives.

Three years later I was speaking to a committee of parliamentarians from Papua New Guinea about changes to their country's
electoral system. While the specific issues facing Papua New
Guinea's fragile post-colonial democracy were very different to
those in Indonesia, the underlying objectives which the politicians on the reform committee hoped to achieve were remarkably

similar. They wanted to construct a more representative electoral process; they wanted to shift politics away from competition between clan and tribal groups to focus more on policy issues; and most of all they wanted to promote more stable and effective government.

My hands-on experience with democratization in the Asia-Pacific region had begun a decade earlier, when I served as a polling station official with the United Nations Transitional Authority in Cambodia—still the largest United Nations peacekeeping mission ever—at the transitional 1993 elections that ushered in a return to constitutional government there. I had also followed attempts to build more representative and effective politics through the introduction of new constitutions in Fiji and Thailand in 1997, and similar but less ambitious reforms in a number of other democracies around the region. The fact that the same core issues and concerns seemed to be driving political change in such vastly different Asian and Pacific countries cried out for explanation.

This book is an analysis of these reforms, and of the political engineering that has taken place in the Asia-Pacific's new or restored democracies over the past decade. It focuses in particular on Korea and Taiwan in Northeast Asia; Cambodia, East Timor, Indonesia, the Philippines, and Thailand in Southeast Asia; as well as Papua New Guinea and Fiji in the Pacific Islands. From Seoul to Suva, reformers in these emerging democracies sought to change the way their political systems operate by refashioning the rules of the democratic game.

In the course of writing this book I have been fortunate enough to spend time in every one of these countries, either as an adviser or an academic. In some cases, such as Taiwan, these visits came via invitations to speak at scholarly conferences; in others, such as East Timor, they were the result of requests to advise on issues of electoral or constitutional reform. In several countries—including Indonesia, Fiji, and Papua New Guinea—I have played both roles. In all cases, I am indebted to many people that have helped me in my work, particularly James Chin, Kevin Evans, Allen Hicken, Yusaku Horiuchi, Paul Hutchcroft, Byung-Kook Kim, Jih-wen Lin, Koji Ono, Walter Rigamoto, Arun Swamy, and Yu-Shan Wu.

I am also grateful to Harold Crouch, John Gerring, Andrea Gleason, Andrew MacIntyre, and Ron May for their close reading and many helpful comments on a draft manuscript of this book. Harold and Andrew in particular saved me from more than a few mistakes and misinterpretations. In Oxford, Laurence

Whitehead and Dominic Byatt were enthusiastic and encouraging from the beginning, and a pleasure to work with as things took shape. I also thank the East-West Center in Hawaii, where a fellowship in 2003 provided me with the opportunity to start thinking seriously about these issues, and the Australian Research Council, which provided a Discovery grant for fieldwork in the region. The Centre for Democratic Institutions and the Crawford School of Economics and Government at the Australian National University provided a stimulating and congenial home base for my research.

Finally, a book like this would not be possible without a happy (and flexible!) home life. I dedicate this book to my two daughters, Madison and Phoebe, whose appearance near the beginning and the end of my research put everything in perspective.

Contents

Contents

List of Figures

List of Tables

....

1

....

Introduction

The closing decades of the twentieth century were years of unprecedented political reform across Asia and the Pacific. Democratizing Asian states such as Indonesia, the Philippines, Korea, Taiwan, and Thailand embarked on sweeping overhauls of their political systems, refashioning their constitutions, legislatures, political parties, and other key institutions of government. So, to a lesser extent, did the region's 'semi-democracies' such as Cambodia, Malaysia, and Singapore. At the same time, in the island Pacific, fragile post-colonial democracies such as Fiji and Papua New Guinea introduced ambitious constitutional reforms of their own in the search for more representative and effective governance.

Diverse coalitions of politicians, academics, the media, and civil society in these countries viewed institutional redesign as the key to overcoming flaws in their systems of government. Incumbent powerholders and opposition movements alike hoped that by changing political institutions, they could change the conduct of democracy itself. They sought to construct a new institutional architecture—one which would be stable enough to deal with economic and political challenges but sufficiently representative to meet popular aspirations. And they saw political restructuring as the key to delivering more effective, predictable, and responsive governance.

Implicit in this was the belief that political institutions and systems can, at some level, be deliberately and purposively designed. But this is a difficult and unpredictable task at the best of times, and one made even more complex by the demographic realities of the Asia-Pacific region. Most Asian and Pacific democracies feature highly diverse societies divided along multiple cleavages of geography, language, history, class, and culture. A core challenge facing many states has thus been the consolidation of democracy in the face of enormous social, political, and territorial diversity.

This book is an analysis of the causes and consequences of
these attempts to bolster democratic prospects in the Asia-Pacific
region via the design or redesign of political institutions. It looks
at the recent experience of democratization across the Pacific rim
of Northeast Asia, Southeast Asia, and the Pacific Islands. Collectively, these include some of the largest and smallest, richest
and poorest, and most and least populous states to be found
anywhere in the world. The Map below shows the geographical
extent of the Asia-Pacific, which collectively contains almost
half the world's population and covers nearly one-third of the
earth's surface.

One reason for writing this book was my dissatisfaction with
the existing scholarly literature. Surprisingly, given the events
of the past two decades, the Asia-Pacific region remains relatively neglected in comparative studies of democratization and
institutional design. Many of the major scholarly studies of
democratic transitions, for example, rely heavily on European

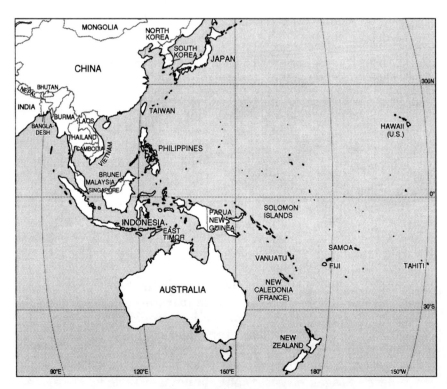

The Asia-Pacific region

and Latin American cases but largely ignore Asia.[1] So, to a lesser extent, do some of the most important works on the causes and consequences of institutions.[2] Only a few recent thematic studies of political institutions place the Asia-Pacific at centre stage.[3] This regional skew in the scholarly literature continues to be influential: while the past decade has seen the publication of much important research on the relationship between political institutions and democracy, most of this has focused on Africa, Latin America, and Europe, rather than the Asia-Pacific.[4]

In addition, most scholarly studies of democratization that do focus on the Asia-Pacific region take the form of edited collections comprising chapter-length studies of a single country.[5] While this has produced many excellent edited volumes, their strength

[1] These include Dankwart A. Rustow, 'Transitions to Democracy: Towards a Dynamic Model', *Comparative Politics*, 2/2 (1970), 337–63; Juan Linz and Alfred Stepan (eds.), *The Breakdown of Democratic Regimes*, 3 vols. (Baltimore, MD: Johns Hopkins University Press, 1978); Guillermo O'Donnell, Philippe Schmitter, and Laurence Whitehead, *Transitions from Authoritarian Rule*, 4 vols. (Baltimore, MD: Johns Hopkins University Press, 1986); Juan Linz and Alfred Stepan, *Problems of Democratic Transition and Consolidation: Southern Europe, South America, and Post-Communist Europe* (Baltimore, MD: Johns Hopkins University Press, 1996).

[2] These include Juan Linz and Arturo Valenzuela (eds.), *The Failure of Presidential Democracy*, 2 vols. (Baltimore, MD: Johns Hopkins University Press, 1994); Arend Lijphart, *Electoral Systems and Party Systems: A Study of Twenty-Seven Democracies, 1945–1990* (New York: Oxford University Press, 1994); Scott Mainwaring and Timothy Scully (eds.), *Building Democratic Institutions: Party Systems in Latin America* (Stanford, CA: Stanford University Press, 1995).

[3] The most important of these are Andrew MacIntyre, *The Power of Institutions: Political Architecture and Governance* (Ithaca, NY: Cornell University Press, 2003); Allen Hicken, *Building Party Systems: Elections, Parties and Co-ordination in Developing Democracies* (forthcoming). Asian cases are also well covered in Stephan Haggard and Robert Kaufman, *The Political Economy of Democratic Transitions* (Princeton, NJ: Princeton University Press, 1995). However, none of these works cover Papua New Guinea or the Pacific Island countries.

[4] These include Michael Bratton and Nicolas van de Walle, *Democratic Experiments in Africa* (Cambridge: Cambridge University Press, 1997); Scott Mainwaring and Matthew Shugart (eds.), *Presidentialism and Democracy in Latin America* (Cambridge: Cambridge University Press, 1997), and Herbert Kitschelt, Zdenka Mansfeldova, Radek Markowski, and Gábor Tóka, *Post-Communist Party Systems: Competition, Representation and Inter-Party Cooperation* (New York: Cambridge University Press, 1999).

[5] These include Larry Diamond, Juan Linz, and Seymour Martin Lipset (eds.), *Democracy in Developing Countries: Asia* (Boulder, CO: Lynne Rienner Publishers, 1989); Kevin Hewison, Richard Robison, and Garry Rodan (eds.), *Southeast Asia in the 1990s: Authoritarianism, Democracy and Capitalism* (Sydney: Allen and Unwin, 1993); Edward Friedman (ed.), *The Politics of*

tends to lie in individual case studies rather than truly thematic comparisons. Book-length comparative analysis of the relationship between social cleavages and democratic institutions in the Asia-Pacific has also been limited.[6]

In taking a different approach, I therefore hope to fill something of a gap in the scholarly literature. As I will show, some of the contemporary world's most ambitious and innovative attempts at institutional crafting have taken place in the Asia-Pacific region. By examining these various examples through a consistent empirical and analytical lens focused on both social and institutional variables, I seek to explain how and why so many Asian and Pacific states have sought to direct the path of democratization through reform of their political systems.

Themes

By analysing political reform in the Asia-Pacific, this book also speaks to a much broader question: what is the best way of 'making democracy work'[7] in new democracies, particularly those with important societal divisions? Some of the greatest

Democratization: Generalizing East Asian Experiences (Boulder, CO: Westview Press, 1994); Gary Rodan (ed.), *Political Oppositions in Industrialising Asia* (London: Routledge, 1996); Robert H. Taylor (ed.), *The Politics of Elections in Southeast Asia* (Cambridge: Woodrow Wilson Center and Cambridge University Press, 1996); Anek Laothamatas (ed.), *Democratization in Southeast and East Asia* (Singapore: Institute of Southeast Asian Studies, 1997); Larry Diamond and Marc F. Plattner (eds.), *Democracy in East Asia* (Baltimore, MD and London: Johns Hopkins University Press, 1998); Ian Marsh, Jean Blondel, and Takashi Inoguchi (eds.), *Democracy, Governance and Economic Performance: East and Southeast Asia* (Tokyo: United Nations University Press, 1999); James W. Morley (ed.), *Driven by Growth: Political Change in the Asia-Pacific Region* (Armonk, NY: M.E. Sharpe, 1999); John Fuh-sheng Hsieh and David Newman (eds.), *How Asia Votes* (New York: Chatham House, 2002).

[6] Partial exceptions include David Brown, *The State and Ethnic Politics in South-East Asia* (London and New York: Routledge, 1994) and Michael R. Vatikiotis, *Political Change in Southeast Asia: Trimming the Banyan Tree* (London: Routledge, 1996), both of which concentrate on Southeast Asia; Michael E. Brown and Šumit Ganguly (eds.), *Government Policies and Ethnic Relations in the Asia-Pacific* (Cambridge, MA and London: MIT Press, 1997), which focuses on policy rather than institutional choices; and Susan J. Henders (ed.), *Democratization and Identity: Regimes and Ethnicity in East and Southeast Asia* (Lanham, MD: Lexington Books, 2004), which draws more on the ethnic conflict literature.

[7] To echo the title of Robert Putnam, *Making Democracy Work: Civic Traditions in Modern Italy* (Princeton, NJ: Princeton University Press, 1993).

political thinkers have argued that stable democracy is incompatible with the presence of communal cleavages.[8] Today, most scholars recognize that it *is* possible to achieve democratic sustainability even in highly diverse societies, but disagree on the optimal institutional arrangements for achieving these goals.[9] A major normative issue for both political scientists and public policymakers thus concerns the design of democratic institutions in fragile states. The core question animating this study speaks directly to this issue: simply put, which form of 'political architecture'—what Andrew MacIntyre calls 'the complex of rules that make up the constitutional structure and party system'[10]—is most conducive to democratic stability in new, restored, or transitional democracies?

To answer this, I begin by examining the interplay between social structure, institutional design and government performance in the Asia-Pacific region. Some states, such as Indonesia and Papua New Guinea, are amongst the world's most culturally diverse, encompassing hundreds of different languages and ethnic groups within their borders. Others, such as Fiji or Malaysia, exhibit more polarized social structures as a result of colonial labour migration and settlement. Still others, such as Taiwan or Korea, feature common cultural foundations but deep ethno-political divisions founded on historical legacies and exacerbated by political competition. These various cleavages have exerted a profound impact upon political development, and hence upon ameliorative strategies of political engineering.

Many of the political reforms examined in this book are, at their heart, the outcome of attempts to cope with the effects of diversity within a democratic framework. Underlying concerns about the performance of political institutions, the stability of democratic politics, and the management of social cleavages were nearly always present. While a response to contemporary

---

[8] See Aristotle, *Politics*; John Stuart Mill, *Considerations on Representative Government* (New York: Liberal Arts Press, 1958 [1861]); Robert A. Dahl, *Polyarchy: Participation and Opposition* (New Haven, CT: Yale University Press, 1971).

[9] See in particular Arend Lijphart, *Democracy in Plural Societies: A Comparative Exploration* (New Haven, CT: Yale University Press, 1977); Donald L. Horowitz, *Ethnic Groups in Conflict* (Berkeley, CA: University of California Press, 1985).

[10] MacIntyre, *The Power of Institutions*, 4.

pressures, these concerns had ancient antecedents: after all, the search for a stable, balanced, and harmonious political order has been a recurring theme in Asian political thought for centuries. However, the very nature of modern representative democracy—characterized as it is by competition, dynamism, and uncertainty—begs the question of how political stability can best be maintained under democratic rather than autocratic rule.

Another theme concerns institutional convergence. While democratizing Asian and Pacific states have responded to the challenges of diversity in a variety of ways, they have often sought to achieve broadly similar objectives. In almost all cases, for example, reforms to electoral and political party systems have sought to foster political aggregation and consolidation. One consequence has been a convergence upon a distinctive regional approach to political engineering and institutional change. This provides a golden opportunity to assess how well particular institutional reform strategies have fared in achieving their objectives—a subject not just of analytical significance, but of considerable practical importance as well. While I examine the evidence for a distinctive Asia-Pacific form of democracy in the second half of this book, it is worth emphasizing at the outset that it bares little relationship to the much-vaunted 'Asian model' of hegemonic one-party rule propagated by former prime ministers Lee Kwan Yew of Singapore and Mahathir Mohamad of Malaysia.[11]

A final distinctive aspect of this book is its geographic scope. Unlike many works on the Asia-Pacific region, this book takes the 'Pacific' part seriously as well as the 'Asia' one. This means that post-colonial Pacific states, such as Fiji and Papua New Guinea, are given coverage along with the more prominent new democracies of East Asia (the South Pacific's two western states, Australia and New Zealand, are excluded on the basis of their status as mature, rather than new, democracies). The Pacific combines some of the longest records of post-colonial democracy with some of the highest levels of societal diversity found anywhere. Papua New Guinea, for example, is on some measures the most ethno-linguistically fragmented country to be found anywhere in the world, and one of the very few post-colonial states to have maintained an unbroken record of democracy since

---

[11] See Daniel A. Bell, *East Meets West: Human Rights and Democracy in East Asia* (Princeton, NJ: Princeton University Press, 2000), 201–13.

independence. Moreover, the Pacific has been the site of some of the most ambitious and creative attempts at political engineering in recent years. But these are little known outside the region, and have attracted limited interest from comparative scholars. I hope this book will help close the gap.

I should also say a few words about this book's intended audience. By looking at the Asia-Pacific in the aggregate, this book by necessity presents a broad and comparative treatment of the region's recent political history, and of the core thematic issues of democratization and institutional reform. It aims primarily to illuminate regional trends across the many young Asian and Pacific democracies, rather than delving deeply into the politics of any one country. While reforms in particular states are covered in some detail, in general this book seeks to highlight connections and commonalities between cases rather than within them. Area specialists may question this approach, given the very different countries and cases gathered here and the need to skate relatively quickly over many important details. However, I am confident that even seasoned regional experts will be surprised by some of the patterns that this broad-brush approach can illuminate, while readers who are interested in the comparative dimension of the Asia-Pacific's experience and its relationship to other world regions should also find much to interest them.

Democratization

A starting point for selecting the country cases examined in this book is the distinction between autocratic and democratic forms of government: My primary focus is on democratic and democratizing states, as it is only in democracies that institutional variables and their interrelationship with competitive politics are really consequential for political outcomes. As it is, the number of Asia-Pacific regimes that can be considered to meet the basic Schumpeterian definition of democracy—that is, governments which are chosen via open and competitive elections—has snowballed over the past twenty years.[12] While at the end of the cold war only Japan and (more tenuously) Papua New Guinea could lay claim to the title of 'established' Asian or Pacific

[12] See Joseph A. Schumpeter, *Capitalism, Socialism and Democracy* (New York: Harper, 1947), 269.

democracies, the years since then have ushered in a new era of liberalization and democratization across the region.[13] In East Asia, for example, major transitions from authoritarian rule towards democracy began with the popular uprising against the flagrantly corrupt Marcos regime in the Philippines in 1986 and the negotiated transitions from autocratic single-party governments in Korea and Taiwan in 1987, before moving on to the resumption of civilian government in Thailand in 1992, the United Nations intervention in Cambodia in 1993, the fall of Indonesia's Suharto regime in 1998, and the international rehabilitation of East Timor which culminated in 2001. As a result of these transitions, more Asia-Pacific governments are today chosen through competitive and freely contested elections than ever before. This represents a dramatic change for East Asia in particular: from what a decade ago was a region dominated by authoritarian rule, there is now a clear trend towards democracy being the accepted means for choosing and changing a country's political leadership in Indonesia, Korea, the Philippines, and Thailand as well as in the established democracy of Japan— five of East Asia's seven largest countries.[14] This marks a truly historic shift in world affairs.

Despite this, there are significant intra-regional variations in the extent and timing of democratization across the region. In Northeast Asia, for instance, Korea and Taiwan are amongst the most successful new democracies in the Asia-Pacific region, and it is unlikely today that democracy could be overturned in either case. It is notable that Korea, for example, showed no sign of flirting with a return to authoritarianism during the severe economic difficulties it suffered as a result of the Asian economic downturn of the late 1990s—and in fact elected the region's foremost democracy activist, Kim Dae Jung, to the presidency in 1997. The election of opposition leader Chen Shui-bian as president of Taiwan in March 2000, the island's first democratic transfer of executive power, was a similar watershed event for Taiwanese democracy.

In Southeast Asia, the Philippines and Thailand are now usually considered the two best-established democracies. While

---

[13] These are the two Asia-Pacific states, along with India in South Asia, categorized as 'established' democracies by Arend Lijphart, *Patterns of Democracy: Government Forms and Performance in Thirty-Six Countries* (New Haven, CT and London: Yale University Press, 1999).

[14] See John Fuh-sheng Hsieh, 'Electoral Politics in New Democracies in the Asia-Pacific Region', *Representation*, 34/3&4 (1997), 157–65.

the Philippines has a considerably longer democratic history than Thailand, both have now experienced over a decade of continuous competitive elections and, importantly, successive (if not always trouble-free) turnovers of government since their reestablishment of democracy in the mid-1980s and early 1990s, respectively. Likewise, Southeast Asia's largest state, Indonesia, has experienced several peaceful transitions of power since the end of the Suharto regime in 1998, and looks set to join this group, as does East Timor—a country born out of the crucible of a liberation struggle and the international intervention which followed its 1999 vote to separate from Indonesia. However, while the democratization of each of these states has proceeded rapidly, there are questions over whether any could yet be said to be truly consolidated, in the sense of democracy being considered the 'only game in town' and any reversion from it unthinkable.[15]

One crude means of assessing this question is Samuel Huntington's 'two-turnover test' of democratic consolidation: that is, when the party or group that takes power in an initial election loses a subsequent election and turns over power, and if those election winners then peacefully turn over power to the winners of a later election.[16] Korea, the Philippines, Taiwan, Thailand, and (more questionably) Indonesia all qualify on this score.[17] By contrast, there have been no turnovers of power in the long-standing semi-democracies of Malaysia and Singapore, and none likely in the immediate future. While both of these states maintain regular and basically fraud-free elections, the fairness of the electoral process is severely compromised in both countries by heavy-handed restrictions on the rights of opposition parties to campaign openly, as well as a compliant judiciary and a pro-government press. A third Southeast Asian state, Cambodia, could be seen as a borderline member of this 'semi-democratic' group also: since its transitional UN-administered elections in 1993 it too has yet to experience a change of government, and elections in 1998 and (to a lesser extent) 2003 were marred by significant voting irregularities and campaign violence.

[15] This is the definition suggested by Adam Przeworski, *Democracy and the Market: Political and Economic Reforms in Eastern Europe and Latin America* (Cambridge: Cambridge University Press, 1991).

[16] Samuel P. Huntington, *The Third Wave: Democratization in the Late Twentieth Century* (Norman, OK: University of Oklahoma Press, 1991), 266–7.

[17] Indonesia has had four turnovers of power since the fall of Suharto, but only one of these (the election of President Susilo Bambang Yudhoyono in 2004) has come as a direct result of the electoral process.

Finally, there are the Asia-Pacific's ongoing and outright authoritarian regimes—Brunei, Burma (which the ruling junta have renamed Myanmar), China, Laos, North Korea, and Vietnam—in which elections are either not held at all, or do not involve a contest for actual political power. Although some democratic reforms and innovations are taking place amongst this group (opposition candidates have been permitted to contest elections in Laos, for example, while competitive village-level elections have been held in China), mass elections in these countries, if they are held at all, are mostly empty and stage-managed exercises. I will therefore not be dealing with the political systems of these countries in this book.

By contrast, in the Pacific Islands, all states bar Tonga, Fiji (intermittently), Solomon Islands (following the 2001 coup) and Samoa (prior to 1991) have maintained an impressive record of unbroken democracy since their emergence as independent entities. The Pacific region thus stands out as something of a democratic oasis not just in comparison to East Asia, but in the post-colonial world more generally. While far from perfect, the competitive and participatory nature of democratic politics in most Pacific Island states is striking when compared to other parts of the developing world.[18] However, the tiny size of many of the island nations, some of which have fewer than 10,000 people, limits their utility for comparative analysis. For reasons of comparability, therefore, in the analyses that follow in subsequent chapters I include only those Pacific states with a population of at least 100,000 over the period of this study—that is, Fiji, Papua New Guinea, Samoa, Solomon Islands, and Vanuatu.

Diversity

Supplementing my focus on new democracies, another important variable for the purposes of this study is the way in which *social cleavages* are manifested across the Asia-Pacific region. These cleavages take multifarious forms, including the clan and tribal allegiances that are a fact of life in Papua New Guinea; the

[18] For example, of the 93 states which became independent between 1945 and 1979, only 15 were still continuous democracies in 1980–9—and one-third of these were in the South Pacific. See Alfred Stepan and Cindy Skach, 'Constitutional Frameworks and Democratic Consolidation: Parliamentarism Versus Presidentialism', *World Politics*, 46/1 (1993), 1–22.

complex cultural, linguistic, regional, and religious identities present in Indonesia; the deepening ethno-nationalist division between 'mainlander' and 'native' origins in Taiwan; and the intense regionalism that continues to afflict party politics in Korea. Political scientists often aggregate these many and various manifestations of cleavage under the collective label of 'ethnicity', so as to cover for analytic purposes a range of identity-based motivators of political behaviour. Under this broad interpretation, ethnic divisions may take the form of essentially ascriptive differences based on race, language, religion, or region of origin, but can also include more instrumental or 'constructed' identities formed in response to colonialism, modernization, and the struggle for political and economic power. In recent years, scholarly discussions of ethnicity have increasingly focused on these constructed cleavages which are not ascribed from birth but which nonetheless constitute important markers of social identity.[19]

The varying scholarly interpretations of ethnicity as a political phenomenon, and the increasing turn in the scholarly literature towards constructed rather than primordial interpretations of ethnicity, are discussed in more detail in Chapter 3. There, I attempt to measure the extent and impact of ethnic diversity between and within Asian and Pacific countries by quantifying their relevant cultural, religious, or linguistic divisions. On most of these measures of diversity, the Asia-Pacific stands out as one of the world's most heterogeneous regions. Its linguistic diversity, for example, far outstrips that of other world regions—in large part because of the thousands of languages spoken in one discrete subregion, Melanesia, the cultures of which stretch from East Timor through eastern Indonesia and into Papua New Guinea and the island Pacific.[20]

Across the Asia-Pacific as a whole, however, there is considerable variation in ethno-linguistic structure, with some states characterized by enormous social diversity and others by corresponding homogeneity. For example, Northeast Asia appears highly homogeneous on most comparative measures. While home to many ethnic minorities, the core civilization of China

[19] See the special issue of the American Political Science Association's comparative politics newsletter devoted to 'Cumulative Findings in the Study of Ethnic Politics', *APSA-CP Newsletter*, 12/1 (2001).

[20] See Michael E. Brown and Sumit Ganguly (eds.), *Fighting Words: Language Policy and Ethnic Relations in Asia* (Cambridge, MA: MIT Press, 2003).

is dominated by one group, the Han Chinese. Likewise, Japan and Korea are two of the most homogeneous states in the world on most indicators of social diversity. Each has a common language, religion, heritage, and culture. However, this does not mean that societal cleavages are absent. For example, despite its cultural homogeneity, Korean politics exhibits at least one distinctive 'ethnic' cleavage: a marked regionalism that dominates much of its democratic politics, and which has been particularly important in determining election outcomes.[21] As Hyug Baeg Im writes, 'Since the democratic transition of 1987, every election has been marked by decisive regional schisms. Korean politics has indeed been reduced to inter-regional rivalries; voters casting votes according to their respective regional self-identification.'[22]

A similar observation applies to Taiwan. Despite a common Sinitic culture, the most important expression of political identity in Taiwan is between mainland-origin and island-origin populations, a division which has become increasingly significant in recent years. This 'national identity' cleavage is now the single most salient political division in Taiwan, and one that is strongly linked to voter behaviour: 'For some, Taiwan is part of China and should be reunited with the mainland. For others, Taiwan is different from China and should be separated from China permanently. Still others hold views somewhere in between. Undoubtedly, the question is a highly emotional issue.'[23] This ethno-political cleavage has been sharpened by the mobilization of identity politics at election time by Taiwan's political parties, for whom the national identity question is both a bedrock issue of political identity and a reliable means of shoring up voter support. Issues of national identity are further complicated in both Korea and Taiwan at the level of inter-national statehood via their complex and confrontational relationships to kin states in North Korea and China, respectively.

In Southeast Asia, by contrast, most states are home to a multitude of distinct ethnic communities, and overt societal diversity is the defining characteristic of the sub-region as a

[21] See Ahn Chung-si and Jaung Hoon, 'South Korea' in Marsh, Blondel and Inoguchi, *Democracy, Governance and Economic Performance*.

[22] Hyug Baeg Im, 'Faltering Democratic Consolidation in South Korea: Democracy at the End of the 'Three Kims' Era', *Democratization*, 11/5 (2004), 187.

[23] See John Fuh-sheng Hsieh, 'Continuity and Change in Taiwan's Electoral Politics', in Hsieh and Newman, *How Asia Votes*, 38.

whole. A number of Southeast Asian countries—especially Indonesia, Malaysia, the Philippines, and Thailand—have also experienced a marked politicization of religion, particularly fundamentalist Islam, in recent years. Again, however, the context of ethno-politics differs markedly from case to case. While the Chinese borderland states of Vietnam, Laos, and Cambodia all contain significant ethnic minorities, particularly in highlands areas, each are dominated by their core populations of Vietnamese, Laotians, and Cambodians respectively. While this ethnic dominance contributes to a strong sense of nationhood, it has not always translated into lower levels of ethnic tension. In Cambodia, for example, the ethnic Vietnamese minority who make up perhaps 5 per cent of the total population are routinely demonized.

Burma and Thailand also feature strong core ethnic allegiances and important lowland–highland divisions which are compounded by other distinctive patterns of ethnic demography. In addition to their core Burman and Thai populations, both countries also contain many smaller indigenous minorities as well as significant Chinese, Indian, and Islamic diasporas. Burma's population profile is truly multiethnic, with over one hundred different ethno-linguistic groups present, and a long and ongoing history of minority insurgency. Thailand is less heterogeneous—but also considerably more diverse than is often appreciated, with numerous regionally concentrated minorities, including the Isan communities in the northeast and the aggrieved Muslim population in the southern provinces bordering Malaysia, where an increasingly bloody confrontation with the central government has escalated sharply since 2001.

Further south, in the greater Malay archipelago encompassing Indonesia, Malaysia, and the Philippines, social diversity becomes particularly acute. Each of these states contains numerous minority ethnic groups and languages, but each is also split along broader cultural, religious, and regional lines as well. Malaysia is divided not only between the majority *bumiputera* (literally, 'sons of the soil') community of Malays and indigenous groups (comprising 62 per cent of the population) and the large Chinese and smaller Indian minorities, but also between peninsula Malaysia and the more fragmented eastern states of Sabah and Sarawak on the island of Borneo. The Philippines is similarly split at a national level between its large Roman Catholic majority and a Muslim minority concentrated in the southern region of Mindanao, and is linguistically fragmented too, with no majority community—the largest group, the Cebuano, make up only 22 per cent of the population.

Southeast Asia's largest state, Indonesia, encompasses significant Islamic, Christian, Hindu, and animist religions, a small but economically powerful Chinese minority, and hundreds of diverse ethno-regional communities. Scattered across 17,000 islands spanning almost 4,000 miles, the Indonesian archipelago is one of the most ethnically complex states in the contemporary world. At the core of Indonesia's 218 million predominantly Muslim population is the island of Java, home to over 40 per cent of the country's population. Long-standing regional divisions between Java and the outer islands are compounded by the ongoing relevance of *aliran*—the cleavage within the Javanese Muslim community between the *santri*, who identify fully with Islam, and those called *abangan*, who retain traditional pre-Islamic beliefs and customs. This continues to exert a profound influence on Indonesian politics, with the *santri* usually supporting Islamic political parties while *abangan* tend to join together with Christians and Hindus in supporting 'nationalist' parties.[24] These cleavages overlap with other regional and cultural markers: *abangan* Muslims, for example, are more influential in Java while *santri* Muslims predominate in western Indonesia. As a result, the more secular parties tend to get much of their support within Java, while Muslim parties often have strong bases in the outer islands. Other major religions are also regionalized: Bali is predominantly Hindu, while Christian and animist faiths remain common in the eastern regions of Maluku and Papua, which are also home to hundreds of smaller ethno-linguistic communities. The result is something of an ethnic kaleidoscope: while most sources put the total number of ethnic communities in Indonesia at around 300, a national census conducted in 2000 identified a total of 1,072 distinct ethnic groups—although most of these were located in the eastern province of Papua, which comprises less than 2 per cent of Indonesia's total population.[25]

Finally, the scattered islands of the Pacific Ocean feature both some of the most homogeneous and most heterogeneous societies in the world. The Polynesian islands of Tonga, Samoa,

---

[24] See Clifford Geertz, *The Religions of Java* (New York: Free Press, 1960).
[25] Gerry van Klinken, 'Ethnicity in Indonesia', in Colin Mackerras (ed.), *Ethnicity in Asia* (London and New York: RoutledgeCurzon, 2003), 69.

and Tuvalu are all classic nation states, each containing core cultures based around a common language, religion, and culture. Micronesia is more diverse, in large part because of the varying influences of colonial rule and migration, but again tend to be characterized by broadly similar cultural practices and identities. By contrast, in the western Pacific, Melanesia is a region of unrivalled diversity: estimates of the total number of discrete ethnic groups in Papua New Guinea alone range from 'more than 1,000' to 'more than 10,000'.[26] A similar micro-ethnic social structure exists in the neighbouring Solomon Islands, which also faces broader regional divisions between the main island groups of Malaita and Guadalcanal that provided the basis for the disastrous internal conflict of 2000–03. Likewise, Fiji is split between indigenous Fijian and Indo-Fijian communities, both of which are themselves internally divided, while Melanesia's other independent state, Vanuatu, is both linguistically diverse and also divided along an overarching Anglophone-Francophone language fissure, the legacy of its colonial status as a joint Anglo-French condominium.

Ethnic Politics

Many Asian and Pacific states have long experience with the problems caused by the interrelationship between democratic government and ethnic diversity. At the end of the Second World War, independent and nominally democratic regimes were installed in post-colonial Burma, Indonesia, Malaysia, the Philippines, and Singapore as well as in Japan. With the exception of Japan, all of these new states were ethnically diverse; by 1972 all of them, Japan again excepted, had also fallen under some form of non-democratic rule. In each case, the adverse consequences of social diversity on competitive electoral politics provides part of the explanation for the shift towards autocracy and the failure of democracy. Weak parties, fragmented legislatures, and an inability to maintain stable government

---

[26] Stephen Levine, 'Culture and Conflict in Fiji, Papua New Guinea, Vanuatu, and the Federated States of Micronesia', in Brown and Ganguly, *Government Policies and Ethnic Relations*, 479; James Griffin, 'Papua New Guinea', in R. Brissenden and J. Griffin (eds.), *Modern Asia: Problems and Politics* (Milton: Jacaranda Press, 1974), 143.

have all been identified as reasons for these ineffective and ultimately unsuccessful initial experiences of democracy.[27]

For example, acute political gridlock and polarization—caused in part by the politicization of social cleavages—is often blamed for the early failure of democracy in Indonesia in the 1950s.[28] Similarly, the quasi-authoritarian political systems of both Malaysia and Singapore evolved partly as a result of a perceived need to control the political expression of ethnicity, and the management of communal relations has remained a cornerstone of politics in both states.[29] In the Philippines, where family, clan, and regional identities are key political commodities, democracy remains fragile and 'candidates for national office have tended to be elected in large part on the basis of their ethno-linguistic and regional ties'.[30] Since 1993, Cambodia too has seen the emergence of significant ethnic and regional cleavages in voting patterns.[31] Even in Thailand, where an assimilative, civic Thai identity has long been present, democratic politics retains a marked ethno-regional dimension, apparent in the growing rural–urban cleavage between the affluent middle classes of Bangkok and the peripheral regions of the north, northeast, south, and west.[32]

As will be discussed in detail in Chapter 3, the political and economic impacts of diversity also provide at least part of the explanation for broader disparities in political development across Asia and the Pacific. Even today, with democracy prevalent in most of the region, the Asia-Pacific's most ethnically heterogeneous states—East Timor, Indonesia, the Philippines, Papua New Guinea, Solomon Islands, and Vanuatu—have higher levels of social conflict, lower per capita incomes and much poorer government performance than their more homoge-

---

[27] Minxin Pei, 'The Fall and Rise of Democracy in East Asia', in Diamond and Plattner, *Democracy in East Asia*, 57–78.

[28] See, for example, Herbert Feith, *The Decline of Constitutional Democracy in Indonesia* (Ithaca, NY: Cornell University Press, 1962).

[29] See Harold Crouch, *Government and Society in Malaysia* (Ithaca, NY: Cornell University Press, 1996); Gary Rodan, 'Elections Without Representation: the Singapore Experience under the PAP', in Taylor, *The Politics of Elections*, 61–89.

[30] Gabriella R. Montinola, 'The Philippines in 1998: Opportunities Amid Crisis', *Asian Survey*, 39/1 (1999), 67.

[31] See Robert B. Albritton, 'Cambodia in 2003: On the Road to Democratic Consolidation', *Asian Survey*, 44/1 (2004), 102–9.

[32] Surin Maisrikrod, 'Political Reform and the New Thai Electoral System', in Hsieh and Newman, *How Asia Votes*, 192.

neous counterparts. While many factors contribute to this pattern, one explanation concerns the way in which ethnic politics impacts on the provision of 'public goods'—that is, goods which benefit everyone without exclusion, such as property rights, the rule of law, public education, health care, roads, and other basic infrastructure.[33] In competing for resources, rival communities in socially diverse states often play an analogous role to interest groups or industry lobbies in the economic realm, diverting potential public goods towards the private enrichment of their communal membership alone.[34] For instance, the provision of public education, a classic form of public good, may be tilted towards the interests of one particular region or ethnic group, thus penalizing others. Such discrimination in access to higher education was an early motivator for the Sinhalese–Tamil conflict in Sri Lanka, fomenting a cycle of escalating ethnic hostilities which led ultimately to civil war.[35]

The broader structure of government also plays a crucial role in determining the extent to which democracies can manage such grievances. Probably the most influential typology of democratic systems is Arend Lijphart's distinction between two ideal types—'majoritarian' and 'consensus' democracies.[36] Majoritarian democracies are characterized by plurality or majority election laws, a few large political parties alternating in power, and governments composed of a single-dominant party. Consensual democracies, by contrast, feature proportional representation elections, numerous parties competing for power, and multiparty coalition governments. The institutional features of each model tend to be self-reinforcing. Thus, in theory, majoritarian electoral rules promote single-party government by systematically over-representing larger parties, while in consensual systems smaller parties are represented proportionately and can play important roles in the formation of governing coalitions. In terms of ethnic politics, therefore, majoritarian

[33] See Alberto Alesina, Reza Baqir, and William Easterly, 'Public Goods and Ethnic Divisions', *Quarterly Journal of Economics*, 114 (1999), 1243–84.

[34] Mancur Olsen, *The Logic of Collective Action: Public Goods and the Theory of Groups* (Cambridge, MA: Harvard University Press, 1971).

[35] See Neil DeVotta, *Blowback: Linguistic Nationalism, Institutional Decay, and Ethnic Conflict in Sri Lanka* (Stanford, CA: Stanford University Press, 2004).

[36] Arend Lijphart, *Democracies: Patterns of Majoritarian and Consensus Government in Twenty-One Countries* (New Haven, CT and London: Yale University Press, 1984).

systems encourage integration across social cleavages into large aggregative parties, while consensual systems encourage different communities to aspire towards separate representation.

As key agents of political articulation, aggregation and representation, political parties are the institution which impact most directly on the extent to which social cleavages are translated into national politics. For example, some parties will adopt 'catch-all' strategies, designed to elicit support from across different segments of the electorate and regions of the country in order to win elections. Others seek to represent ethnic cleavages explicitly, and appeal for votes predominantly along communal lines. Drawing upon Robert Putnam's work on social capital, Pippa Norris has characterized these divergent approaches as 'bridging' versus 'bonding' strategies. Bridging parties, she writes, 'bring together heterogeneous publics into loose, shifting coalitions, linking different generations, faiths, and ethnic identities, thereby aggregating interests and creating cross-cutting allegiances'. By contrast, bonding parties 'focus on gaining votes from a narrower home-base among particular segmented sectors of the electorate . . . promoting the interests of their own members, and developing tightly knit social networks and clear one-of-us boundaries'.[37]

Party systems thus impact decisively on the extent to which social cleavages are replicated in the organs of representative government, and hence in public policy. Fragmented party systems composed predominantly of 'bonding' parties offer few incentives towards political integration, instead encouraging direct appeals to a relatively narrow support base for votes. Rather than supplying public goods, these kinds of parties optimally focus on winning and maintaining voter support by providing private or 'club' goods to their supporters—goods which benefit their own communal group rather than the broader electorate. Roads, health care, government services, and other kinds of public goods may be provided unequally (or not at all) to some groups or regions over others. As I will discuss in Chapter 3, this kind of distributive politics, whereby state resources are diverted towards narrow ethnic constituencies in return for electoral support, lies at the heart of the developmental malaise affecting contemporary Melanesia.[38]

---

[37] Pippa Norris, *Electoral Engineering: Voting Rules and Political Behavior* (Cambridge: Cambridge University Press, 2004), 10.

[38] Benjamin Reilly, 'State Functioning and State Failure in the South Pacific', *Australian Journal of International Affairs*, 58/4 (2004), 479–93.

Although the relationship between social cleavages and party formation is far from axiomatic, diverse societies which foster a multitude of 'bonding' parties representing distinct social cleavages are especially prone to the negative impacts of party multiplicity upon governance. Comparative studies have found that the most socially diverse states tend to have less cohesive parties, more fragmented party systems, and higher turnover of elected politicians than their more homogeneous counterparts.[39] They also tend to have relatively low levels of political stability, as measured by the durability of executive governments.[40] This instability of cabinets, party allegiances, and parliamentary majorities all contributes to uncertainty in terms of government tenure, leading to a lack of predictability in decision-making, an inability to make credible policy commitments, and incoherent public policy more generally.

The tendency towards political instability in fragmented societies has long been evident in the Asia-Pacific. Democracy in Indonesia, for instance, has been hampered recurrently by the consequences of party fragmentation—both in recent years following the collapse of the Suharto regime, but also earlier, during the country's initial democratic interlude in the 1950s, when shifting coalitions of secular, Islamic, nationalist, communal, and regional parties led to six changes of government in seven years, providing a ready pretext for the overthrow of democracy and the declaration of martial law by President Sukarno in 1957. In Papua New Guinea, ethno-linguistic fragmentation is one of several factors that have stymied the development of a cohesive party system since independence in 1975. Since returning to democracy in 1986, the Philippines has also suffered from the consequences of a fragmented social landscape: weak and personalized parties, patrimonial politics, unstable government, and an ongoing crisis of underdevelopment.

Problems of political fragmentation can also afflict relatively unstratified societies. For instance, despite Thai-speaking Buddhists comprising over 90 per cent of the population, Thailand until recently had a highly unstable political system, with frequent changes of governing coalitions, small parties holding larger ones to ransom under the threat of withdrawing support,

[39] See G. Bingham Powell, *Contemporary Democracies: Participation, Stability, and Violence* (Cambridge, MA: Harvard University Press, 1982), 101.
[40] See Michael Taylor and V. M. Herman, 'Party Systems and Government Stability', *American Political Science Review*, 65/1 (1971), 28–37.

and no government lasting the full length of its parliamentary term.[41] This instability exacerbated underlying problems of vote-buying and corruption: since the outcome of elections was usually unclear, with all administrations coalitions of five or more parties, money became an essential lubricant for both politicians and those seeking political favours. As Duncan McCargo put it, 'the electoral system had become a massive exercise in benefit-sharing, the slicing up of a cake which grew larger and more sumptuous with each election. Most of the eating, however, was done by elites.'[42]

Even in highly homogeneous societies such as Korea, regionally based parties can present a major impediment to national economic and political development: because most Korean parties continue to be associated with distinct territorial strongholds, 'regionalism is the key mobilizing element on which politicians base their appeal and to which the voters respond'.[43] The political consequences of such regionalism are not unlike those of ethnic diversity: a focus on sectoral interests rather than national ones, to the detriment of the country as a whole. Thus Korean scholars Ahn Chung-Si and Jaung Hoon lament how 'the legacy of authoritarian rule, regional cleavages, and the lack of institutionalization of political parties has blocked Korea's path towards a mature democracy'.[44]

As will be discussed in some detail in Chapters 5–7, many Asian and Pacific states have recently taken steps to counter the political impact of these kinds of social cleavages. In Indonesia, for example, the reinstatement of democracy was accompanied by new party registration laws which discourage narrow regionally based parties from competing in elections, while revised arrangements for presidential elections make it impossible for candidates to win without cross-regional support. In Fiji, the desire to promote 'multiethnic politics' was the stated objective of a new constitution promulgated in 1997 containing electoral and legislative provisions designed to foster inter-ethnic cooperation. In Papua New Guinea, a raft of political reforms passed in 2002 aimed to promote more stable governing coalitions and

[41] David Murray, 'Thailand's Recent Electoral Reforms', *Electoral Studies*, 17/4 (1998), 527.

[42] Duncan McCargo, 'Introduction: Understanding Political Reform in Thailand', in Duncan McCargo (ed.), *Reforming Thai Politics* (Copenhagen: Nordic Institute of Asian Studies, 2002), 7.

[43] Chung-Si and Hoon, 'South Korea', 152.

[44] Ibid, 162.

cohesive parties, making it difficult to win elections on the basis of ethnic appeals alone. All of these attempts to 'engineer' political outcomes by institutional reform are discussed in more detail later in this book. But can democratic politics be engineered in the first place?

Political Engineering

A central theme of this book concerns the potential of 'political engineering': that is, the conscious design of political institutions to achieve certain specified objectives. A core premise of political engineering is that underlying problems of government stability and effectiveness in democratic systems can be addressed via the design of political institutions—parties, elections, presidents, parliaments, and so on. Changing the institutional incentives facing political actors so as to induce particular outcomes (such as party consolidation) while constraining others (such as political fragmentation) is a common strategy. While potentially applicable in both established and emerging democracies, advocacy of political engineering in recent years has been most prominent in transitional or post-conflict states, often as part of broader attempts to construct sustainable political systems in deeply divided societies.

Tinkering with the institutional 'rules of the game' to influence outcomes is not a new idea: indeed, the possibilities of influencing political development via institutional design has ancient antecedents. Its contemporary articulation, however, began in the late 1960s with scholars, such as Giovanni Sartori, who argued that new democracies could be strengthened by the adoption of institutions to constrain the centrifugal pressures unleashed by democratization.[45] Today, it is widely accepted that some institutions can be purposively designed so as to reward or constrain particular kinds of behaviour. Many political engineering strategies focus on the creative manipulation of electoral systems for achieving these aims.[46] Similarly, there is a long and ongoing debate on the relative merits of presidential and

[45] Giovanni Sartori, 'Political Development and Political Engineering', *Public Policy*, 17 (1968), 261–98.
[46] See, for example, Arend Lijphart and Bernard Grofman (eds.), *Choosing an Electoral System: Issues and Alternatives* (New York: Praeger, 1984); Rein

parliamentary systems of government,[47] devolution of power
via decentralization, federalism, or autonomy,[48] the development of political parties and party systems,[49] and the design
of constitutional structures more generally.[50] As Sartori put it,
'the central question of political engineering is: How can we
intervene *politically* in steering and shaping a process of political development?'[51]

While there is today widespread agreement amongst political
scientists that institutions matter to political development, there
is profound disagreement as to which institutional prescriptions
are most likely to promote sustainable democracy in diverse
societies. Of the several contending schools of thought, the
most important and influential approaches can be boiled down
to two: consociationalism and centripetalism. Both approaches
tend to concentrate on the design or reform of democratic institutions that mediate between state and society, such as
political parties and party systems; on institutions which determine how these parties and groups will be represented, particularly the electoral system; and (in part as a consequence of
the interaction of party and electoral engineering) on the
composition of inclusive cabinets and executive governments.
The two approches, however, have different strategic logics:
centripetalism attempts to encourage moderate and centrist
political outcomes through explicit institutional designs to
depoliticize ethnic divisions, while consociationalism sees minority influence as a poor substitute for minority representation

Taagepera and Matthew S. Shugart, *Seats and Votes: the Effects and Determinants of Electoral Systems* (New Haven, CT and London: Yale University
Press, 1989).

[47] See Juan Linz, 'The Perils of Presidentialism', *Journal of Democracy*, 1
(1990), 51–69; Matthew S. Shugart and John M. Carey, *Presidents and Assemblies: Constitutional Design and Electoral Dynamics* (Cambridge: Cambridge
University Press, 1992).

[48] See Graham Smith (ed.), *Federalism: The Multiethnic Challenge* (London
and New York: Longman, 1995); Yash Ghai (ed.), *Autonomy and Ethnicity:
Negotiating Competing Claims in Multi-ethnic States* (Cambridge: Cambridge
University Press, 2000).

[49] For an example see Benjamin Reilly, 'Political Parties and Political
Engineering in the Asia-Pacific Region', *Asia Pacific Issues: Analysis from the
East-West Center*, 71 (December 2003), 1–8.

[50] Giovanni Sartori, *Comparative Constitutional Engineering: An Inquiry
Into Structures, Incentives and Outcomes* (London: Macmillan, 1994).

[51] Sartori, 'Political Development and Political Engineering', 272.

and hence advocates 'bonding' parties representing distinct communal segments or ethnic groups, as opposed to the cross-communal 'bridging' parties favoured by centripetalism.

This scholarly debate on political engineering has lately found real-world expression in the Asia-Pacific region. While consociational approaches were once prominent in a number of states, and remain important in semi-democracies such as Malaysia, political reforms by Asian and Pacific governments in recent years have more often followed centripetal strategies. For instance, fragile democracies such as Indonesia, Fiji, and Papua New Guinea have adopted explicitly centripetal institutions in order to promote bridging parties which can foster political aggregation. Other states including Korea, Taiwan, Thailand, and the Philippines have introduced highly majoritarian mixed-member electoral systems which penalize minority or cleavage-based parties. Across the region, informal ethnic power-sharing and oversized cabinets have increasingly supplanted the formal power-sharing rules and grand coalitions recommended by consociationalists. All of these cases will be discussed in detail in the following chapters.

In some respects, the prominence of institutional crafting in the Asia-Pacific over the past decade echoes the way East Asia's newly industrializing states attempted to shape the growth of key industries through targeted sectoral strategies of economic development in the 1970s and 1980s. Implementing highly interventionist economic policies rather than more orthodox, laissez faire approaches, countries such as Japan, Korea, and Taiwan become exemplars of this distinctive model of state-led development which relied on strategic industrial policy rather than the invisible hand of the market. Academic studies hailed the success of this unorthodox policy of government-led growth by coining a now widely used term to describe it: the 'developmental state'.[52] With the democratic transitions of the 1990s, this interventionist approach to economic development began to be replicated in the political arena as well—by deliberate

---

[52] Chalmers Johnson is usually credited with establishing the developmental state model with his *MITI and the Japanese Miracle: The Growth of Industrial Policy* (Stanford, CA: Stanford University Press, 1982). See also Stephan Haggard, *Pathways from the Periphery: the Politics of Growth in the Newly Industrializing Countries* (Ithaca, NY: Cornell University Press, 1990), and Meredith Woo-Cumings (ed.), *The Developmental State* (Ithaca, NY: Cornell University Press, 1999).

strategies of political engineering. Mirroring their interventionist economic strategies, Asian elites sought to strategically
retool their political architecture through technocratic reform
of democratic institutions. These attempts to craft what has
been called a 'democratic developmental state' thus represent
an extension of successful economic strategies into the political
arena.[53]

Common to both these economic and political interventions
was the metaphor of engineers and engineering. Just as East
Asian technocrats pursued economic growth under the developmental state model, the region's 'developmental democrats' tried
to engineer political outcomes such as promoting the interests of
national parties at the expense of fringe movements, or constructing broad-based governing coalitions which could be insulated from sectoral groups seeking particularistic policy
concessions. As the late Gordon White wrote,

[when] 'designing' a state which is both democratic and developmental,
it is useful to see 'democratization' not merely as a relatively sudden
political rupture caused by regime transition, but also as a process of
institutional accumulation, built up gradually like layers of coral... a
contemporary developmental democrat can be seen as a modern
Machiavelli who is constantly seeking to reconcile the democratic
and developmental imperatives through conscious, incremental institutional innovation.[54]

Structure

Because much of this book deals with the interrelationship
between democracy and diversity, the cases examined necessarily reflect the considerable variation in these phenomena across
the Asia-Pacific region. Taking a broad interpretation of both,
I will therefore focus on the following new, restored, or transitional democracies: Korea and Taiwan (in Northeast Asia); East
Timor, Indonesia, the Philippines, and Thailand (in Southeast
Asia); as well as Papua New Guinea and the larger Pacific
Island states of Fiji, Samoa, Solomon Islands, and Vanuatu. For

---

[53] See Mark Robinson and Gordon White (eds.), *The Democratic Developmental State* (Oxford: Oxford University Press, 1998).

[54] Gordon White, 'Constructing a Democratic Developmental State' in
Robinson and White, *The Democratic Developmental State*, 32.

comprehensiveness, the illiberal semi-democracies of Cambodia, Malaysia, and Singapore will also be included where appropriate. Furthermore, as it is the fledgling democracies of Indonesia, Thailand, and the Philippines—as well as Fiji and Papua New Guinea in the Pacific—that have been most active in terms of political engineering, I will give special attention to these cases.

I recognize at the outset that such a classification means some important cases are squeezed out. By focusing thematically on new democracies, the region's long-standing Western democracies, Australia and New Zealand, are necessarily omitted, as is Japan, East Asia's sole 'established democracy' (although discussion of the Japanese case will be included when relevant). Similarly, my regional focus on the Asia-Pacific means that the huge and varied subcontinent of South Asia and key states such as India—the world's largest democracy and the foremost example of an enduring democratic state in the developing world—are also neglected. While recognizing the importance of all of these cases, by way of explanation I offer not just the usual constraints of space and time, but also the need to bring some coherence to what is a huge and enormously diverse region. My conceptualization of the Asia-Pacific region as Northeast and Southeast Asia and the island states of the Southwest Pacific is identical to what is sometimes called 'Pacific Asia'.[55]

Structurally, the book is divided into two main parts. The first part, comprising Chapters 2 through 4, is concerned with the impacts of democracy and diversity upon different dimensions of governance. Chapter 2 looks at the democratization of Asian and Pacific states in more detail, and the relationship between democracy and ethnic conflict across the region. It shows how the political openings provided by democratization, combined with external shocks like the Asian economic crisis and increasing recognition of the weakness of inherited political systems, opened the door for major institutional reform. Chapter 3 examines the theoretical and empirical relationship between social diversity and political outcomes throughout Asia and the Pacific. Drawing on both regional and comparative studies, it details the impact that different patterns of ethnic heterogeneity have had upon patterns of democracy and development across the region. Chapter 4 looks squarely at the problems of democracy-building in ethnically divided societies, and at the various schemes

---

[55] See David Drakakis-Smith, *Pacific Asia* (London and New York: Routledge, 1992).

devised for managing social divisions through the design of democratic institutions.

Building on these thematic chapters, the second part of this book looks at how Asia-Pacific states have engineered their political institutions in order to enhance political stability, protect incumbent elites, and limit the impacts of social cleavages upon democratic development. Chapter 5 examines the reform of the region's electoral systems, and how the swing to majoritarian electoral rules has changed the conduct of democratic politics. Chapter 6 investigates the way governments have tried to influence the development of their party systems by changing the institutional environment in which political parties form and function. Chapter 7 explores the relationship between political engineering and power-sharing, and the way different approaches to cabinet formation and political devolution have been used to share or divide governing power.

Chapter 8, the conclusion, pulls these various threads together in order to assess the impact of political engineering across the Asia-Pacific region compared with other world regions such as Europe, Latin America, and the Anglo-American democracies. One conclusion that stands out is the increasing convergence in regards to both institutional designs and political outcomes within the Asia-Pacific over the past decade. Despite significant variations from country to country, across the region as a whole the gravitation towards convergent forms of political engineering in the three main arenas surveyed—political parties, electoral systems, and executive government—is quite striking in comparative terms. The final chapter of this book thus examines whether the democratic reforms enacted in these areas can be said to constitute a distinctive 'Asian model' of democracy.

·····················
2
·····················

Democratization and Internal Conflict
in the Asia-Pacific

The Asia-Pacific today stands at the forefront of two worldwide
trends that have come to dominate the international security
agenda: the ongoing spread of democracy as the only legitimate
form of government, and the ever-growing prominence of intrastate rather than interstate manifestations of violent conflict.
Between them, these countervailing patterns have defined
world politics for much of the post-cold war period.[1]

   Beginning with the collapse of authoritarian regimes in Spain
and Portugal in 1974 and working its way through Eastern
Europe, Latin America, Africa, and Asia, what Samuel Huntington dubbed the 'third wave' of democracy has led to a threefold
increase in the number of democracies around the globe. At the
same time, however, the world has also witnessed a drastic
change in the expression of large-scale conflict, towards internal
violence, rather than the wars between states of the past. As a
consequence, democratization and internal conflict comprise two
of the most important currents of political change in the contemporary world.

---

[1] This process has naturally encouraged a considerable literature dealing
with democratization and its consequences. See, for example, Huntington, *The
Third Wave*; Larry Diamond, Juan Linz, and Seymour Martin Lipset (eds.),
Politics in Developing Countries: Comparing Experiences with Democracy
(Boulder, CO: Lynne Rienner Publishers, 1995); Larry Diamond and Mark F.
Plattner (eds.), *The Global Resurgence of Democracy* (Baltimore, MD: Johns
Hopkins University Press, 1996); Larry Diamond, *Developing Democracy: To-
wards Consolidation* (Baltimore, MD: Johns Hopkins University Press, 1999);
Laurence Whitehead, *Democratization: Theory and Experience* (Oxford: Oxford
University Press, 2002); Robert Pinkney, *Democracy in the Third World*, 2nd
edn. (Boulder, CO and London: Lynne Rienner, 2003).

These parallel phenomena are also deeply intertwined. In many cases, rising levels of internal conflict have accompanied, or been precipitated by, transitions from authoritarian to democratic rule. The vast majority of violent conflicts today occur not between states, but within them: by one count, of the 116 'major armed conflicts' that took place around the world between 1989 and 2002, only 7 were traditional interstate conflicts. The remaining 109 took place within existing states and nearly all displayed a clear ethnic identity dimension.[2] According to Ted Robert Gurr, the Asia-Pacific had both the highest incidence of internal conflict and the highest number of independent ethno-political groups involved in such struggles of any region in the world in the post-cold war period.[3] Another study found the Asia-Pacific also suffered the largest number of major armed conflicts of any world region in every year between 1989 and 1997—all bar one of which were intrastate conflicts.[4] These findings were reinforced by Gurr's recent evaluation of 'minorities at risk', which reported that Asia had 'a larger absolute and proportional number of high-risk groups than any other world region'.[5]

This chapter examines the interrelationship between democratization and ethnic conflict in the Asia-Pacific region. It begins by considering the divergent paths from authoritarian rule to democracy that different Asian and Pacific states have followed. It then examines the various internal conflicts afflicting states of the region. It concludes by considering which political strategies and institutional choices may be most appropriate for states facing the twin challenge of democratization and conflict management.

Democratization

The democratization of the Asia-Pacific region has taken place over several different periods as a result of quite distinct

[2] Mikael Eriksson, Peter Wallensteen, and Margareta Sollenberg, 'Armed Conflict, 1989–2002', *Journal of Peace Research*, 40 (2003), 593–607.
[3] Ted Robert Gurr, 'Peoples Against States: Ethnopolitical Conflict and the Changing World System', *International Studies Quarterly*, 38/3 (1994), 349–53.
[4] See Margareta Sollenberg, Peter Wallensteen, and Andrés Jato, 'Major Armed Conflicts', in Stockholm International Peace Research Institute, *SIPRI Yearbook 1999: Armaments, Disarmament and International Security* (Oxford: Oxford University Press, 1999).
[5] Ted Robert Gurr, *Peoples Versus States: Minorities at Risk in the New Century* (Washington, DC: United States Institute of Peace Press, 2000), 244.

historical circumstances. The settler societies of Australia and New Zealand introduced fully democratic regimes with near-universal adult suffrage in the first decade of the twentieth century, making them the oldest democracies in the world on these measures.[6] Elsewhere, the region's longer-lasting democracies—Japan, the Philippines (omitting the Marcos years of 1972–86), and Papua New Guinea—initially acquired their democratic systems as a result of foreign occupation or colonial rule. Independent Burma and Indonesia also began as democratic regimes.

East Asia's oldest and most stable democracy, Japan, first introduced a written constitution in 1889, but the advent of modern democratic government was a consequence of American occupation at the end of the Second World War. Universal suffrage and parliamentary government came in 1947 under a new post-war constitution which stripped the Japanese military, bureaucracy, and nobility of their powers and transformed the emperor into a figurehead. In the Philippines, similarly, the emergence of presidential democracy based around two broad-based centrist parties on the American model (the Nacionalistas and the Liberals) was a colonial transplant by the United States. This system remained relatively stable from 1946 until 1972, when President Ferdinand Marcos declared martial law. More recently, in Papua New Guinea and some of the Pacific Islands, departing colonial powers in the 1960s and 1970s, such as Australia, Britain, and France, helped to promulgate written constitutions, responsible parliamentary government, and other democratic institutions—but paid less attention to the task of developing competent bureaucracies and state capacity, paving the way for the inherent weakness of many island states today.[7]

Elsewhere democracy had to be fought for, often violently. From the mid-1980s onwards, authoritarian regimes in the Philippines, Taiwan, Korea, and Indonesia came under pressure from an array of domestic and international forces, including a changing regional environment, increasing internal political

[6] See Lijphart, *Democracies*, 37.
[7] Papua New Guinea achieved democratic self-government in 1973 and full independence in 1975. Of our Pacific Island cases, Samoa was the first to attain independence in 1962, followed by Fiji in 1970, but restrictions on the franchise remained in both states.

opposition, and pressure for liberalization following the end of the cold war. In many cases, demand for the end of authoritarian rule was driven to a significant extent by popular pressure from below.

The 1986 'people power' revolution in the Philippines that deposed the decaying and corrupt Marcos regime is a classic example of this civil society-led resumption of democracy. First elected president in 1965, Marcos assumed quasi-dictatorial powers in 1972 and indulged in an increasingly patrimonial, oligarchic, and ultimately kleptocratic form of authoritarian rule. In 1986, amidst burgeoning political repression, institutional decay, and mounting domestic and international pressure, Marcos sought to demonstrate the legitimacy of his regime by calling a snap election—of which, despite clear evidence to the contrary, he was initially declared the winner. The large-scale and well-documented fraud involved in this attempt to 'steal' the election outcome inspired massive popular protests, as well as a significant revolt by some elements of the military. Amid a mounting national civil disobedience campaign, Marcos's regime collapsed in February 1986. People power returned as a decisive force in Filipino politics in 2001, when the ailing presidency of Joseph Estrada was overturned by a combination of middle-class street protests, congressional impeachment, and judicial action.

Elsewhere, incumbent autocratic regimes handled their exit from power more skilfully. In Taiwan and Korea especially, the dominant parties of the authoritarian period played a crucial role in opening up the political system to competitors. In Taiwan, the incumbent Kuomintang (KMT) party, which had ruled unchallenged since Taiwan's liberation from Japanese forces in 1945, itself initiated decisive steps towards political liberalization in the late 1980s. Opposition parties such as the Democratic Progressive Party (DPP) were legalized, media restrictions lifted, and constitutional reforms enacted, resulting in the direct election of the Taiwanese parliament, the Legislative Yuan, for the first time in 1991. Voters rewarded the KMT's skilful handling of this graduated political opening by re-electing them to office—an unusual outcome for a transition from authoritarian rule. Further constitutional reforms saw the first direct presidential elections under Taiwan's unusual form of semi-presidentialism in 1996, which was also won by the KMT. It was not until March 2000 that a clear transfer of power across party lines occurred, when the DPP's Chen Shui-bian scored a narrow victory in presidential elections, ending more than five decades of unbroken KMT rule.

In Korea, political liberalization in the lead-up to the Seoul Olympics of 1988 began a chain reaction that ended with the collapse of the military regime and the transition to democracy. The authoritarian government of Chun Doo-Hwan and the Democratic Justice Party, which had been in power since the proclamation of Korea's Fifth Republic in 1980, had come under increasing domestic and international pressure to liberalize politics and legalize opposition parties. By 1987 the regime was facing a powerful political opposition, as well as the mass mobilization of religious groups, social movements, and other civil society actors. The death of a university student at the hands of the national police sparked massive street protests which forced Chun to step down in June 1987. His successor, Roh Tae-woo, introduced a sweeping programme of political liberalization, including direct presidential elections, press freedom, and human rights reforms, and negotiated a phased transition to democracy which led to a new constitution and Korea's first competitive presidential elections later that same year. As in Taiwan, political reforms sponsored by the incumbent autocrats which legalized opposition parties and provided for free elections to presidential and legislative offices were a central part of the transition. Korea's first competitive presidential elections (won by Roh) in December 1987, and the subsequent victories of democracy campaigners Kim Young Sam in 1992 and Kim Dae Jung in 1997—both former dissidents who had been subject to arrest and, in the latter's case, assassination attempts—constituted further landmarks in the ongoing consolidation of Korean democracy.

Another wave of Asia-Pacific democratization occurred in the late 1990s, precipitated to a significant degree by the Asian economic crisis that swept across the region in 1997. While the impact of the crisis was economically devastating, particularly in the hardest-hit states such as Indonesia and Thailand, it also proved to be politically liberating, stimulating fundamental political reform in both countries. The crisis also dealt a grievous blow to proponents of the much-heralded Asian model of restrictive one-party politics with open competitive markets. More importantly, by exposing social cleavages, isolating incumbent elites, and providing opportunities for new entrants, the crisis had a profound effect on the domestic politics of the region, stimulating an intense struggle for reform in Indonesia, Thailand, Korea, and (to a lesser extent) Malaysia and the Philippines.[8]

In Indonesia, where concerns about poor governance, high-level corruption, and 'crony capitalism' were most pronounced, the crisis brought about the end of the Suharto era, paving the way for long-awaited leadership transition and the possibility of large-scale political reform. Again, student protests and mass public rallies were critical events precipitating the fall of the New Order regime, which had monopolized power since 1966. Indonesia's *reformasi* movement was an unlikely and in many ways chaotic combination of opposition campaigners, non-government organizations, and student activists, as well as influential political leaders such as Amien Rais. In 1998, with the Indonesian economy crippled by the effects of the Asian crisis, fatally undermining the regime's main claim to legitimacy, Suharto's fate was sealed. A combination of popular discontent, military pressure, and mass riots that left over 1,000 people dead and many commercial centres in Jakarta destroyed saw him step down on 21 May 1998, to be replaced by his almost equally unpopular vice-president, B. J. Habibie, whose interim government began the process of serious democratic reform.[9]

In June 1999, Indonesia's first genuinely competitive elections since 1955 were held amidst great excitement and not a little trepidation at the uncertain consequences that might attend the liberalization of national politics. The election itself passed relatively peacefully, and resulted in a powerful new role for Indonesia's legislature, the DPR (*Dewan Perwakilan Rakyat*, or People's Representative Assembly), and broader national assembly, the MPR (*Majelis Permausyawaratan Rakyat*, or People's Consultative Assembly). Previously a compliant servant of the president, the post-Suharto MPR was a much more activist

---

[8] See MacIntyre, *The Power of Institutions*; Stephan Haggard, 'The Politics of the Asian Financial Crisis', in Laurence Whitehead (ed.), *Emerging Market Democracies: East Asia and Latin America* (Baltimore, MD and London: Johns Hopkins University Press, 2000). For a discussion of the impact of the crisis on ethnic politics, see Jungug Choi, 'Ethnic and Regional Politics After the Asian Economic Crisis: A Comparison of Malaysia and South Korea', *Democratization*, 10/1 (2003), 121–34.

[9] For accounts and analyses, see Geoff Forester and R. J. May (eds.), *The Fall of Soeharto* (Bathurst, NSW: Crawford House Publishing, 1998); Edward Aspinall, *Opposing Suharto: Compromise, Resistance, and Regime Change in Indonesia* (Stanford, CA: Stanford University Press, 2004).

body which flexed its muscles in 2001 by impeaching Indonesia's first democratically chosen president, Abdurrahman Wahid, only eighteen months after voting him into office. Newly empowered legislators passed a series of major constitutional amendments, including direct presidential elections; a new house of review, the DPD (*Dewan Perwakilan Daerah*, or Regional Representative Assembly) to represent the country's provinces; revised electoral arrangements for both houses; and a shift in the balance of powers between the president and the legislature.[10] At the same time, previously moribund provincial and local assemblies were empowered via a massive decentralization of functions and responsibilities to the regional level. The result of these changes has been a major reorientation of the Indonesian political system, which are examined in more detail in subsequent chapters.

After Indonesia, it was the fragile new democracies of Thailand and Korea that were most affected by the region's economic emergency, mostly due to the inability of their elected governments to respond appropriately and quickly to the crisis when it first erupted. Thailand, which had experienced decades of sporadic political liberalization followed by military coups, appeared to have unpromising foundations for democracy, with no less than sixteen constitutions introduced and then discarded since 1932. Over the course of the 1980s, however, demands for meaningful democracy gained ascendancy in the Thai political fabric—to the point that by the end of military involvement in politics in 1992, Thailand was widely considered to have one of Southeast Asia's most competitive and participatory political systems.[11] However, Thai democracy remained fragile. When the economic crisis struck in 1997, the incumbent government of Prime Minister Chavlit Yongchaiyut was, like its predecessors, a shaky coalition comprising six different parties, making for chronic political instability. Pressure for major political reform, which had been growing since the early 1990s but successfully stonewalled to that point, was thrust to centre stage as the economic collapse exposed deep structural weaknesses in Thailand's governance architecture. Within the space of a few weeks, Thai politicians began to openly embrace demands for a new constitution, justifying the need for change

[10] See Stephen Sherlock, *Struggling to Change: The Indonesian Parliament in an Era of* Reformasi (Canberra: Centre for Democratic Institutions, 2003).

[11] See Kevin Hewison (ed.), *Political Change in Thailand: Democracy and Participation* (London: Routledge, 1997).

by reference to the financial crisis.[12] With Thailand's currency and stock market both plunging, the Chavlit government collapsed, opening the way for a diverse coalition of reformers to shepherd through a radical reform agenda which represented a distinct break with the politics of the past.

Thailand's 1997 Constitution established a number of independent watchdog bodies beyond the reach of the traditional political apparatus, including an anti-corruption commission, a constitutional court, human rights monitoring bodies, and a muscular new electoral commission empowered to oversee candidate spending and campaigning and overturn fraudulent outcomes. Other changes included 'anti-hopping' provisions designed to restrict legislators' ability to switch parties, restrictions on the use of no-confidence votes in parliament, an elected but non-partisan Senate, and—most influential of all— new electoral and political party laws, all of which are examined in subsequent chapters.[13] Some of these measures were without precedent in Asia; indeed the 'self-restraining' nature of Thailand's new institutional apparatus makes it an important and potentially influential example of institutional reform in the region.[14]

While less dramatic than in Thailand, the Asian crisis also exacted political casualties in other countries. The fragile foundations of political order in Korea—which as a presidential system should have been able to respond more rapidly as the crisis loomed—were exposed by the speed and severity of the economic meltdown. Despite Kim Young Sam's government looking relatively secure when the crisis first hit, popular concerns about the economy's robustness and a looming presidential election quickly fragmented his support base. One faction of the ruling party switched support to opposition leader Kim Dae Jung, who went on to win the 1997 elections. In Malaysia, by

---

[12] Thus a former opponent of reform chose to vote for the new constitution, saying: 'There are some clauses that I don't like, but because of the economy, we have to accept it.' Said another: 'I changed my position because when the constitution was finished the economic crisis broke out.' Quoted in MacIntyre, *The Power of Institutions*, 121.

[13] For a good overview of the reforms, see Sombat Chantornvong, 'The 1997 Constitution and the Politics of Electoral Reform', in Duncan McCargo (ed.), *Reforming Thai Politics* (Copenhagen: Nordic Institute of Asian Studies, 2002).

[14] Andreas Schedler, Larry Diamond, and Marc F. Plattner (eds.), *The Self-Restraining State: Power and Accountability in New Democracies* (Boulder, CO and London: Lynne Rienner Publishers, 1999).

contrast, a more institutionalized form of semi-democracy dominated by the long-ruling alliance government allowed for a more flexible response to the crisis, and the succession issue was effectively postponed by Prime Minister Mahathir Mohamad crushing the rising challenge of Anwar Ibrahim.[15] Having seen off this challenge, in 2003 Mahathir retired, to be replaced by his less controversial deputy, Abdullah Ahmad Badawi.

Junhan Lee has argued that these various examples of post-cold war democratization in Asia share four basic characteristics. First, in almost all cases, university students played a central incendiary role in sparking demonstrations against incumbent regimes, which then spread to encompass labour movements, religious organizations, and other social groups. Second, the role of the middle classes was critical. In the Philippines, Korea, Taiwan, Thailand, and Indonesia, middle-class citizens formed the backbone of the political protests, relaying information and organizing public gatherings via mobile phones to the point where more than one transition was later dubbed the 'mobile phone revolution'. Third, this combination of student activism and middle-class support enabled pro-democracy organizations to organize highly visible and effective nationwide street demonstrations. Finally, these popular protests continued unabated until the pro-democracy movement's demands were met—which in most cases meant the departure of the incumbent government.[16]

The one transition to democracy in the region that did not share these characteristics was the case of East Timor. There, democratization came about as a result of a number of factors—a prolonged independence struggle against Indonesian military forces, which had invaded in 1975; the transition from Suharto to Habibie in Jakarta, which opened the door for a referendum on the disputed entity's future; and mounting pressure on the new Habibie regime from international actors—but was facilitated primarily by direct international intervention and the subsequent state-building efforts of the United Nations. East Timor's August 1999 popular vote to reject Habibie's offer of autonomy and thereby register a demand for independence unleashed a wave of violence, destruction, and looting by pro-Indonesian

---

[15] MacIntyre, *The Power of Institutions*, 104.
[16] See Junhan Lee, 'Primary Causes of Asian Democratization', *Asian Survey*, 42/6 (2002), 821–37.

militias. Frantic international negotiations resulted in an Australian-led regional military intervention which restored basic security and placed East Timor under the control of the United Nations. Two years later, in its final act before handing back power to the East Timorese people, the UN organized East Timor's first free elections—to a constituent assembly which then drafted a constitution for the new state. As with the constituent assemblies held in the Philippines (1986) and Thailand (1996–7), this constitution-writing exercise was itself an important part in the democratization process, acting as both a drafting exercise and a civic education process. The resulting constitution provided for a semi-presidential system of government for the new nation, renamed Timor-Leste. With the drafting process completed, the constituent assembly was transformed into the nation's first democratic parliament. To complete this transformation, presidential elections took place in April 2002, won by the former resistance leader Xanana Gusmão.[17]

How successful have these various transitions proved to be in consolidating democracy? One way of answering this question is to look at the comparative rankings given to each country by independent bodies such as the US private foundation Freedom House, which conducts an annual survey of political freedom and civil rights around the world. Table 2.1 presents some basic geographic, demographic, economic, and political data for all Asian and Pacific states, including the latest Freedom House scores. These are measured on a scale of 1 to 7, with 1 representing the highest degree of freedom and 7 the lowest. (Countries whose political rights and civil liberties scores fall between 1.0 and 2.5 are designated 'free'; between 3.0 and 5.5 'partly free'; and between 5.5 and 7.0 'not free'.)[18]

Five Asian states—Japan, the Philippines, Korea, Taiwan, and Thailand—have been consistently ranked as free for most of the past decade. East Timor, Indonesia, Malaysia, and Singapore are classified as partly free, although their trajectories run in different directions, with Indonesia and East Timor improving their rankings in recent years while Malaysia and Singapore have regressed. The others—Brunei, Burma, Cambodia, China,

---

[17] See Dionisio da Costa Babo Soares, Michael Maley, James J. Fox, and Anthony J. Regan, *Elections and Constitution Making in East Timor* (Canberra: State, Society, and Governance in Melanesia Project, 2003).
[18] See Freedom House, www.freedomhouse.org.

TABLE 2.1. *Basic indicators for Asia-Pacific countries*

Country	Population 2004	Total land area (1000 sq. km)	Per capita GNI 2003 ($US)	Freedom House ranking 2005
Northeast Asia				
China	1,299,900,000	9,327.4	1,100	6.5 (Not free)
Republic of Korea	48,100,000	98.7	12,030	1.5 (Free)
North Korea	22,800,000	120.4	440	7.0 (Not free)
Taiwan	22,700,000	36.2	13,140	1.5 (Free)
Southeast Asia				
Brunei	440,000	5.2	13,724	5.5 (Not free)
Burma/Myanmar	54,300,000	657.6	1,170	7.0 (Not free)
Cambodia	13,500,000	176.5	300	5.5 (Not free)
East Timor	925,000	14.9	460	3.0 (Partly free)
Indonesia	216,400,000	1,811.6	810	3.0 (Partly free)
Laos	5,800,000	230.8	340	6.5 (Not free)
Malaysia	25,600,000	328.6	3,880	4.0 (Partly free)
Philippines	83,500,000	298.2	1,080	2.5 (Free)
Singapore	4,200,000	0.7	21,230	4.5 (Partly free)
Thailand	64,200,000	510.9	2,190	2.5 (Free)
Vietnam	82,000,000	325.5	480	6.5 (Not free)
Pacific Islands				
Fiji Islands	840,000	18.3	2,240	3.5 (Partly free)
Kiribati	89,700	0.7	860	1.0 (Free)
Marshall Islands	61,200	0.2	2,710	1.0 (Free)
Micronesia	108,000	0.7	2,070	1.0 (Free)
Nauru	12,000	<0.1	3,740	1.0 (Free)
Palau	20,600	0.5	5,740	1.0 (Free)
Papua New Guinea	5,800,000	452.9	500	1.0 (Free)
Samoa	180,900	2.8	1,440	3.0 (Partly free)
Solomon Islands	521,000	28.0	560	3.0 (Partly free)
Tonga	101,800	0.7	1,490	3.0 (Partly free)
Tuvalu	11,200	<0.1	—	1.0 (Free)
Vanuatu	213,300	12.2	1,180	2.0 (Free)

Source: Asian Development Bank, *Key Indicators 2005* (www.adb.org/statistics); Freedom House, *Freedom in the World 2005* (www.freedomhouse.org).

North Korea, Laos, and Vietnam—are all adduced as being not free, although again there is enormous variation within this group, with some countries having held relatively free elections at times (e.g. Cambodia) while others remain under totalitarian rule (e.g. North Korea). By contrast, in Papua New Guinea and the Pacific Island states, there is less diversity of experience and a better record of democracy, with no countries ranked as not free, and four classified as partly free due to ongoing franchise restrictions (in Samoa and Tonga), or recent coups (in Fiji and Solomon Islands).

Of course, these judgements on the civil and political liberties of particular states are open to argument. Yet other rankings of democracy produced by political scientists looking at the competitiveness of electoral processes, levels of popular participation, recognition of civil and political rights, and so on produce broadly similar classifications.[19] In general, these various studies confirm the same upwards trend in the Asia-Pacific's political rights and civil liberties over the past decade, as well as the emergence of East Timor, Indonesia, Korea, the Philippines, Taiwan, and Thailand as clear examples of transitions from authoritarian to democratic rule.

Conflicts

In most of the Asia-Pacific region, the recent advent of democracy was preceded by a much longer period of state-building. This was not a peaceful process. While democratic transitions were often accompanied by—and in cases such as East Timor, a result of—considerable violence, intrastate conflict in the Asia-Pacific has much older antecedents. Much of this can be traced to the struggle for independence of Asian and Pacific peoples during the final stages of the Second World War. Since the 1940s, these societies struggled to achieve independence from centuries of colonial rule by Europe and America, and in some cases from other states within Asia. With independence, many of these same states faced new conflicts stemming not from the impacts of external colonizers, but from their own internal diversity. As a result, some of the bloodiest and most persistent episodes of violence in the region have been conflicts between central governments and peripheral regions in which ethnic minorities are concentrated.

The range of internal conflicts currently afflicting Indonesia is a case in point. By population the world's fourth-largest state

---

[19] See Tatu Vanhanen, *Prospects of Democracy: A Study of 172 Countries* (London and New York: Routledge, 1997); Lijphart, *Patterns of Democracy*; Lawrence LeDuc, Richard G. Niemi, and Pippa Norris (eds.), *Comparing Democracies 2: New Challenges in the Study of Elections and Voting* (Thousand Oaks, CA: Sage, 2002).

and largest Muslim country, Indonesia's two most persistent secessionist struggles—in Aceh and Papua, at the western and eastern extremities of the country, respectively—both have a strong self-determination focus. There have also been violent inter-ethnic clashes in other Indonesian outer regions such as Maluku, Kalimantan, Sulawesi, and Riau. Tension between 'local' and 'migrant' groups have often also been influential: between Islamic migrants and local Christians in Maluku; indigenous resistance to in-migrants from other Indonesian provinces in Papua; and Dyak attacks on Madurese migrants in Kalimantan, to name a few.

Centre–periphery conflicts are common elsewhere in Southeast Asia as well. Secessionist struggles in the Philippines, for example, have centred on the predominantly Muslim southern islands of Mindanao and Sulu which stand apart from the Christian affiliation of the rest of the country. The campaign for a Muslim homeland in Mindanao has resulted in successive cycles of violent armed conflict followed by peace talks between the Philippines government and the Moro National Liberation Front, leading to a peace agreement and the establishment of an autonomous regional government in 1996. Despite this, militant groups have continued to campaign for a separate Islamic state based around the Mindanao region. The Philippines also continues to suffer the effects of a three-decade old communist insurgency led by the New People's Army, which draws on the deep and persistent inequalities of Philippines society.

Elsewhere, violent conflicts have been of a lower intensity. In Malaysia, with its relatively effective state apparatus and more pluralistic regime, there have been no large-scale ethnic conflicts since the race riots of 1969. However, centre–periphery tensions are again present in the eastern provinces of Sabah and Sarawak, and are of growing importance in parts of peninsula Malaysia as well due to calls by some state governments for the introduction of Islamic law. Similarly, Thailand, another relatively strong state, has experienced decades of ethno-regional violence on its northern and southern extremities. In addition to ongoing tensions between the central government and the many hill peoples of the country's north, the far southern region of Pattani on the Thai–Malaysia border has experienced sporadic conflicts between government forces and the local population. These escalated significantly in 2004, after a violent altercation between local Islamic activists and the Thai military which left over 100 people dead. Finally, since its emergence under UN auspices as an independent state in 2002, East Timor has had to deal with its own internal problems of poverty, lawlessness, and underdevelopment fuelled by cross-border raids from pro-Indonesian militias in West Timor.

Major internal conflicts also afflict a number of the Pacific Island countries. The most serious of these, in the Solomon Islands, resulted in the overthrow of the government in June 2000, amid violent quasi-criminal attacks by local militias representing rival communities from the islands of Guadalcanal and Malaita. In June 2003, a regional military intervention initiated and led by Australia resulted in the re-establishment of legitimate government, although the rebuilding of state institutions will take much longer. Papua New Guinea also suffers from a score of ongoing local inter-ethnic conflicts—many of them the product of traditional tribal animosities combined with competition over modern resources, compounded by the widespread availability of high-powered weapons. While most such conflicts have a limited impact on the state, recent armed conflict in the Southern Highlands led to the abandonment of the 2002 elections there. By contrast, the long-running separatist struggle in Papua New Guinea's eastern island of Bougainville appears to have been resolved for the time being by a series of peace deals brokered between 1997 and 2001 which culminated in the establishment of an autonomous local government in 2005. Elsewhere in the South Pacific, inter-group tensions and sporadic low-level conflicts remain a factor in Fiji following the May 2000 coup, and in the French overseas territory of New Caledonia, both of which are divided along racial lines. Indeed, the prevalence of such internal conflicts, all of which have a clear ethnic dimension, is one of the hallmarks of what I have previously called the 'Africanization' of the South Pacific.[20]

What explains the prominence of internal ethnic conflicts in such a varied range of Asia-Pacific countries and contexts? While causes are clearly complex and multidimensional, several common themes stand out, including the uncertain effects of modernization and democratization; the problems of weak and artificial state structures imposed on diverse and fragmented societies; and the distinctive geographic and demographic factors

---

[20] Benjamin Reilly, 'The Africanization of the South Pacific', *Australian Journal of International Affairs*, 54/3 (2000), 261–8.

of the region. The following section discusses these various factors in more detail.

Modernization, Democratization, and Conflict Management

Many Asia-Pacific states are in the throes of enormous social, economic, and political change: from tradition to modernity, from rural to urban-based societies, from command to market economies, and, of course, from authoritarian to democratic government. This process of transformation is itself conflict-creating.[21] One of the great failures of the modernization paradigm of economic and political development that dominated academic thinking about non-Western countries in the 1960s and 1970s was the expectation that traditional allegiances to clan, tribe, and region would gradually wither away as modernization proceeded, to be replaced by new forms of identity such as class interests. In reality, modernization often led not to a withering away but rather a reformulation and strengthening of ethnic, linguistic, religious, and other forms of group identity, in part as a reaction to the pace of change and social upheavals. Because economic modernization creates winners and losers, traditional allegiances provide a way of mobilizing coalitions of common interest in the competition for scarce natural or economic resources.

Today, scholars and policymakers often suffer from a similar blindness to the modernization theorists of the past when they expect that democratic governance will naturally lead to peaceful communal relations and lower levels of conflict—the so-called 'democratic peace' thesis much cited in speeches by former US President Bill Clinton during his term in office.[22] In fact, while long-term democracies are, on average, both less prone to internal conflict and much less likely to go to war with each other than their authoritarian counterparts, comparative research has repeatedly found that countries undergoing the

---

[21] This is the core argument of Samuel P. Huntington, *Political Order in Changing Societies* (New Haven, CT: Yale University Press, 1968) and of Walker Connor, *Ethnonationalism: The Quest for Understanding* (Princeton, NJ: Princeton University Press, 1994).

[22] Bruce Russett, *Grasping the Democratic Peace* (Princeton, NJ: Princeton University Press, 1993).

wrenching process of *democratization* are neither. As one study concluded, 'while mature, stable democracies are safer, states usually go through a dangerous transition to democracy. Historical evidence from the last 200 years shows that in this phase, countries become more war-prone, not less.'[23] As a consequence, many indicators of conflict—both inter- and intrastate varieties—tend to *rise* in the initial period of democratization.[24] A major insight of political science scholarship in recent years— harking back to an earlier literature from the 1960s and 1970s on post-colonial state-building in Africa—thus concerns the dangers of early democratization in fragile states.

A recent book-length study of this phenomenon contends that democratization is most likely to stimulate ethno-nationalist conflict when elites are threatened by rapid political change and when the expansion of popular participation precedes the formation of strong political institutions.[25] The failure of Indonesia's first abortive experience of democracy in the 1950s provides a good example of this dilemma of early democratization preceding the development of robust civic institutions. Indonesia's fall into authoritarian rule was largely a response to the chaotic democratic period between 1950 and 1957, when 'ethnic conflict of two kinds, religious-based, and cultural/ regional-based, threatened to tear apart the infant republic'.[26] Today, some scholars see new Southeast Asian democracies like Indonesia, Thailand, and the Philippines as suffering a similar legitimacy crisis, whereby 'invocation of primordial loyalties by political leaders for their own ends ... [is] compounded by the key features of the democratic system (universal suffrage, freedom of association, free expression, participation, and contestation)— making for bitter conflict, turmoil, and generally a zero sum political game in these countries'.[27]

[23] Edward Mansfield and Jack Snyder, 'Democratization and War', *Foreign Affairs*, 74/3 (1995), 79–97.

[24] See Renée de Nevers, 'Democratization and Ethnic Conflict', in Michael Brown (ed.), *Ethnic Conflict and International Security* (Princeton, NJ: Princeton University Press, 1993).

[25] Jack Snyder, *From Voting to Violence: Democratization and Nationalist Conflict* (New York and London: W.W. Norton, 2000).

[26] R. William Liddle, 'Coercion, Co-optation, and the Management of Ethnic Relations in Indonesia', in Brown and Ganguly, *Government Policies and Ethnic Relations*, 311.

[27] Muthiah Alagappa, 'Contestation and Crisis', in Muthiah Alagappa (ed.), *Political Legitimacy in Southeast Asia: The Quest for Moral Authority* (Stanford, CA: Stanford University Press, 1995), 63.

One explanation for this legitimacy deficit lies in the distinctive impact of ethnic politics in weakly institutionalized new democracies. While the mere presence of ethnic differences does not mean that these will necessarily become the basis of political competition, they do tend to have relatively predictable impacts on the conduct of competitive politics, particularly in new democracies. In such cases, political parties often form around ethnic identities and respond to popular insecurities by 'playing the ethnic card' to attract support. Because these parties depend on the mobilization of communal interests and identities for their ongoing existence, their appearance can trigger a cascading tit-for-tat of escalation on ethnic issues. As elections become little more than ethnic censuses, the risk of group conflict increases—threatening, ultimately, the failure of democracy itself as majority group hegemonic 'control', often aided by the assumption of martial law or outright military rule, are justified by the need to restore order and stability.[28] The erosion of competitive democracy in Malaysia, in which the party system has always been based along communal lines, is an example of this process in action.

None of this means that democracy is necessarily a negative factor for the management of internal conflict. Indeed, the very survival of complex multiethnic states, such as Indonesia, depends to a large extent on the success of their democratic experiment. By providing the institutional framework through which aggrieved social groups can gain access to government and influence policy outcomes, democracies are capable of responding to societal conflicts with accommodation rather than repression, in sharp contrast to authoritarian regimes. This is one reason why democratic theorists like Adam Przeworski characterize democracy as a political arrangement which processes, but never definitely resolves, social conflicts.[29] Under this interpretation, a functioning democracy serves as a system of *conflict management*, with potential disputes channelled into constitutional arenas such as non-violent competition between political parties rather than armed conflict on the streets. These

---

[28] See Horowitz, *Ethnic Groups in Conflict*. Recent research on India has generated important new insights into this process: see Steven I. Wilkinson, *Votes and Violence: Electoral Competition and Ethnic Riots in India* (New York: Cambridge University Press, 2004) and Kanchan Chandra, *Why Ethnic Parties Succeed: Patronage and Ethnic Headcounts in India* (New York: Cambridge University Press, 2004).

[29] Przeworski, *Democracy and the Market*, 10–14.

arguments have been buttressed by empirical studies which emphasize the success of consolidated democracies in accommodating ethnic differences through peaceful means.[30]

But despite these benefits, it is clear that democratization can also sow the seeds for the possible break-up of countries previously held together by force. As the case of East Timor graphically demonstrates, the logic of democratization is also the logic of self-determination: both are based on the idea of people freely choosing their political status and government through fundamental freedoms of movement, speech and assembly. A recurrent feature of rapid democratization in multiethnic states is therefore the outbreak of ethnic self-determination movements—a phenomenon that has been evident in a number of emerging Asia-Pacific democracies. Thus while democratization in countries such as Indonesia has opened up new possibilities of managing conflicts, it has also enabled secessionist movements to organize and campaign in a way that was impossible under authoritarian rule. For instance, in 1999 Indonesia's Papua province, which borders Papua New Guinea, held a mass-participation congress of regional leaders which culminated in a declaration of the province's independence on the basis of its unwilling incorporation into Indonesia in 1962. While Papua remains firmly under Indonesian control, such events would have been unthinkable during the Suharto era.

Another fundamental problem facing parts of Southeast Asia and the island Pacific in particular is the basic weakness of state structures in the face of resurgent regional, religious, and ethnic identities—what have been called strong societies in weak states.[31] While countries like Thailand and Cambodia have historical claims to 'stateness', others are amongst the more artificial creations of the twentieth century. For example, the combination of peninsula and eastern Malaysia is a product of British colonialism, as is the territorial manifestation of modern Burma. Indonesia, a country created by Dutch colonialism's amalgamation of quasi-independent sultanates and stateless

---

[30] See Ted Robert Gurr, 'Ethnic Warfare on the Wane', *Foreign Affairs*, 79/3 (2000), 52–64; Håvard Hegre, Tanja Ellingsen, Scott Gates, and Nils Petter Gleditsch, 'Towards a Democratic Civil Peace? Democracy, Political Change and Civil War, 1816–1992', *American Political Science Review*, 95/1 (2001), 33–48.

[31] Joel S. Migdal, *Strong Societies and Weak States: State–Society Relations and State Capacities in the Third World* (Princeton, NJ: Princeton University Press, 1988).

communities, has famously been described by Benedict Anderson as a 'a territorially specific imagined reality' of post-colonial nationalism.[32] Concepts of the nation are even more artificial in Papua New Guinea and Solomon Islands, where stateless traditional societies were aggregated into modern states by the external impetus of colonialism rather than by internal nation-building movements.

Conclusion

The Asia-Pacific experience highlights the general point that democratization in ethnically plural societies can be a violent, difficult, and dangerous process. Because democracies explicitly acknowledge the presence of varied and conflicting interests and enable different groups to organize, mobilize supporters, and campaign for votes to advance their respective interests, they tend to highlight social cleavages. While many theories of political change contend that the introduction of democratic politics is inherently destabilizing, democratization in diverse societies can be a particularly difficult process to manage. This makes democratic transitions a high risk exercise in many Asia-Pacific states, most of which are internally divided along multiple cleavages of geography, language, religion, and culture.

Once unleashed, ethnic conflicts tend to be extremely difficult to solve. Because of the deep-seated nature of communal identities, they are unsuited to cake-cutting, split-the-difference solutions. They also tend to be immune to traditional state-based approaches to security based on international law, diplomacy, and intergovernmental organizations such as the United Nations. Such institutions were designed for the maintenance of interstate peace and order, and are often impotent or irrelevant in the face of internal disputes. For the same reason, intrastate conflicts present problems for those attempting to resolve disputes via traditional remedies such as 'preventive diplomacy', 'early warning', and 'multilateral intervention'. These paradigms have so far had little real impact on contemporary intrastate conflicts in the Asia-Pacific region, most of which are not amenable to external involvement

---

[32] Benedict Anderson, *Imagined Communities: Reflections on the Origin and Spread of Nationalism* (London: Verso, 1983), 122.

(in part because such involvement conflicts with the paradigm of state sovereignty) and do not, unusual cases like East Timor aside, attract direct international intervention. Particularly in East Asia, where the concept of a strong state continues to be highly valued by regimes of all persuasions, governments routinely oppose even benign attempts at external interference in their internal affairs.

All of this underscores the reality that workable solutions to internal conflicts in Asia and the Pacific must inevitably rely in large part on internal political reforms rather than external interventions. Designing political institutions which can respond to the underlying grievances driving internal conflict thus stands as a major policy priority, and one in which Asian and Pacific governments have invested heavily in recent years. Generally speaking, political reformers have tended to focus their efforts on three broad institutional arenas: *representational* institutions covering the formal structures of elections, legislatures, and assemblies; *mediating* institutions, such as political parties and party systems, which aggregate popular preferences and play an intermediary function between state and society; and what might be called *power-sharing* institutions—that is, institutions which attempt to divide, devolve, or share power between different groups both vertically, via the formation and composition of executive government, and horizontally, via the devolution of political power.

The recognition that each of these institutional arenas can impact on democratic consolidation, political stability, and effective government has served to underscore the potential of political engineering amongst Asia-Pacific reformers. The second part of this book therefore examines cases of institutional innovation in each of these three arenas, looking sequentially at reforms to electoral systems, political parties, and cabinet formation practices across the region. Before doing so, however, there is a need to move away from the broad subject of democratization and conflict management and shift focus to a much more specific issue: the impact of social cleavages upon governance, both within individual Asian and Pacific states and across the region as a whole. This is the subject of the next chapter.

Diversity, Democracy, and Development in the Asia-Pacific

A central concern of this book is the impact of social cleavages on the conduct of democratic politics. Such cleavages take different forms in different countries. For example, some Asia-Pacific states are highly diverse in ethno-linguistic terms: Papua New Guinea is a case in point. Others are not so much diverse as divided, comprising two or three large and relatively autonomous communities: for instance, Fiji and Malaysia. Other states are less heterogeneous but feature distinct and aggrieved ethnic minorities, such as the Muslim communities in the southern regions of Thailand and the Philippines. Still others are culturally fairly homogeneous but have deep ethno-political divisions based around regional or ancestral ties, as in Korea and Taiwan. Finally, some states display various combinations of the above: Indonesia, for example, faces multiple overlapping communal, religious, linguistic, and regional cleavages.

One way of quantifying these differences is to measure the structure of such cleavages across different states. In recent years, a growing body of cross-national research has investigated the effect of ethnic fragmentation on political and economic outcomes. Focusing on ethnicity as an independent variable in this way has generated some striking findings. For example, comparative studies by economists have found that states with high levels of ethnic or linguistic diversity tend to have lower economic growth, deliver fewer public services, more corruption, and lower overall development than their more homogeneous counterparts. Conversely, and contrary to conventional wisdom, other studies by political scientists have found that ethno-linguistic fragmentation can also be associated with other, more positive, political indicators, such as lower chances of civil war and other threats to regime survival.

Drawing on this rich comparative literature, this chapter examines the impact of social diversity on state development across the Asia-Pacific region. It argues that variation in ethnic structure both between and within states helps to explain some of the distinctive features of political and economic development across the region. However, these vary across different dimensions of governance. In regards to public policy, highly diverse societies almost inevitably face difficulties of government coordination and policy implementation due to competing ethno-regional demands. On the other hand, in certain situations such diversity may also assist democratic continuity by necessitating cross-ethnic power-sharing and making challenges to the existing order difficult to organize and sustain. The differential impacts of social structure on a state's political and economic performance are thus complex, strengthening some dimensions of governance as they weaken others.

Before proceeding, an important caveat needs to be emphasized: ethnicity is one of the most slippery and difficult social phenomena to capture and measure effectively. For the purposes of this chapter, an 'ethnic group' can be defined as a collectivity within a larger society which has real or putative common ancestry, memories, and common cultural traits such as language, religion, kinship, region of residence, or physical appearance.[1] This definition clearly leaves much room for interpretation, ranging from situations in which group boundaries are relatively defined, as with the Chinese, Indian, and Malay communities in Malaysia, to those where there may be no obvious indicator of ethnic allegiance, as with the issue of mainlander versus native ancestry in Taiwan. In addition, the expanded definitions of ethnicity that have become common in the scholarly literature typically include a range of psychological and relational aspects of identity which are by their very nature difficult to gauge and quantify with confidence.[2] As a result, there is no scholarly consensus on how to measure ethnicity or ethnic diversity, and all approaches that attempt to do so suffer

---

[1] See Anthony D. Smith, *The Ethnic Origins of Nations* (Oxford: Blackwell, 1986).

[2] See, for example, Henry Hale, 'Explaining Ethnicity', *Comparative Political Studies*, 37/4 (2004), 458–85.

from a number of more or less obvious limitations. Mindful of these difficulties, this chapter attempts to assess and analyse the impact of ethnic diversity across Asia and the Pacific.

Diversity and Development

For the purposes of this book, I am interested primarily in ethnicity not as an anthropological or cultural phenomenon but as a political one. This is now common to many social science analyses of the effects of ethnic identity, but it remains relatively unusual when examining these phenomena in the Asia-Pacific region, where anthropology has traditionally dominated many scholarly investigations of ethnicity. Today, there is increasing recognition across disciplinary boundaries of the way in which communal ties can be utilized to achieve political and economic objectives. Under this 'instrumental' approach, ethnicity is viewed not as a manifestation of cultural or ascriptive identity (although it often will be), but rather as a social construct which enables individuals to act collectively to achieve desired outcomes. These can range from community-based objectives, such as the building of a local school, to economic objectives, such as securing a monopoly over a particular resource, to overtly political objectives, such as seeing a chosen candidate elected to parliament. In each case, the key is not the content of ethnic identity but rather the way it is used to achieve desired ends.

Ethnicity's usefulness as a means for achieving such desired ends relies upon individuals' understanding of their collective interests. Where communal ties and other social bonds are weak, the interests of an individual and his or her broader community will often diverge because of the difficulty of achieving coordinated collective action. For example, it may make more sense for an individual to 'free ride' on the work of others rather than to invest a lot of time and energy in something that is going to happen anyway. Conversely, when a good or service can potentially be monopolized by one group alone, there is a strong incentive for that group to engage in 'rent seeking'— 'the socially costly pursuit of wealth transfers'[3]—in order to capitalize on the scarcity value of that good or service. Both activities, free riding and rent seeking, are individually

[3] Robert D. Tollison, 'Rent Seeking', in Dennis Mueller (ed.), *Perspectives on Public Choice: A Handbook* (New York: Cambridge University Press, 1997), 506.

rational and rewarding, but detrimental for society as a whole. As a result, collective action dilemmas are one of the fundamental problems afflicting the provision of public goods in a wide variety of circumstances and contexts.[4]

Commonality of language and cultural identity should, ostensibly, provide a means of surmounting some of these collective action problems. Information and communication flows, for instance, are likely to be much more efficient in monocultural areas where almost everyone speaks the same language—as, for example, in Korea or Samoa—and where leaders can monitor and enforce behavioural norms and punish free riders or other transgressors who attempt to stray from the group line. Problems arise, however, when there is not one ethnic group but many, each attempting to achieve the best outcomes for its own members. Much of eastern Indonesia and Melanesia, for example, comprises hundreds of small ethno-political units based around clan, tribe, and kinship ties. As a result, while coordinated action *within* each group may be possible, collective action dilemmas afflict relations *between* groups. In the absence of external enforcement mechanisms, such as a strong state, ethnic cliques have incentives to act like interest groups for their own members, investing time and resources to secure access to public goods and rent-seeking opportunities for their group alone.

Comparative studies into the impact of linguistic fragmentation enable some quantification of the impact of such collective action problems on state performance. In one of the earliest studies of the impact of linguistic fragmentation, Joshua Fishman found that linguistically more heterogeneous countries had, on average, higher rates of mortality, lower Gross National Product, lower government revenues, fewer students in higher education, lower literacy, and fewer radios, televisions, and newspapers than more homogeneous countries.[5] More recent analyses have confirmed these results and reported similar trends on other development indicators.[6] For instance, looking mostly at Africa,

---

[4] Olson, *The Logic of Collective Action*.

[5] Joshua Fishman, 'Some Contrasts Between Linguistically Homogeneous and Linguistically Heterogeneous Polities', in J. Fishman, C. Ferguson, and J. Das Gupta (eds.), *Language Problems of Developing Nations* (New York: Wiley, 1968).

[6] Daniel Nettle, 'Linguistic Fragmentation and the Wealth of Nations: The Fishman-Pool Hypothesis Reexamined', *Economic Development and Cultural Change*, 49/2 (2000), 335–48.

William Easterly found that more linguistically diverse societies had half the schooling years, one-thirteenth the telephones per worker, twice as many electric power losses, and less than half as many paved roads as more homogeneous ones.[7] These patterns appear to hold true within countries as well as between them: ethnically fragmented municipalities in the United States, for instance, tend to be poorer and provide fewer public goods to their citizens than other, less diverse jurisdictions.[8]

A similar but not identical pattern is evident when many political parties are competing for votes at election time. In such circumstances, the size of each party's support base—specifically, the proportion of the electorate each party relies on for votes—will often be relatively small. Such parties can thus succeed by wooing voters on the basis of particularistic policy platforms that promise to reward specific groups or regions. In such circumstances, parties can concentrate on mobilizing their supporters by providing clientelistic rewards and selective incentives rather than broader public policies. By contrast, larger parties that appeal for votes on a bridging basis in order to win elections outright need a different strategy: they can best reward their many supporters by investing available resources in public, rather than private, goods. When this happens, everyone benefits. Thus, larger coalitions of groups or parties 'encourage attention to the quality of public policy' and, by extension, to development.[9]

The findings of the burgeoning academic literature on this subject tend to be reinforcing. Whether the focus is on ethnic, linguistic, regional or political divisions, scholarly studies by developmental economists and political scientists alike find consistently that greater social fragmentation leads to lower provision of public goods. Under this interpretation, diversity hinders development in part because of its impact on the conduct of competitive politics. These findings have considerable relevance for the Asia-Pacific region—particularly, Southeast Asia and the Pacific Islands, where social cleavages not only have great political salience but also vary greatly both between and

---

[7] William Easterly, *The Elusive Quest for Growth: Economists' Adventures and Misadventures in the Tropics* (Cambridge, MA and London: MIT Press, 2001).

[8] See Alesina, Baqir, and Easterly, 'Public Goods and Ethnic Divisions'.

[9] See Bruce Bueno de Mesquita, James D. Morrow, Randolph Silverson, and Alastair Smith, 'Political Competition and Economic Growth', *Journal of Democracy*, 12/1 (2001), 58–72.

within states. To assess the differential impact of social fragmentation on the region's political and economic development, we therefore need to consider how to measure meaningfully the level of diversity across and within different Asia-Pacific states—a subject to which I now turn.

Measuring Diversity

Studying the independent impact of social diversity on state performance is no straightforward task. For one thing, measuring the diversity of any given state requires choices to be made about what measure of social fragmentation is most appropriate and which identities and cultural distinctions are considered to be salient at a particular point in time.[10] In addition, ethnicity itself is a notoriously slippery concept, widely considered to be manifested as a mixture of primordial and constructed factors.[11] In other words, it can be seen both as an ascriptive phenomenon, based on socio-biological traits, such as race, tribe, and language—a position often characterized in the scholarly literature as 'primordialism'—as well as an adaptive expression of more malleable or constructed identities formed in reaction to external pressures and incentives—'constructivism', to use the academic shorthand.[12]

Studying the cross-national effects of diversity also requires a common measurement of relevant social cleavages in order to undertake cross-country comparisons. However, the complexities and subtleties of quantifying such cleavages have bedevilled attempts to arrive at a uniform measure of social diversity. The most widely used measure to date has been an index of ethnic and linguistic fractionalization (ELF) compiled by a Russian

[10] For a convincing analysis of the way different identities can be utilized for political gain, see Daniel N. Posner, *Institutions and Ethnic Politics in Africa* (New York: Cambridge University Press, 2005).

[11] The term primordialism is usually associated with Clifford Geertz (ed.), *Old Societies and New States: The Quest for Modernity in Asia and Africa* (New York: Free Press, 1967). For a discussion of this typology, see Milton Esman, *Ethnic Politics* (Ithaca, NY: Cornell University Press, 1994), 9–16.

[12] There is a considerable literature on ethnicity and ethnic identity. See Crawford Young, *The Politics of Cultural Pluralism* (Madison, WI: University of Wisconsin Press, 1976); Paul Brass (ed.), *Ethnic Groups and the State* (London: Croom Helm, 1985); Smith, *The Ethnic Origin of Nations*; Horowitz, *Ethnic Groups in Conflict*; Esman, *Ethnic Politics*.

anthropological survey in the 1960s, *Atlas Narodov Mira* ('The Atlas of the Peoples of the World'), which claimed to measure the salient ethnic cleavages in 129 different countries.[13] The *Narodov Mira* data was used as a source by Charles L. Taylor and Michael C. Hudson in their 1972 *World Handbook of Political and Social Indicators*, and subsequently by dozens of scholarly studies which used this data source as their principal reference point.[14]

Researchers have found a consistent negative relationship between ELF and development. In one prominent case, a World Bank study of economic growth in Africa found that ELF was negatively correlated with economic growth, per capita schooling attainment, availability of public infrastructure, and sound government policies, prompting the authors to identify ethnic fragmentation as the key to Africa's 'growth tragedy'.[15] Another study by the economist Dani Rodrik, which looked at all regions of the world, found that ethnic fragmentation was independently associated with a range of negative outcomes, including lower economic growth rates and higher levels of income inequality.[16] Incorporating social and political indicators as well as economic ones, other economists reported similar findings.[17] Paolo Mauro, for instance, concluded that fragmented societies had a strong tendency towards corruption in part because of the tendency of members of ethnic groups to favour their own kin.[18]

Why should social diversity be associated with so many poor outcomes? Whilst a number of competing theories have been put forward, most explanations boil down to the deleterious effects of

[13] See *Atlas Narodov Mira* (Moscow: The N.N. Miklukho-Maklaya Institute of Ethnography for the Academy of Sciences, Department of Geodesy and Cartography of the State Geological Committee of the USSR, 1964).
[14] See Charles L. Taylor and Michael C. Hudson, *World Handbook of Political and Social Indicators* (New Haven, CT: Yale University Press, 1972); Charles L. Taylor and David A. Jodice, *World Handbook of Political and Social Indicators* (New Haven, CT: Yale University Press, 1983).
[15] William Easterly and Ross Levine, 'Africa's Growth Tragedy: Policies and Ethnic Divisions', *Quarterly Journal of Economics*, 112/4 (1997), 1203–50.
[16] Dani Rodrik, 'Where Did All the Growth Go? External Shocks, Social Conflict, and Growth Collapses', *Journal of Economic Growth*, 4/4 (1999), 385–412.
[17] Johannes Fedderke and Robert Klitgaard, 'Economic Growth and Social Indicators: An Exploratory Analysis', *Economic Development and Cultural Change*, 46/3 (1998), 455–89.
[18] Paolo Mauro, 'Corruption and Growth', *Quarterly Journal of Economics*, 110/3 (1995), 681–712.

ethnic fragmentation on economic growth. Linguistic explanations focus on the coordination problems created by many different languages, thereby limiting trade, handicapping efficient markets, and undermining prospects for social cooperation. Explanations focused on communal divisions add to these several specific effects of economic and political competition for power and resources. First, in more ethnically heterogeneous states, sound macroeconomic policy is often made subservient to the rent-seeking ambitions of communal cliques, who focus their energies on wealth redistribution rather than wealth creation. Second, growth-promoting public infrastructure like health and education will often be undersupplied in more heterogeneous states because of the difficulties of reaching agreement on the provision of such public goods across ethnic lines. Third, ethnically-diverse societies typically spawn fragmented or personalized party systems—which have important independent impacts of their own. Finally, ethnic and linguistic fragmentation is negatively related to the development of 'social capital', the network of civic bonds and associations increasingly posited as underpinning good economic and political performance.[19]

Despite its widespread use, increasing doubts have been raised about the utility of measuring ethno-linguistic fragmentation via the Russian data. The ELF index is prone to numerous errors of both omission and commission, and has come under sustained criticism by political scientists due to the inadequacy of the often idiosyncratic *Naradov Mira* data-set, as well as the problems inherent in any attempt to capture a dynamic and socially-constructed phenomena such as ethnicity in a single, static index.[20] This has led to a revised focus by scholars on the adequacy of existing data sources on this subject, and the development of a number of new indices of ethnic and cultural diversity in recent years.

Probably the most useful such index for our purposes is the one produced by James Fearon of Stanford University. Fearon uses a

---

[19] On this final point, see Putnam, *Making Democracy Work*. For an influential application of social capital theory to the ethnic conflict literature, see Ashutosh Varshney, *Ethnic Conflict and Civil Life: Hindus and Muslims in India* (New Haven, CT and London: Yale University Press, 2002).

[20] See Benjamin Reilly, 'Democracy, Ethnic Fragmentation, and Internal Conflict: Confused Theories, Faulty Data, and the "Crucial Case" of Papua New Guinea', *International Security*, 25/3 (2000), 162–85; Daniel N. Posner, 'Measuring Ethnic Fractionalization in Africa', *American Journal of Political Science*, 48/4 (2004), 849–63.

range of contemporary sources and a new coding methodology combining both 'prototypical' (such as a group's belief in their common descent and history) and 'objective' (such as language, religion, or custom) characteristics to arrive at a new index of 'ethnic and cultural diversity' covering some 160 countries.[21] Like ELF, Fearon's diversity index effectively measures the probability of two randomly drawn citizens within a country being members of different ethnic or linguistic groups, represented as a measure of ethnic heterogeneity ranging from 0 (completely homogeneous) to 1 (completely heterogeneous).[22]

In the following analysis of the relationship between diversity and development in the Asia-Pacific, I use Fearon's data-set as the independent variable measuring the overall level of social diversity in each country. For the dependent variable, measuring each country's level of development, again a range of data is available. One of the simplest is per capita gross national income (GNI), as presented in Table 2.1, which is widely available and easily understood. However, a better, more comprehensive measure for our purposes is each country's level of 'human development', as calculated by the UNDP's human development index (HDI). The HDI is an aggregate collection of social and economic indicators, such as life expectancy, literacy, education, and per capita income which together provide a composite measure of a country's overall human development.[23] The following analysis therefore uses Fearon's index of social diversity as the independent variable, and the HDI as the dependent variable.

Again, a cautionary note is in order: while these may be the best measures of diversity and development available, neither is perfect. In countries such as Korea, for instance, social cleavages are not based around ethno-linguistic variables but around other issues, such as regionalism, which are not captured by this measure. In other cases such as Taiwan, these cleavages are relevant to the extent that they reflect deeper political divisions over national identity.[24] As with all such exercises,

---

[21] James D. Fearon, 'Ethnic and Cultural Diversity by Country', *Journal of Economic Growth*, 8 (2003), 195–222.

[22] A measure first developed by Douglas W. Rae and Michael Taylor, *The Analysis of Political Cleavages* (New Haven, CT: Yale University Press, 1970).

[23] United Nations Development Programme, *Human Development Report 2004* (New York: United Nations Development Programme, 2004).

[24] As it happens, there does appear to be a clear correlation between ethnic and national identity issues in Taiwan. See Hsieh, 'Continuity and Change', 48 (fn).

Fearon's index also includes some questionable classifications: the majority population in the Philippines, for instance, is categorized as 'lowland Christian Malays', which effectively elides many salient subnational ethno-linguistic cleavages. Finally, Fearon's data, like most comparative data-sets on ethnic and linguistic diversity, ignores some smaller countries such as Brunei and most of the Pacific Islands.[25]

To deal with these shortcomings, I have re-calculated diversity figures for the Philippines and Brunei from other reliable data sources.[26] For the Pacific Islands, I have constructed my own index of ethno-linguistic diversity based on each country's level of linguistic fragmentation in the *Ethnologue* database of languages spoken around the world.[27] Again, this information is captured in a 'diversity index' measuring the probability of two random strangers speaking a different language, which ranges from 0 (a completely homogeneous country where every individual speaks the same language) to 1 (a completely heterogeneous country where every individual speaks a different language). While crude, this information is relatively easy to quantify, and is a good way of capturing each country's *relative* degree of homogeneity or heterogeneity when used as a comparative measure. Table 3.1 therefore makes use of Fearon's data for all Asian countries bar the Philippines and Brunei, but uses data from the *Ethnologue* ranking of linguistic diversity for the five Pacific countries of Fiji, Papua New Guinea, Samoa, Solomon Islands, and Vanuatu.

As Table 3.1 shows, there is enormous variation in diversity levels across the Asia-Pacific region as a whole. At one extreme, classic nation states such as Japan, Korea, and Samoa are all highly homogeneous in societal terms, with a 1 per cent chance or less of any random individual being from a different group to his or her compatriots. At the other extreme, there is a 99 per cent probability that any two randomly chosen individuals in Papua New Guinea will hail from different ethno-linguistic

---

[25] Fiji and Papua New Guinea are the only Pacific countries included in Fearon's paper. Papua New Guinea's fragmentation level is such that Fearon excludes it from his analysis altogether, acknowledging instead that 'Papua New Guinea approximates a perfectly fractionalized state' ('Ethnic and Cultural Diversity', 205).

[26] Data from Asian-Pacific Cultural Center, *A Handbook of Asian-Pacific Countries and Regions* (Taipei: Asian-Pacific Cultural Center, 1995).

[27] See Barbara Grimes (ed.), *Ethnologue: Languages of the World* (Dallas, TX: SIL International, 2002).

TABLE 3.1. *Diversity and development in Asia and the Pacific*

Asian states	Ethnic and cultural diversity	Human development 2004
Brunei	0.265	.867
Burma	0.522	.551
Cambodia	0.186	.568
China	0.154	.721
East Timor	0.880	.436
Indonesia	0.766	.692
Japan	0.009	.938
Korea	0.004	.888
Laos	0.481	.534
Malaysia	0.596	.793
Philippines	0.740	.753
Singapore	0.388	.902
Taiwan	0.274	—
Thailand	0.431	.768
Vietnam	0.233	.691
Pacific states	Linguistic diversity	Human development 2004
Fiji	0.600	.758
Papua New Guinea	0.990	.542
Samoa	0.010	.769
Solomon Is.	0.970	.624
Vanuatu	0.970	.570

Sources: Fearon, 'Ethnic and Cultural Diversity'; Grimes, *Ethnologue*; Asian-Pacific Cultural Center, *Handbook*; United Nations Development Program, *Human Development Report 2004*.

groups, and similarly high rates of diversity in East Timor, Indonesia, the Philippines, Solomon Islands, and Vanuatu.

Strikingly, when the two measures of social diversity and human development are compared, there is a very clear relationship between them. As the scattergram at Figure 3.1 shows, across the Asia-Pacific region social diversity is negatively related to human development. The Pearson correlation between these two variables is $-.61$, statistically significant at the 1 per cent level—a strong and significant relationship by contemporary social science standards. Moreover, although questions of causality remain open, the most plausible explanation for this relationship is clearly that human development is affected by the degree of social diversity in each state rather than development somehow causing variation in objective measures of heterogeneity. Overall, the model suggests that over one-third of the variance in human development in the Asia-Pacific can be explained simply by differences in social diversity from state to state.

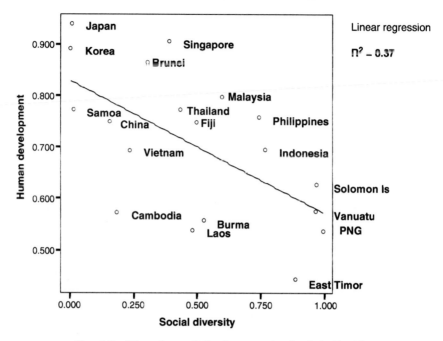

FIG. 3.1. *Diversity and development in the Asia-Pacific*

This pattern is repeated at a subnational level too. In almost all the cases investigated in this book, regions with higher levels of ethnic diversity display appreciably lower development than more homogeneous ones, even within the same country. Thus, Malaysia's eastern states of Sabah and Sarawak, which are more fragmented than other parts of the country due to the inter-mixture of Malays, Chinese, Dyaks, and other indigenous communities, score lower on almost every indicator of prosperity than those of peninsula Malaysia.[28] In Indonesia, levels of per capita income, educational attainment, adult literacy, and human development fall as one moves from west to east through the archipelago, tracking almost exactly the corresponding rise in ethnic diversity as the Malay hegemony of Sumatra and Java give way to the increasingly fragmented regions of Nusa Tenggara, Maluku, and Papua.[29] In Thailand, the urbanized central

[28] James Chin, 'Politics of Federal Intervention in Malaysia, with Reference to Kelantan, Sarawak, and Sabah', *Journal of Commonwealth and Comparative Politics*, 35/2 (1997), 96–120.

[29] See United Nations Development Programme, *Indonesia Human Development Report 2001* (Jakarta: BPS-Statistics Indonesia, Bappenas and UNDP, 2001), 72.

part of the country is considerably more prosperous than the fragmented highland peripheries of the north and north-east— the same areas where vote-buying and patron-client politics have traditionally been most pronounced.[30] In Papua New Guinea, more ethnically-diverse provinces have significantly lower development levels than the norm, even when controlling for factors such as population, geographic size, government per- formance, and land resources.[31]

The scattered island states of the South Pacific also appear to follow this pattern. Thus small, isolated but socially homoge- neous Polynesian states, such as Samoa, fare better on almost every development indicator than larger but more heteroge- neous Melanesia states such as Vanuatu and the Solomon Islands. Of course, a range of alternative explanations could be advanced to explain this disparity: the differences in both population and geographic size of different countries, the much larger natural resource endowments of Melanesia, proximity to potential markets in Asia and Australia, and so on. However, on most of these measures the larger, better-resourced Melanes- ian states should be at an advantage compared to their smaller and more isolated Polynesian counterparts. Yet despite these inherent advantages, the relatively large, populous and resource-rich states of Melanesia have performed more poorly across the board (with the exception of Fiji, with its large Indo-Fijian population).[32]

How do we account for this consistent negative relationship between social diversity and government performance? One explanation already alluded is the difficulty of delivering public services and infrastructure in the face of competing ethno-linguistic demands. In Papua New Guinea, for example, ethno-political units based upon traditional clan allegiances often form the basis of rival electoral 'vote banks', meaning that in many cases politicians see their primary role not as members of a national government but more as clan delegates, whose main responsibility is to channel government resources back to their own ethnic supporters. In such cases, they have less incentive to invest in genuinely public infrastructure—that is, infrastructure

---

[30] Anek Laothamatas, 'A Tale of Two Democracies: Conflicting Perceptions of Elections and Democracy in Thailand', in Taylor, *The Politics of Elections*, 201–33.
[31] See Benjamin Reilly, 'Ethnicity, Democracy and Development in Papua New Guinea', *Pacific Economic Bulletin*, 19/1 (2004), 46–54.
[32] See Reilly, 'State Functioning and State Failure'.

which benefits everyone, regardless of their ethnic ties—than would be the case in a more homogeneous society. The result is lower provision of many public resources, and hence poorer developmental outcomes, for society as a whole.

Understanding the underlying impact of ethnic fragmentation on state capacity thus helps to explain the relatively poor developmental performance of the socially diverse states of maritime Southeast Asia and the Southwest Pacific. Despite abundant resource endowments, it should therefore be no surprise that these states have struggled to deliver national development in the face of a multitude of competing ethno-political demands. Of course, there are many other explanations for this pattern as well: the 'resource curse' literature, for example, argues that it is the bountiful resource endowments of these countries that leads to rent-seeking behaviour rather than their ethnic divisions.[33] Nonetheless, this initial inquiry does suggest that social structure is an important part of the explanation for the enormous disparities in human development across the Asia-Pacific.

Ethnicity and Democracy

While the consequences of ethno-linguistic fragmentation are apparently detrimental to human development, what about the *political* impacts of heterogeneity—that is, the impact of social diversity on a country's regime type and its propensity for democratic or autocratic government? Here, the comparative literature is more nuanced. Although few scholars argue that ethnic divisions are a positive attribute for stable politics, there is an ongoing debate about whether ethnic heterogeneity serves to help or hinder democracy.

A common contention in the scholarly literature for many years has been that increasing ethnic fragmentation makes democratic government more difficult. Since at least the 1960s, a series of cross-national investigations into the effect of ethnic heterogeneity on political stability concluded that as the number of ethnic groups in a state increases, the prospects for sustainable democracy falls. One of the first such studies, Robert Dahl's *Polyarchy*, concluded that although democracy in highly

[33] See Michael L. Ross, *Timber Booms and Institutional Breakdown in Southeast Asia* (New York: Cambridge University Press, 2001).

fragmented countries was not impossible, 'pluralism often places a dangerous strain on the tolerance and mutual security required for a system of public contestation', and hence 'a competitive political system is less likely in countries with a considerable measure of subcultural pluralism'.[34] Around the same time, Alvin Rabushka and Kenneth Shepsle found that one of the 'striking regularities' amongst ethnically fragmented societies was that 'democracy frequently gives way to forms of authoritarian rule'.[35] Lijphart argued in his work on consociational democracy, *Democracy in Plural Societies*, that the optimal number of groups for peaceful conflict management is three or four, with conditions becoming progressively less favourable as numbers rise because 'co-operation among groups becomes more difficult as the number participating in negotiations increases'.[36] In a cross-national multivariate analysis of factors affecting democratic prospects, G. Bingham Powell similarly found a strong relationship between ethnic fractionalization and government instability, with less stability correlated with higher ethnic fractionalization.[37]

More recent cross-national studies have also found a negative correlation between ethnic diversity and democratic persistence.[38] In general, there is still a common presumption that 'ethnic hatreds' created by communal cleavages are the chief cause of ethnic conflict, making it 'reasonable to suppose that, *ceteris paribus*, the extent of intra-societal ethnic and religious hatred is related to the extent of their respective degrees of fractionalization'.[39] This presumption extends across the social sciences: 'Both economists and social scientists have postulated that such fractionalization is unambiguously conflict-enhancing.'[40] For example, Freedom House has claimed that 'countries without a predominant ethnic majority are less successful in establishing open and democratic societies than

---

[34] Dahl, *Polyarchy*, 109–11.

[35] Alvin Rabushka and Kenneth Shepsle, *Politics in Plural Societies: A Theory of Democratic Instability* (Colombus, OH: Merrill, 1972), 177–8.

[36] Lijphart, *Democracy in Plural Societies*, 56.

[37] Powell, *Contemporary Democracies*, 44–6.

[38] See Jan-Erik Lane and Svante Ersson, *Comparative Political Economy* (London: Pinter, 1990), 138; Axel Hadenius, *Democracy and Development* (Cambridge: Cambridge University Press, 1992), 116–17.

[39] Paul Collier, *The Economics of Civil War* (Washington, DC: World Bank Monograph, 1998), 3.

[40] Paul Collier and Anke Hoeffler, 'On Economic Causes of Civil War', *Oxford Economic Papers*, 50/4 (1998), 571.

ethnically homogeneous countries', and that mono-ethnic countries are twice as likely to be ranked 'free' as multi-ethnic ones.[41]

By contrast, other scholars argue that ethnic fragmentation may in some circumstances actually assist prospects for democracy in multi-ethnic states. In cases where there are many small and geographically concentrated groups, for example, it may make little sense for them to devote energy to political activity much beyond their locality—meaning that, 'from the standpoint of ethnic conflict, much of the pressure is off the center'.[42] Thus one explanation for the democratic success of India has in large part been the product of that diversity itself, 'for at the national level...no single ethnic group can dominate'.[43] Others have interpreted the democratic record of the Philippines as being facilitated 'by ethnic compositions which make it difficult for any single ethnic group to predominate', thereby encouraging the formation of multi-ethnic alliances.[44] In the same manner as those who contend that ethnic fragmentation and democracy are negatively related, these scholars can also point to large-N confirming studies, such as one statistical analysis that reported 'little sign of any particularly detrimental effects of ethnic and religious fragmentation on state stability and performance'.[45]

There are several ways to test this debate in the Asia-Pacific region. An obvious starting point is to examine the extent of correlation between the two variables. Using the Freedom House political rights and civil liberty scores from Table 2.1, Table 3.2 compares those Asia-Pacific countries which can be classified as 'democratic' (those with an average Freedom House score of less than 3.5) to those classed as 'non-democratic' (average scores of 3.5 and over).[46] Each country is also classified

[41] See Adrian Karatnycky, 'The 1998 Freedom House Survey: The Decline of Illiberal Democracy', *Journal of Democracy*, 10/1 (1999), 117–18; Freedom House, *Freedom in the World: The Annual Survey of Political Rights and Civil Liberties 1998–1999* (New York: Freedom House, 1999), 9–10.

[42] Horowitz, *Ethnic Groups in Conflict*, 37.

[43] Robert L. Hardgrave Jr., 'India: the Dilemmas of Diversity', in Larry Diamond and Marc F. Plattner (eds.), *Nationalism, Ethnic Conflict and Democracy* (Baltimore, MD: Johns Hopkins University Press, 1994), 72.

[44] Harold Crouch, 'Democratic Prospects in Indonesia', *Asian Journal of Political Science*, 1/2 (1993), 83.

[45] Jan-Erik Lane and Svante Ersson, *Comparative Politics: An Introduction and a New Approach* (Cambridge: Polity Press, 1994), 204.

[46] Freedom House ranks each country's political rights and civil liberties on a scale of 1 to 7, with 1 representing the highest degree of freedom present and 7 the lowest.

TABLE 3.2. *Democracy and ethnic structure in Asia and the Pacific*

	Homogeneous (diversity <0.33)	Polarized (diversity 0.33–0.67)	Fragmented (diversity >0.67)
Democratic (FH <3.5)	Japan Korea Taiwan Samoa	Thailand	East Timor Indonesia Papua New Guinea Philippines Solomon Islands Vanuatu
Non-democratic (FH >3.5)	Brunei China Cambodia Vietnam	Burma Fiji Laos Malaysia Singapore	

Source: Tables 2.1 and 3.1.

according to its level of social diversity from the Fearon index into three categories: 'homogeneous' (those countries with a diversity score of less than 0.33), 'polarized' (those between 0.33 and 0.67), and 'fragmented' (those with a score greater than 0.67).

As the table shows, the Asia-Pacific offers little support for the claim that ethnic heterogeneity hampers democracy. Indeed, the opposite appears to be the case: the region's most socially diverse states are all democracies, as are many of the more homogeneous cases. The problems for democracy appear to be greatest in polarized societies—which suggests that the most dangerous situation for democracy is not one of ethnic fragmentation, but rather where there is at least one group which can potentially control power alone, as in Fiji or Malaysia. Such a bi-polar social structure is also, as it happens, one of the strongest comparative predictors of civil war.[47] Overall, Table 3.2 suggests that the relationship between democracy and diversity in the Asia-Pacific is essentially U-shaped: while there are a number of examples of ethnically homogeneous countries in both the democratic and non-democratic categories, there are no democracies in the polarized category and no non-democracies in the fragmented category (the one exception, Thailand, falls into the polarized

[47] Collier and Hoeffler, 'On Economic Causes of Civil War'.

category on the basis of the Fearon data, but in reality contains a core majority of Buddhist Thais and a number of smaller ethno-religious minorities).

In sum, the evidence suggests that the ethnic structure of some countries is more favourable for the maintenance of democracy than others. In particular, a balanced form of ethnic diversity, where no group can command an absolute majority of the population and assume the capacity to dominate others, appears to be a positive feature for democratic continuity. Such an ethnic structure may contribute to interethnic harmony by making national government dependent on inter-ethnic bargaining—a process inherently compatible with democracy. As David Wurfel argues, this means that poor but diverse states such as the Philippines or East Timor may be at a structural advantage in ethno-political terms: in both cases, no group constitutes more than about a quarter of the population, and in neither is there a history of one ethnic group dominating others. Rather, the fragmented ethnic arithmetic of both states may enable a 'supra-ethnic' sense of nationhood based on civic rather than communal identity to emerge.[48]

Given that we have already established that social fragmentation is negatively related to most indicators of development, it may be surprising that this same factor also appears to be positively related to democratic continuity. There is, after all, a strong connection more generally between regime type and economic development: most of the world's long-term democracies are wealthy countries, and rising per capita income is one of the best predictors of a transition to democracy.[49] How then is it possible that democracy can co-exist with poor government effectiveness, persistent economic underperformance, and declining prosperity?

Case Study: Papua New Guinea

To answer this question, consider the case of Papua New Guinea, one of the most ethno-linguistically diverse and least-developed

---

[48] David Wurfel, 'Democracy, Nationalism and Ethnic Identity: The Philippines and East Timor Compared' in Henders, *Democratization and Identity*, 204.
[49] The classic statement of this is Seymour Martin Lipset, *Political Man: The Social Basis of Politics* (New York: Doubleday, 1960). For an application of this argument to the Asia-Pacific see Morley, *Driven by Growth*.

countries in the Asia-Pacific region. Despite this Papua New Guinea has one of the longest democratic records of any developing country, with over forty years of continuous democratic elections, all of them characterized by high levels of participation and candidature, as well as numerous peaceful changes of government. However, the per capita income of the average citizen is lower today than it was at independence over thirty years ago. One reason for this lies in the way the political system works. Electoral politics in Papua New Guinea, as in many other developing countries, is primarily a competition for access to the state. In combination with its exceptionally high number of ethno-linguistic groups and a plurality electoral system, this results in frantic and often violent competition for elected office. At the 2002 elections, for example, an average of twenty-seven candidates stood in each constituency, and most winners gained office on less than 20 per cent of the vote as supporters split along clan and tribal lines.[50] Most voters expect that these successful candidates will use political office to extract resources from the government and deliver them back to their supporters—not to the country at large or even to all of their electorate, but to the much smaller group of clan members who voted for them and to whom they now need to distribute the rewards of office to maintain support for the next election.[51]

Such naked ethno-political clientelism has created a vicious cycle of particularistic politics in Papua New Guinea, as ethno-linguistic units play the role of interest groups seeking to secure benefits for their members, thus undermining the broader prospects for the country as a whole. Rent-seeking has flourished, as tribal groups attempt to monopolize any potential public good for their own ends. Political time horizons are short, with most parliamentarians lasting only a single term in office, so productive investments are curtailed as newly elected politicians focus their energies on short-term wealth distribution to shore up their supporter base rather than long-term wealth creation. The result is that public goods are increasingly diverted towards the private enrichment of political entrepreneurs

[50] Results from the PNG Electoral Commission, www.pngec.gov.pg.

[51] For a useful discussion, see Henry Okole, 'Papua New Guinea's Brand of Westminster: Democratic Traditions Overlaying Melanesian Cultures', in Haig Patapan, John Wanna, and Patrick Weller (eds.), *Westminster Legacies: Democracy and Responsible Government in Asia and the Pacific* (Kensington: University of New South Wales Press, 2005).

and the small ethnic interest groups they represent. For example, in November 2002, it was revealed that a former finance minister had granted approval to seven major new national road projects during his term in office—six of which were in his own electorate![52]

The acute fragmentation of Papua New Guinea's electorate thus has direct public policy implications. Beneficial outcomes for society at large are overwhelmed by a collective action problem created by several thousand small ethnic collectives competing with each other for resources, prestige, and public goods. By my calculations, the members elected to Papua New Guinea's 2002 parliament under plurality rules received the support of just 16 per cent of the electorate: 84 per cent of voters cast their ballot for losing candidates. Voter support levels for the government (i.e. the ruling coalition) are lower still, at less than 10 per cent—compared to an average of around 45 per cent across other established democracies.[53] Again, this has policy implications: regimes which rely on the support of only a small proportion of the population in general display much weaker economic growth rates than more broadly supported ones, as governments need to reward only a small proportion of the electorate to secure their re-election.[54] Encouraging the election of more broadly supported candidates is thus an issue that touches directly on wider issues of economic growth and development. In response to this ongoing institutional decay, in 2002 the Papua New Guinea government passed a package of electoral and party reforms (discussed in more detail later in this book) to encourage more broadly supported candidates, cohesive political parties, and stable executive coalitions.

In summary, Papua New Guinea's forty years of continuous democracy has not brought development to the majority of its people—quite the contrary. Rather, the imposition of modern

[52] See 'Kumbakor Gets Tongue Lashing', *PNG Post-Courier*, 15–17 November 2002.

[53] G. Bingham Powell, *Elections as Instruments of Democracy: Majoritarian and Proportional Visions* (New Haven, CT and London: Yale University Press, 2000), 236.

[54] See Bueno de Mesquita et al., 'Political Competition and Economic Growth'. Although this piece focuses on the link between economic stagnation and non-democratic regimes dependent for their support on a small 'winning coalition', its basic arguments can also be applied to democratic countries like Papua New Guinea, in which the government's electoral support comes from only a small fraction of the electorate.

representative politics onto a fragmented, clan-based society has led to a retribalization of political life, as clan and linguistic allegiances become the primary vehicle for attaining and maintaining political power, leading to a precipitous decline in prosperity. In most countries, such a decline usually leads to some kind of coup or other overthrow of the existing regime.[55] However, Papua New Guinea's extraordinary level of ethno-linguistic diversity makes all forms of collective action difficult, with the consequence that even though there may be widespread dissatisfaction with the way the political system works, it is nevertheless unlikely that any one group will ever be able to amass sufficient collective support to overthrow the state. Although it has not delivered much in the way of development, Papua New Guinea's democratic political system therefore persists—in part through its own inertia and the formidable problems in producing a realistic alternative. The Papua New Guinea case thus provides a striking example of how a dysfunctional political system can nonetheless come to comprise something of an inefficient equilibrium. As Douglas North has observed, just as successful institutions help create the conditions for their own persistence, so 'institutions that provide disincentives to productive activity will create organizations and interest groups with a stake in the existing constraints. They will shape the polity in their interests.'[56]

Conclusion

The accumulated evidence of this chapter raises several challenges to our understanding of the relationship between ethnicity, democracy, and development. First, it suggests that the conventional wisdom positing a link between social diversity and democratic instability—what Lane and Ersson typified as 'the common sense notion' that ethno-linguistic heterogeneity and democracy are negatively related—is misconceived.[57] In some circumstances, a high degree of ethnic pluralism may actually *assist* democratic continuity if no group can act as a hegemon and control power alone. As the Papua New Guinea

[55] See John B. Londregan and Keith T. Poole, 'Poverty, the Coup Trap, and the Seizure of Executive Power', *World Politics*, 42 (1990), 151–83.

[56] Douglas North, *Institutions, Institutional Change and Economic Performance* (Cambridge: Cambridge University Press, 1990), 99.

[57] Lane and Ersson, *Comparative Politics*, 204.

case illustrates, even as it undermines effective governance, a highly fragmented society can also help to safeguard democratic regimes from extra-constitutional threats, such as coups, if no group has the organizational capacity to threaten the state. Reinforcing this conclusion, the comparative analysis of Asia-Pacific democracies presented in this chapter suggests that the broader relationship between ethnic fragmentation and democracy is U-shaped rather than linear, with both low (i.e. homogeneous) and high (i.e. heterogeneous) levels of social diversity more conducive to democracy than those in between. All of this casts doubt on the conventional wisdom that ethnic diversity undermines stable democracy.

The evidence of this chapter also presents something of a challenge to facile presumptions about the relationship between democracy and development, which tend to assume that all good things go together, and that a functioning democracy will, over time, generate increasing economic development or, if not, will be overthrown and replaced by another form of regime. As the Papua New Guinea example indicates, neither of these outcomes is likely in situations where the electoral process facilitates the mobilization of social cleavages and the victory of ethnic representatives who seek to divert public goods to their own narrow support base.

This suggests two potentially relevant insights. First, competitive democracy will not generate public goods if social groups can use the electoral process to secure their own interests at the expense of others. Second, formal democracy can survive in the face of both ethnic fragmentation and underdevelopment, but without necessarily overcoming or generating solutions to either of these afflictions. In fact, the three can co-exist as long as the logic of collective action leads to divergent outcomes at the local and national levels. Papua New Guinea is one example of this kind of inefficient equilibrium; the Philippines provides perhaps another. There, democracy in both its pre- and post-Marcos manifestations has been dominated by a self-serving elite who have milked the resources of the state for their own benefit, and maintained power through the politics of patronage, while delivering precious little in the way of development.[58] Instead,

---

[58] For an analysis of the Philippines' 'democratic deficit', see Paul D. Hutchcroft and Joel Rocamora, 'Strong Demands and Weak Institutions: The Origins and Evolution of the Democratic Deficit in the Philippines', *Journal of East Asian Studies*, 3 (2003), 259–92.

elections have reinforced patterns of ethnic clientelism, with targeted side-payments to key electoral constituencies supplanting the provision of genuinely public goods.[59]

These observations have important implications for political engineers, and specifically for the engineering of democratic institutions such as electoral systems and political parties. By 'distributing things of value', politicians in any democratic system must form coalitions to win office, but as the size of winning coalitions increase, incumbents face increasing incentives to pour resources into public rather than private goods. Where a small number of large, nationally focused political parties compete for office, they need the support of different social groups and classes to secure victory. Any winning coalition of their supporters is thus likely to comprise a substantial proportion of the electorate as a whole. As a result, such arrangements 'create a stronger push for leaders to provide good policies than do other systems with smaller winning coalitions'.[60] Under conditions of party fragmentation, by contrast, a lesser proportion of votes is needed to win a seat, winning coalitions can thus be smaller—sometimes, much smaller—and some parties may be able to achieve office simply by mobilizing their own narrow base and providing private goods to their supporters alone. Supporting these conclusions, comparative research has found that fragmented party systems are associated with lower overall levels of economic development than more aggregated party constellations.[61]

This insight into the different developmental trajectories of aggregative versus fragmented political systems implies several potential institutional reform strategies to counter and combat these perverse outcomes. Most obviously, it suggests that the best way to facilitate development in new democracies may be to encourage the development of broad, aggregative, catch-all political parties—parties 'oriented to programmatic rather than particularistic goals, policy rather than pork'[62]—while

---

[59] See Carl Landé, *Leaders, Factions and Parties: The Structure of Philippine Politics* (New Haven, CT: Yale University Southeast Asia Monograph No. 6, 1965).

[60] Bruce Bueno de Mesquita, James D. Morrow, Randolph Silverson, and Alastair Smith, 'Political Institutions, Political Survival, and Policy Success', in Bruce Bueno de Mesquita and Hilton L. Root (eds.), *Governing for Prosperity* (New Haven, CT: Yale University Press, 2000), 67.

[61] Powell, *Comparative Democracies*, 101.

[62] Hutchcroft and Rocamora, 'Strong Demands and Weak Institutions', 259.

discouraging parties based around narrow ethnic, regional, or other cleavages. In practical terms, this means that electoral and party laws should be relatively majoritarian in practice, so as to encourage parties to widen their voter appeals via broad-based campaign strategies. Hence Norris argues that 'moves towards more majoritarian arrangements should mitigate some of the problems experienced in countries suffering currently from the dangers of excessively unstable, undisciplined, and fragmented party competition'.[63] However, in a move away from classic majoritarian theory, the evidence of this chapter also suggests that winning coalitions—and executive governments— in ethnically diverse societies should be as inclusive as possible, so as to secure broader representation of social interests within government, and hence enhance political stability.

As we shall see in the second part of this book, these are precisely the strategies adopted by many Asian and Pacific governments in their democratic reforms of recent years. The experience of these states also highlights some of the strengths and weaknesses of the different approaches to political engineer- ing advocated in the scholarly literature. To investigate these, the following chapter examines the various approaches to political engineering in more detail. It looks at the theoretical and empirical record of the three most influential scholarly models of political engineering for ethnically diverse societies— consociationalism, centripetalism, and communalism—and evaluates the claims made by proponents and opponents of each. It also looks at how Asian and Pacific states have contrib- uted directly to the evolution of these various institutional models through their own distinctive approaches to political engineering.

---

[63] Norris, *Electoral Engineering*, 254–5.

4

Political Engineering:
Consociationalism, Centripetalism,
and Communalism

Asia-Pacific regimes have responded in different ways to the reality of ethnic diversity in their societies. The most draconian political response has been outright oppression: some regimes have tried to suppress ethnic mobilization and threats of separatism by maintaining authoritarian control of the political system. Burma is the classic example: with the exception of a brief period of democracy following independence in 1948, Burma has remained under oppressive military rule, and the country's ruling generals have consistently and ruthlessly suppressed demands for ethnic self-determination while using the threat of ethnic conflict to justify their ongoing control of power.

A second response to ethnic diversity has been the evolution of 'semi-democratic' models of government, which permit a degree of political competition but attempt to quarantine ethnicity as a political issue by depoliticizing social life and bending electoral rules in favour of the majority community. Malaysia, Singapore and, intermittently, Fiji are all examples of this approach. Long-serving leaders such as Lee Kwan Yew in Singapore and Mahathir Mohamad in Malaysia regularly justified the erosion of civil liberties and competitive democracy under their leadership by alluding to the dangers of unrestricted ethnic politics if political control was loosened.[1] While the retirement of these resilient strongmen in 1990 and 2003, respectively, led to small

---

[1] See Fareed Zakaria, 'Culture is Destiny: A Conversation with Lee Kwan Yew', *Foreign Affairs*, 73/2 (1994), 109–26; 'East Beats West', *Asiaweek*, 8 September 1995.

gains for liberalism in both states, dire warnings of ethnic chaos in the event of a change of government remained commonplace. In Indonesia, similar claims about the need for strong military leadership to prevent ethnic disorder and violence were used to justify Sukarno's original policy of 'Guided Democracy'. Its successor doctrine, 'Pancasila Democracy', was first propagated by Sukarno as a means of bridging social cleavages, and later enshrined as a kind of state ideology by Suharto in order to delegitimize communist and ethnic challenges to his regime.

A final approach to the governance of ethnically plural societies has been to accept both the reality of ethnic diversity and the principles of open democratic politics, allowing political parties to form and campaign freely for public office without restriction through competitive elections and universal suffrage. However, this approach is also problematic due to the interaction between ethnic politics and the electoral process. As Rabushka and Shepsle observed over thirty years ago, the presence in new democracies of self-conscious ethnic communities will often spur the formation of ethnic political parties; the proliferation of ethnic parties, in turn, can incite inter-group tensions and inhibit cooperative behaviour, turning electoral campaigns into a competition between rival extremist visions. In extreme cases, the basic procedures of electoral democracy can themselves represent a danger to peaceful state-building.[2]

Political engineering is thus intimately associated with issues of conflict management and polarization. According to Timothy Sisk:

The central question of political engineering is this: In deeply divided societies, which kinds of institutions and practices create an incentive structure for ethnic groups to mediate their differences through the legitimate institutions of a common democratic state? Alternatively, how can the incentive system be structured to reward and reinforce political leaders who moderate on divisive ethnic themes and to persuade citizens to support moderation, bargaining, and reciprocity?[3]

This chapter addresses both of these questions. It begins by looking briefly at some of the overarching theoretical issues confronting the field of institutional design and the rival approaches to political engineering on which they are based. It then assesses the merits of the three most coherent models

---

[2] Rabushka and Shepsle, *Politics in Plural Societies*, 187.

[3] Timothy D. Sisk, *Power Sharing and International Mediation in Ethnic Conflicts* (Washington, DC: United States Institute of Peace Press, 1996), 33.

of political engineering in the contemporary world: consociation-alism, centripetalism, and communalism. It concludes by assess-ing the empirical record of each approach in the Asia-Pacific region.

The Theory of Institutional Design

The past decade has seen a burgeoning scholarly and policy interest in the design of political institutions, examining how institutions function, why they develop, and the reasons behind their success or failure. In the 1980s, as the limits of behavioural approaches to political science became increasingly apparent, formal institutions of government increasingly became the focus of study in their own right. In 1984, James March and Johan Olsen heralded the appearance of a 'new institutionalism' in political science. Political institutions, they argued, were gaining a more autonomous role as subjects of academic study: 'democracy depends not only on economic and social conditions but also on the design of political institutions ... They are polit-ical actors in their own right.'[4] 'Institutionalism', concluded one survey of the field a decade later, 'constitutes the bedrock of comparative politics'.[5]

The expanded interest in institutions was fired in part by the belated recognition that institutional reform could, under cer-tain circumstances, change political behaviour and hence political outcomes. Studies of both established and emerging democracies increasingly emphasized the importance of institu-tional variables.[6] Summarizing this new orthodoxy, Lijphart characterized the rebirth of interest in the institutional aspects of politics as being:

based on the conviction that institutions do matter, that they are not merely weak and inconsequential superstructures dependent on a

---

[4] James March and Johan P. Olsen, 'The New Institutionalism: Organiza-tional Factors in Political Life', *American Political Science Review*, 78 (1984), 738.

[5] David E. Apter, 'Comparative Politics, Old and New', in Robert E. Goodin and Hans-Dieter Klingemann (eds.), *A New Handbook of Political Science* (Oxford: Oxford University Press, 1996), 374.

[6] See, for example, R. Kent Weaver and Bert A. Rockman (eds.), *Do Institu-tions Matter? Government Capabilities in the United States and Abroad* (Washington, DC: The Brookings Institution, 1993); Diamond, *Developing Democracy*; Zielonka, *Democratic Consolidation*.

'truly' determinant socioeconomic, cultural, or other non-institutional base. For political engineers, and democratic political engineers in particular, this new approach means that different institutional forms, rules, and practices can have major consequences both for the degree of democracy in a democratic system and for the operation of the system.[7]

To the political engineer, then, institutions change outcomes, and changing formal political institutions can result in changes in political behaviour and political practice. As another leading figure in the political engineering literature, Donald Horowitz, put it: 'Where there is some determination to play by the rules, the rules can restructure the system so the game itself changes.'[8]

This revival of interest was not restricted to the academy. By the early 1990s, the collapse of communism and the 'third wave' of democratization had resulted in a threefold increase in the number of competitive democracies around the world.[9] As third wave states drafted new constitutions and forged new political systems, there was a tremendous upsurge of interest in the possibilities of institutional designs for democracy. Accompanying this was a change in the dynamics of international development assistance and the role of multilateral institutions such as the United Nations. Spurred by the liberalization of previously autocratic states in Africa, Asia, Eastern Europe, and Latin America, the international community began to invest heavily in concepts of democracy promotion, electoral support, and 'good governance' as essential elements of both economic development and the creation of stable and peaceful states.

The 1990s thus saw an explosion in political engineering as institutions were borrowed, adapted, or created afresh for transitional democracies. Developments which took decades and in some cases centuries in Western countries—such as the development of a stable political party system—were expected to be achieved in the space of a few short years. Concluding that 'solutions to the problem of democratization consist of institutions', an increasing number of political scientists argued that careful and purposive institutional design was

---

[7] Arend Lijphart, 'Foreword: "Cameral Change" and Institutional Conservatism', in Lawrence D. Longley and David M. Olson (eds.), *Two Into One: The Politics and Processes of National Legislative Cameral Change* (Boulder, CO: Westview Press, 1991), ix.

[8] Horowitz, *Ethnic Groups in Conflict*, 601.

[9] Huntington, *The Third Wave*.

not only possible but *necessary* to consolidate fragile new democracies.[10] Scholars looking at the management of ethnic conflict came to the same conclusion, advocating overt and explicit 'constitutional engineering' as a means of promoting stable democracy in deeply divided societies such as South Africa.[11] This message was echoed by other studies, reflecting a growing consensus on the importance of institutional design.[12] By contrast, sceptics who saw political engineering as inevitably more art than science expressed caution at this new enthusiasm for political engineering. Laurence Whitehead, for example, maintained that 'the idea that human subjects will simply conform to a structure of incentives bestowed on them by designers is untenable'.[13] Others went further: Jon Elster thought it 'impossible to predict with certainty or even quantified probability the consequences of a major constitutional change'.[14]

Amongst advocates, two contrasting approaches to political engineering for the management of social cleavages have dominated much of the academic literature. One is the scholarly orthodoxy of *consociationalism*, which relies on elite cooperation between leaders of different communities. Under this model, inter-ethnic harmony is maintained via mechanisms which collectively maximize the independence and influence of each main ethnic community, such as grand coalition cabinets, proportional representation elections, minority veto powers, and communal autonomy. An alternative approach, sometimes typified as *centripetalism*, eschews consociational formulas and instead advocates institutions which encourage inter-communal moderation by promoting multi-ethnic political

---

[10] Adam Przeworski, 'Democracy as the Contingent Outcome of Conflicts', in Jon Elster and Rune Slagstad (eds.), *Constitutionalism and Democracy* (Cambridge: Cambridge University Press, 1988), 304.

[11] See Donald L. Horowitz, *A Democratic South Africa? Constitutional Engineering in a Divided Society* (Berkeley, CA: University of California Press, 1991).

[12] See, for example, Andrew Reynolds (ed.), *The Architecture of Democracy: Constitutional Design, Conflict Management and Democracy* (Oxford: Oxford University Press, 2002). For a policy-focused approach to these issues, see Peter Harris and Ben Reilly (eds.), *Democracy and Deep-Rooted Conflict: Options for Negotiators* (Stockholm: International Institute for Democracy and Electoral Assistance, 1998).

[13] Whitehead, *Democratization*, 98.

[14] Jon Elster, 'Arguments for Constitutional Choice: Reflections on a Transition to Socialism' in Elster and Slagstad, *Constitutionalism and Democracy*, 304.

parties, cross-cutting electoral incentives, and inter-group accommodation. The former approach is based on the strategy of clarifying ethnic identities and 'making plural societies more truly plural',[15] the latter on the opposite strategy of diluting the ethnic character of competitive politics and promoting multi-ethnic outcomes in its place. A third approach, *communalism*, uses explicit ethnic criteria of representation, and has largely been abandoned as a political engineering strategy in most of the contemporary world, but retains some vestigial support in a few Asia-Pacific states. This chapter looks at each of these models of political engineering in turn, and concludes with an assessment of the empirical record of each approach in the Asia-Pacific.

Consociationalism

As noted in the first chapter, one basic typology of democratic systems begins with the distinction between majoritarian and consensual democracies.[16] Because majoritarian models can lead to ethnic minorities being denied parliamentary representation, it is often argued that they are unsuitable for ethnically diverse societies. For example, simple majority rule can easily entrench one party or group's dominance over all others. Processes of competitive electoral democracy can, under these circumstances, result in a situation of permanent inclusion and exclusion, a zero-sum game. Because of this, the scholarly orthodoxy of institutional design for plural societies typically advocates the adoption of 'consensual' institutions and practices which encourage inter-ethnic balancing in public office, proportional representation of all significant cleavages in parliament, and sharing of power between these various segments in government. Consociationalism is the most well-developed of such models.[17]

[15] Lijphart, *Democracy in Plural Societies*, 42.

[16] Lijphart, *Democracies*.

[17] There is a voluminous literature on consociationalism. Major works include Arend Lijphart, *The Politics of Accommodation: Pluralism and Democracy in the Netherlands* (Berkeley, CA: University of California Press, 1968); Eric A. Nordlinger, *Conflict Regulation in Divided Societies* (Cambridge, MA: Center for International Affairs, Harvard University, 1972); Kenneth McRae (ed.), *Consociational Democracy: Political Accommodation in Segmented Societies* (Toronto: McLelland and Stewart, 1974); Lijphart, *Democracy in Plural*

Consociational prescriptions are based on the principle that each ethnic polity should enjoy a significant degree of autonomy and a right of veto over matters directly affecting the welfare of its members. Emphasizing the need for elite cooperation if democracy is to survive in ethnically cleaved societies, consociational agreements entail a balance of power within government between clearly defined social segments, brokered by identifiable ethnic leaders. Lijphart, the scholar most associated with the consociational model, developed this prescription from a detailed examination of power-sharing democracy in European countries such as the Netherlands, Belgium, and Switzerland, and there is disagreement over the extent to which these measures can be applied to other regions.[18] However, there is little doubt that consociationalism represents the dominant model of power-sharing for 'plural societies'—that is, in Lijphart's terminology, 'societies that are sharply divided along religious, ideological, linguistic, cultural, ethnic, or racial lines into virtually separate subsocieties with their own political parties, interest groups, and media of communication'.[19] This definition points both to the European provenance of consociationalism, and to some of the inherent difficulties in applying this model to developing countries in Asia and the Pacific, which in many cases are not divided into 'separate subsocieties' but comprise more of an ethnic mélange, in which groups 'mix but do not combine'.[20]

In terms of political engineering, consociationalists focus on core democratic institutions such as political parties, electoral systems, and cabinet governments, and on the territorial division of state powers. In each case, the focus is on defining and strengthening the autonomy of communal components of the society in question. In terms of political parties, for example, consociational approaches presuppose the existence of functional political organizations led by communal elites representing a country's main ethnic groups. The ideal form of party system

---

Societies; Sisk, *Power Sharing*; Philip G. Roeder and Donald Rothchild (eds.), *Sustainable Peace: Power and Democracy after Civil Wars* (Ithaca, NY and London: Cornell University Press, 2005).

[18] See Lijphart, *Democracy in Plural Societies*; Sisk, *Power Sharing*; cf. Horowitz, *A Democratic South Africa?*

[19] Lijphart, *Democracies*, 22.

[20] J. S. Furnivall, *Colonial Policy and Practice: A Comparative Study of Burma and Netherlands India* (Cambridge: Cambridge University Press, 1948), 304.

for consociationalists is one based around clear social cleavages in which all significant groups, including minorities, 'define themselves' into ethnically based parties. Only through leading parties based around segmental cleavages, consociationalists contend, can political elites negotiate delicate ethnic issues effectively. Ethnic parties are thus an integral part of a functioning consociational package.[21]

To ensure the fair representation of such ethnic parties, consociational prescriptions invariably recommend proportional representation (PR) electoral systems, particularly party list systems which ensure a close parity between the proportion of the vote won by a party and its parliamentary representation. Lijphart, for instance, has consistently maintained that 'the electoral system that is optimal for segmented societies is list PR'.[22] This contention is based on PR's tendency to produce multi-party systems and hence multi-party parliaments in which all significant segments of the population can be clearly represented. Optimally, 'closed' party lists which do not enable voters to select individual candidates (thus strengthening the autonomy of party leaders) and large multi-member electoral districts (to maximize proportionality of outcomes) are favoured. Majoritarian systems, by contrast, are seen as 'deeply flawed and dangerous'.[23]

As their widespread adoption around the world indicates, PR systems have many advantages for new democracies: they are equitable, transparent, and provide a clear correlation between votes cast in the election and seats won in parliament. By giving minorities a stake in the political process and fairly representing parties in the legislature, PR is often seen as an integral component of inclusive and legitimate post-authoritarian democracy. Indeed, almost all of the major transitional elections conducted since the end of the cold war

[21] See Arend Lijphart, 'Self-determination Versus Pre-determination of Ethnic Minorities in Power-sharing Systems', in Will Kymlicka (ed.), *The Rights of Minority Cultures* (Oxford: Oxford University Press, 1995).

[22] Arend Lijphart, 'Electoral Systems, Party Systems and Conflict Management in Segmented Societies', in R. A. Schreirer (ed.), *Critical Choices for South Africa: An Agenda for the 1990s* (Cape Town: Oxford University Press, 1990), 2, 13.

[23] Arend Lijphart, 'Prospects for Power-Sharing in the New South Africa', in Andrew Reynolds (ed.), *Election '94 South Africa: the Campaigns, Results and Future Prospects* (Claremont: David Phillip Publishers, 1994), 224.

have been held under some form of PR. For instance, elections in Namibia (1989), Nicaragua (1990), Cambodia (1993), South Africa (1994), Mozambique (1994), Bosnia (1996, 1998, 2000), Indonesia (1999), Kosovo (2001), East Timor (2001), Afghanistan (2005), and Iraq (2005) were all conducted under party-list PR, which appears to have become a de facto norm for United Nations-sponsored elections in particular. However, the adoption of such systems has often been dictated more by administrative concerns, such as the need to avoid demarcating local electoral districts and producing separate ballot papers, than by wider political considerations. Particularly in post-conflict situations, party-list PR is often the only feasible means of holding an election quickly, as a uniform national ballot can be used in one national district, and the process of voter registration, vote counting, and the calculation of results is consequently simplified.[24]

Despite this, PR systems also have some clear disadvantages, particularly the highly-proportional variants favoured by consociationalists. By ensuring fair representation of all significant parties, such systems can enable minority movements to gain crucial footholds in power. The tendency of highly proportional PR to entrench small extremist parties in parliament is a recurring problem.[25] Comparative studies have found that smaller 'district magnitude'—the number of members elected from each electoral district—can play a role in blocking the rise of extremist parties and encouraging the development of more broad-based party systems, implying that *less* proportionality may be preferable for new democracies.[26] Finally, because parties elected under PR rules can succeed by mobilizing niche sectors of the electorate rather than broad heterogeneous coalitions, PR tends to be associated with party fragmentation. Some scholars have therefore concluded that 'plurality systems

[24] I discuss this point in more detail in 'Elections in Post-Conflict Societies', in Edward Newman and Roland Rich (eds.), *The UN Role in Promoting Democracy: Between Ideals and Reality* (Tokyo: United Nations University Press, 2004).

[25] George Tsebelis, 'Elite Interaction and Constitution Building in Consociational Democracies', *Journal of Theoretical Politics*, 2/1 (1990), 5–29.

[26] Joseph Willey, 'Institutional Arrangements and the Success of New Parties in Old Democracies', in Richard Hofferbert (ed.), *Parties and Democracy* (Oxford and Malden, MA: Blackwell, 1998).

perform better than proportional representation with respect to the consolidation of fragile democracies'.[27]

Because they need large, multi-member electoral districts to work effectively, highly proportional PR can also weaken the geographic link between voters and their representatives, creating difficulties of political accountability and responsiveness. While this may not be a problem in advanced industrial democracies like the Netherlands (where the entire country forms one 120-member electoral district), many new democracies—particularly those in rural societies—have much higher demands for constituency service at the local level than they do for representation of all shades of ideological opinion in the legislature.[28] Several developing countries which have made the transition to democracy under list PR rules have subsequently found that the large, multi-member districts required to achieve proportionality weakens the relationship between elected politicians and voters. In both Indonesia and Cambodia, for instance, demands for greater accountability led to modification of PR systems and reductions in district size to encourage closer links between elected politicians and voters—as discussed in more detail in Chapter 5.

In addition to PR, consociationalism also advocates 'grand coalition' governments, in which all significant parties are given a share of executive power, and in which minorities have the right of veto over important issues directly affecting their own communities. Lijphart has described South Africa's interim 1994 constitution, which featured a formal requirement that all parties with at least 5 per cent of seats in the legislature be offered commensurate positions in the cabinet, as 'close to the optimal power-sharing system that could have been devised'.[29] In 1997, Fiji adopted a similar system, with a 10 per cent seat threshold, based on the South African model. Other experiments with grand coalition cabinets have occurred in Cambodia (where the constitution requires a two-thirds vote of confidence in new governments), Indonesia (during the 1950s and again under

[27] André Blais and Stephanie Dion, 'Electoral Systems and the Consolidation of New Democracies', in D. Ethier (ed.), *Democratic Transition and Consolidation in Southern Europe, Latin America and Southeast Asia* (London: Macmillan, 1990), 262.

[28] See Joel D. Barkan, 'Elections in Agrarian Societies', *Journal of Democracy*, 6/4 (1995), 106–16.

[29] Lijphart, 'Prospects for Power-Sharing', 222.

Abdurrahman Wahid's presidency between 1999 and 2001) and, to a lesser extent, in Malaysia (although significant opposition parties have always been present there). All of these cases will be discussed in more detail later in this book.

A final model of institutional design favoured by consociationalists is ethnic federalism. When ethnic groups are territorially concentrated, the consociational principle of group autonomy can be achieved by the devolution of power so as to enable 'rule by the minority over itself in the area of the minority's exclusive concern'.[30] As with political parties, a key presumption is that constituent units should be as ethnically homogeneous as possible in order to maximize each group's control over their own interests and resources. While there are no examples of pure ethnic federalism in the Asia-Pacific, schemes for regional autonomy in the Philippines (in Mindanao and the Cordilleras), Indonesia (in Aceh and Papua), and Papua New Guinea (in Bougainville) have all been justified by reference to the language (if not always the reality) of group autonomy.

Lijphart has consistently claimed that consociationalism represents the *only* means of making democracy work in divided societies.[31] While there is no doubt that consociational theories have had a major impact not just on scholarly approaches but also in the real world of institutional design, consociationalism has a decidedly mixed record in practice, and rests on several key assumptions that may not always hold in divided societies. The most important of these is the assumption that ethnic leaders will be more moderate on key sectarian issues than their supporters. While this may hold true in some cases, the experience of ethnic civil wars in countries like Bosnia, Sri Lanka, and Rwanda suggests that it is ethnic leaders who often have the most to gain by maintaining or fomenting ethnocentric politics.[32] Other critics point to consociationalism's potential for inflexibility and rigidity, its infringement of basic democratic assumptions, and its inefficiency in terms of decisive decision-making.[33]

---

[30] Lijphart, *Democracy in Plural Societies*, 41.

[31] Lijphart, 'Prospects for Power-Sharing', 222.

[32] For a survey of academic studies of this phenomenon, see Donald L. Horowitz, 'Self-determination: Politics, Philosophy, and Law', *Nomos*, 39 (1997), 421–63.

[33] See, for example, Brian Barry, 'The Consociational Model and its Dangers', *European Journal of Political Research*, 3 (1975), 393–412; Horowitz, *A Democratic South Africa?*, 137–45; Paul Dixon, 'Consociationalism and the Northern Ireland Peace Process: A Glass Half Full or Half Empty?', *Nationalism and Ethnic Politics*, 3/3 (1997), 20–36.

The empirical record of consociationalism in the Asia-Pacific is patchy. Malaysia's ethnically defined political system has often been identified as a consociational arrangment.[34] Other Asia-Pacific states which have been claimed to operate according to consociational principles are Fiji and Singapore.[35] Another example is Burma under its 1948 constitution, which provided for a combination of ethnically based states, reserved parliamentary seats for specified groups, and ethnic 'councils' to look after the interests of inter-mixed or dispersed minorities.[36] Lijphart has also cited the case of post-colonial Indonesia during its original democratic incarnation in the 1950s as an example of consociationalism in practice.[37] During this period, Indonesian ethnic and religious groups formed their own parties and were included in a grand coalition government, on the assumption that 'ethnic and other demands would be articulated through the party system and conflicts would be settled through negotiation and compromise in the parliament'.[38]

The one feature all these examples of consociationalism in Asia have in common is that they proved incompatible with open, competitive democracy. In Indonesia, the 1950–7 parliament represented virtually the full spectrum of the country's social diversity, but its inability to maintain a stable political centre led directly to the end of democracy in 1957 and four decades of authoritarian rule. Burma's post-independence democracy survived for fourteen turbulent years until 1962, before being overthrown in a military coup which had strong ethnic motivations. In Malaysia and Singapore, as noted earlier, the need to manage ethnic tensions has been the primary justification for the increasing restrictions on democratic competition. The eclipse of democracy in each of these cases, and its replacement with forms of semi-democracy (in Singapore and Malaysia) or outright authoritarianism (in post-colonial Indonesia and Burma), represents an important empirical challenge to advocates of consociationalism. On the other hand, consociationalists may

[34] William Case, *Elites and Regimes in Malaysia: Revisiting a Consociational Democracy* (Monash: Monash Asia Institute, 1996).

[35] See R. S. Milne, '"The Pacific Way"—Consociational Politics in Fiji', *Pacific Affairs*, 48/3 (1975), 413–31; N. Ganesan, 'Democracy in Singapore', *Asian Journal of Political Science*, 4/2 (1996), 63–79.

[36] Furnivall, *Colonial Policy and Practice*, 169.

[37] Lijphart, *Democracy in Plural Societies*, 198–201.

[38] Liddle, 'Coercion, Co-optation, and the Management of Ethnic Relations in Indonesia', 286.

well question if any alternative approach would have worked better in these countries.

More contentiously, Lijphart has recently claimed India, with its combination of long-lasting democracy with exceptional ethnic diversity, as another example of consociationalism in Asia.[39] However—as with Malaysia, Singapore, Fiji, and post-colonial Burma—this has led to accusations of 'conceptual stretching' and raised serious questions about the clarity of the consociational model, in institutional terms at least.[40] Specifically, while each of these states may have employed consociational *practices* at various times, none has adopted key consociational *institutions* such as grand coalitions, proportional elections, minority vetoes, or segmental autonomy. For example, neither Malaysia, Fiji, and Singapore nor India has ever employed proportional representation elections or minority vetoes, while (as will be discussed in Chapter 7) true grand coalition governments have been rare and, for the most part, short-lived. Rather, the main institutional features these countries have in common derive from their shared British colonial heritage: plurality elections, responsible parliamentary government, and adversarial politics.

Centripetalism

Despite claims to the contrary, alternative prescriptions for divided societies to those of consociationalism do exist. *Centripetalism* is one such approach to political engineering—so called 'because the explicit aim is to engineer a centripetal spin to the political system—to pull the parties towards moderate, compromising policies and to discover and reinforce the centre of a deeply divided political spectrum'.[41] Centripetalism emphasizes the importance of institutions that can encourage cooperation, accommodation, and integration across ethnic divides, and can thus work to break down the salience of ethnicity rather than

---

[39] Arend Lijphart, 'The Puzzle of Indian Democracy: A Consociational Interpretation', *American Political Science Review*, 90/2 (1996), 258–68. For a critique, see Steven Wilkinson, 'India, Consociational Theory, and Ethnic Violence', *Asian Survey*, 40/5 (2000), 767–91.

[40] Ian Lustick, 'Lijphart, Lakatos, and Consociationalism', *World Politics*, 50 (1997), 81–117.

[41] See Timothy D. Sisk, *Democratization in South Africa: The Elusive Social Contract* (Princeton, NJ: Princeton University Press, 1995), 19.

fostering its representation institutionally. In direct opposition to consociational recommendations, centripetalists maintain that the best way to manage democracy in divided societies is not to simply replicate existing ethnic divisions in the legislature and other representative organs, but rather to *depoliticize* ethnicity by putting in place institutional incentives for politicians and their supporters to act in an accommodatory manner towards rival groups. Institutions which encourage parties and candidates to 'pool votes' across ethnic lines, centripetalists contend, can promote cooperative outcomes and, in so doing, take the heat out of ethnic politics. This is an argument that Horowitz has made consistently in his writings on strategies for ethnic conflict moderation.[42]

In an earlier book on electoral engineering for divided societies, I defined centripetalism as a shorthand for a political system or strategy designed to focus competition at the moderate centre rather than the extremes, and identified three facilitating components:

1. the presentation of *electoral incentives* for campaigning politicians to reach out to and attract votes from a range of ethnic groups other than their own, thus encouraging candidates to moderate their political rhetoric on potentially divisive issues and forcing them to broaden their policy positions;
2. the presence of multi-ethnic *arenas of bargaining* such as parliamentary and executive forums, in which political actors from different groups have an incentive to come together and cut deals on reciprocal electoral support, and hence perhaps on other more substantial policy issues as well; and
3. the development of *centrist, aggregative, and multiethnic political parties* or coalitions of parties which are capable of making cross-ethnic appeals and presenting a complex and diverse range of policy options to the electorate.[43]

[42] In addition to vote-pooling electoral systems, Horowitz identifies four other mechanisms which characterize his approach to moderating the potentially harmful effects of inter-ethnic competition: arrangements which proliferate the points of power 'so as to take the heat off a single focal point', such as a constitutional separation of powers or federalism; devolution or ethnically reserved offices to foster intra-ethnic conflict at the local level; public policies which encourage the growth of less damaging 'cross-cutting cleavages', such as class identification, to act as counterweights to ethnic identification; and measures which serve to reduce inter-ethnic inequalities and disparities 'so that dissatisfaction declines' (*Ethnic Groups in Conflict*, 597–600).

[43] Benjamin Reilly, *Democracy in Divided Societies: Electoral Engineering for Conflict Management* (Cambridge: Cambridge University Press, 2001), 11.

Like consociationalism, centripetal proposals for conflict manage-ment thus focus on parties, elections, and parliaments as the institutions which offer the most potential for effective political engineering. However, the specific institutional recommenda-tions made by centripetalists often run sharply counter to those of consociationalists. For instance, rather than focusing on the fair representation of ethnically defined political parties, centri-petalists place a premium on promoting multi-ethnic parties and cross-ethnic activity. This means that, in contrast to the consocia-tional focus on proportional elections, centripetal approaches fa-vour an aggregative majoritarianism, with more emphasis on the *process* by which different groups work together than strict fair-ness of *outcomes*. Thus, in relation to elections, centripetalists advocate institutional designs which encourage negotiation and accommodation between opposing political forces in the context of political competition rather than strict proportionality. They argue that if the rules of the game are structured so as to reward cooperative political strategies with electoral success, candidates representing competing interests can be presented with incen-tives to negotiate across ethnic lines for reciprocal support and to bargain across cleavages for political deals and policy concessions.

How can such cooperative behaviour be promoted in divided societies, where cooperation across social cleavages is, by defin-ition, lacking? One approach is to use institutions that encourage cross-ethnic deal-making and accommodative behaviour be-tween competing groups and their representatives. Again, elect-oral systems are crucial: centripetalists advocate electoral arrangements that make politicians reciprocally dependent on the votes of members of groups other than their own, and present campaigning politicians with incentives to court voter support across ethnic lines. To achieve this, electoral processes can be structured so as to require successful candidates to gain support across different regions of a country, thus helping to break down the appeal of narrow parochialism or regionalism. The 'distribu-tion requirement' introduced for the 2004 presidential elections in Indonesia, where candidates had to gain at least 20 per cent of the vote in 16 provinces in the first round of elections to avoid a run-off, is an example of such a system.

Other approaches attempt to undercut the logic of ethnic politics by requiring political parties to present ethnically mixed slates of candidates for 'at-large' elections, thus making voter choice contingent upon issues *other* than ethnicity. In the Philippines, for example, senators are elected on a nationwide basis, making cross-national support essential. In East Timor, similarly, most parliamentarians are similarly elected from across the country as a whole rather than local districts, a process which can encourage a focus on national rather than regional or sectoral interests.[44] In Singapore, parties and alliances contesting the fourteen multi-member districts designated as 'Group Representation Constituencies' must include candidates from designated ethnic minorities on their ticket, and voters must choose between competing party slates rather than individual candidates—arrangements which effectively require a degree of cross-ethnic voting while guaranteeing that at least nine of the ninety-three seats in the Singaporean parliament will be occupied by Malays, and five by Indians or other minorities.

A more direct and more powerful centripetal approach to electoral system design is to use preferential, rank-order electoral systems such as the alternative vote, which require voters to declare not only their first choice of candidate, but also their second, third, and subsequent choices amongst all candidates standing. If no-one gains an outright majority, these votes are transferred according to their rankings in order to elect a majority-supported winner. Because they make politicians from different parties reciprocally dependent on preference transfers from their rivals, such systems present candidates who wish to maximize their electoral prospects with an incentive to try to attract secondary preference votes from other groups, so as to ensure the broadest possible range of support for their candidacy. As will be discussed in more detail in Chapter 5, the Pacific states of Papua New Guinea and Fiji have both adopted such systems in recent years.[45]

Another important difference between consociational and centripetal approaches to conflict management is their contrasting recommendations regarding political parties. As already noted, consociational prescriptions advocate the presence of ethnically-based parties and party systems, and see a virtue in having a multiplicity of parties representing all significant social groups. By contrast, centripetalists ideally favour an aggregative party system, in which 'one or two broadly based, centrist parties fight for the middle ground',[46] and therefore endorse

---

[44] See Wurfel, 'Democracy, Nationalism and Ethnic Identity', 220.

[45] See Reilly, *Democracy in Divided Societies*.

[46] Larry Diamond, 'Toward Democratic Consolidation', in Larry Diamond and Marc F. Plattner (eds.), *The Global Resurgence of Democracy* (Baltimore, MD and London: Johns Hopkins University Press, 1996), 239.

the development of multiethnic parties or coalitions. Over time, it is argued, the presence of such party constellations can serve to depoliticize social cleavages and foster more fluid, cross-cutting affiliations.

The distinction between 'bridging' and 'bonding' political parties is again important here. Classically, political scientists have believed that majoritarian electoral rules will, over time, encourage the development of two large, aggregative parties.[47] This reductionist tendency occurs through a combination of 'mechanical' and 'psychological' electoral system effects. Mechanically, because they award seats on the basis of individual 'winner-take-all' contests in single-member districts, majoritarian elections tend to over-represent large parties and under-represent small ones, particularly those with a dispersed share of the vote. This tendency is compounded by the psychological impact of this process on voters, many of whom choose not to 'waste' their vote on a minor party, but instead switch their support to one with a reasonable chance of success. The cumulative effect of these mechanical and psychological factors is to systematically advantage large parties and discriminate against small ones. The pay-off for this discrimination is, in theory, more decisive and effective government, characterized by stable, responsible, and predictable majority rule.[48]

A separate theoretical approach, derived from basic game theory, argues that the presence of two parties competing for office should promote a convergence towards the political centre, thus helping avoid ideological and other kinds of polarization. Anthony Downs famously showed that under plurality electoral rules and a unidimensional (e.g. left-right) policy spectrum, the winning strategy will focus on the 'median voter' who has an equal number of fellow voters to both the left and the right.[49] In a two-party system, the most successful parties will therefore be those that command the middle ground. As a consequence, office-seeking candidates in such systems need to adopt centrist policies that appeal to the broadest possible array of interests, avoiding extreme positions and focusing instead on widely shared demands: for example, the need for economic growth,

---

[47] The classic statement of this is Maurice Duverger, *Political Parties: Their Organization and Activity in the Modern State* (New York: Wiley, 1954).

[48] See Sartori, *Comparative Constitutional Engineering*.

[49] Anthony Downs, *An Economic Theory of Democracy* (New York: Harper and Row, 1957).

competent bureaucracy, clean government, and so on. Thus, in theory, majoritarian elections and two-party systems should produce centripetal politics focused on the political centre. As with consociationalism, supporting empirical evidence for this contention varies. While critics argue that supporting evidence is thin on the ground, a number of comparative studies have found an association between more majoritarian electoral laws and weaker cleavage politics across both emerging and established democracies.[50]

The formation of governing coalitions is another area of contrast between consociational and centripetal approaches. Just as Lijphart and other consociationalists advocate the formation of inclusive executive governments, centripetalists such as Horowitz argue that multiethnic coalitions are a near-essential element of conflict management for divided societies. But while both favour executive power-sharing underpinned by multi-ethnic coalition governments, again there is disagreement on the optimal application of these models. As noted earlier, consociationalists advocate 'grand coalitions' in which all significant parties (and hence ethnic groups) are included in the cabinet—if necessary, by constitutional fiat, such as the mandatory power-sharing provisions in the Cambodian and Fijian constitutions. By contrast, centripetalists see grand coalitions as being only weakly harnessed to political incentives, and hence prone to falling apart when contentious decisions affecting group interests have to be taken. Truly multi-ethnic parties or coalitions of parties founded on common interests and vote-pooling electoral arrangements are, they contend, more likely to endure than forced cooperation between erstwhile enemies. Thus Horowitz favours pre-election pacts to build enduring 'coalitions of commitment' in government, as opposed to the weak and tenuous 'coalitions of convenience' which characterize post-election grand coalitions.[51]

Similarly, consociationalism assumes that enlightened elites will not just represent the interests of their own communities but will also act moderately towards their rivals, thus becoming a driving force for inter-ethnic moderation in divided societies. By contrast, centripetalism places less faith in elite moderation—a contention based on the evidence that ordinary voters are often

[50] See Willey, 'Institutional Arrangements'; Norris, *Electoral Engineering*, Chapter 5.
[51] Horowitz, *Ethnic Groups in Conflict*, 365–95.

the main bulwark against political extremism and democratic breakdown.[52] For centripetalists, communal moderation is more dependent on the behaviour of campaigning politicians and their supporters on the ground, and it is assumed that voters will follow the lead of their political leaders and pool votes across ethnic lines when asked to. The willingness of Chinese voters to support ethnically Malay candidates as part of the ruling multi-ethnic coalition in Malaysia is often cited as an example of this kind of vote-pooling in action.[53] More generally, whereas consociational prescriptions are seen as relying predominantly on constraints (such as minority vetoes) against inter-ethnic hostility, the centripetal approach focuses on the need for incentives to motivate accommodative behaviour via the search for secondary support. This further distinguishes the centripetal model from that of consociationalism.

A final important point of contrast concerns territorial schemes such as federalism, devolution, and autonomy. The competing logics of consociational and centripetal approaches to conflict management mean that ethnic federalism is the natural choice for consociationalists, as already noted. The cross-ethnic logic of centripetalism, by contrast, suggests that a unitary state or non-ethnic federation would be a more appropriate choice, given the centripetal focus on multi-ethnicity as the key to conflict management. Unfortunately for comparative purposes, the Asia-Pacific region offers limited possibilities for testing these debates. Only one country in the region, Malaysia, is clearly federal; despite significant variation in their levels of decentralization, all the other countries included in this study are formally unitary in nature; while autonomy for aggrieved regions in the Philippines, Indonesia, and Papua New Guinea has been dogged by problems, including a number of cases in which offers of substantial regional autonomy have failed to be implemented in practice.

Like consociationalism, centripetalism has attracted significant criticism on both empirical and conceptual grounds. Empirically, critics point to the paucity of centripetal models in

---

[52] See Nancy Bermeo, *Ordinary People in Extraordinary Times: The Citizenry and the Breakdown of Democracy* (Princeton, NJ: Princeton University Press, 2003).

[53] See Donald L. Horowitz, 'Making Moderation Pay: the Comparative Politics of Ethnic Conflict Management', in J. V. Montville (ed.), *Conflict and Peacemaking in Multiethnic Societies* (New York: Lexington Books, 1991), 464–7.

the real world; the limited application of cross-voting electoral systems, distribution requirements, and other favoured devices; the difficulty in both forming and sustaining multi-ethnic polit- ical parties and coalitions in divided societies; and the ambigu- ous real-world experience of particular institutions such as the alternative vote.[54]

Conceptually, centripetalism is also criticized for being essen- tially majoritarian in nature. As the logic of centripetalism is focused above all on the potential benefits of *aggregation*—of votes, of opinions, of parties—at one level, this is correct. Powell, for example, notes that political aggregation lies at the heart of what he calls the 'majoritarian vision' of democracy: 'the major- itarian view favours much greater aggregation, while the pro- portional view emphasizes the importance of equitable reflection of all points of view into the legislature'.[55] For this reason, critics of centripetalism have often identified the majoritarian nature of its institutional recommendations as a key weakness.[56] Centri- petalists respond that they favour 'a majoritarian democracy that will produce more fluid, shifting majorities that do not lock ascriptive minorities firmly out of power'.[57] In other words, while centripetalism is indeed a majoritarian model, it is a majoritar- ianism of broad-based parties and inclusive coalitions—not a majoritarianism of 'ins' and 'outs', of ethnically defined majorities and minorities.

Interestingly, the majoritarian themes of the centripetal ap- proach and their emphasis on aggregative, bridging political parties are echoed by and find support in a quite separate schol-

---

[54] See Arend Lijphart, 'The Alternative Vote: A Realistic Alternative for South Africa?', *Politikon*, 18/2 (1991), 91–101; Andrew Reynolds, 'Constitu- tional Engineering in Southern Africa', *Journal of Democracy*, 6/2 (1995), 86–100; Jon Fraenkel, 'The Alternative Vote System in Fiji: Electoral Engin- eering or Ballot-Rigging?', *Commonwealth and Comparative Politics*, 39/1 (2001), 1–31; Arend Lijphart, 'Constitutional Design for Divided Societies', *Journal of Democracy*, 15/2 (2004), 96–109; Jon Fraenkel and Bernard Grof- man, 'A Neo-Downsian Model of the Alternative Vote as a Mechanism for Mitigating Ethnic Conflict in Plural Societies', *Public Choice*, 121 (2004), 487–506.

[55] Powell, *Elections*, 26.

[56] See, for example, Arend Lijphart, 'Multiethnic Democracy', in Seymour Martin Lipset (ed.), *The Encyclopedia of Democracy* (Washington, DC: Con- gressional Quarterly Press, 1995), 863–4; Andrew Reynolds, *Electoral Systems and Democratization in Southern Africa* (Oxford: Oxford University Press, 1999), 108–110.

[57] Horowitz, *A Democratic South Africa?*, 176.

arly literature, on the political economy of development. In the course of writing this book I have been struck by the extent to which institutional preferences and priorities are shared between political economists and centripetalists. Both literatures, for example, advocate aggregative political institutions, majoritarian electoral processes, and broad-based 'catch-all' parties or coalitions.[58] These same recommendations are also prominent in discussions of the optimum political arrangements for promoting economic development in new democracies.[59]

Political economists, for instance, often extol the virtues of settled, aggregative party systems for generating public goods, social welfare, and economic development. Thus, various works co-authored by Stephan Haggard have consistently argued that a system of two large parties or coalitions is the most propitious arrangement for democratic durability during periods of economic adjustment, while fragmented or polarized party systems represent a major barrier to achieving economic reform.[60] Similarly, in his exegesis of the optimum conditions for a democratic developmental state, Gordon White stressed the importance of party systems that are 'relatively well developed, concentrated rather than fragmented, broadly based, and organized along programmatic rather than personalistic or narrowly sectional lines'.[61] Such recommendations suggest a growing convergence amongst different political science sub-disciplines on the benefits of aggregative and centripetal institutions for political development and stability.

Communalism

A third approach to building stable democracy in ethnically divided societies is to explicitly recognize the importance of group identity in politics by making social cleavages a fundamental building block of the entire political system—for example, by ensuring that ethnic representation and ratios are preset according to explicit communal criteria in the electoral

[58] See Stephan Haggard and Steven B. Webb, *Voting for Reform: Democracy, Political Liberalization and Economic Adjustment* (New York: Oxford University Press, 1992).

[59] See Robinson and White, *The Democratic Developmental State*.

[60] See Haggard and Webb, *Voting for Reform*; Haggard and Kaufman, *The Political Economy of Democratic Transitions*.

[61] See White, 'Constructing a Democratic Developmental State', 46.

system, the parliament, and other key institutions. Under such schemes, legislative seats are often allocated communally and in some cases the entire political system is based on communal considerations—distinguishing it from the 'self-determined' model of ethnic representation favoured by consociationalists.[62] In New Zealand, for example, Maori electors can choose to have their names registered on either the national electoral roll or a specific Maori roll, from which seven indigenous representatives are chosen. A related approach is to explicitly *reserve* some seats so as to ensure the legislative representation of specific communal groups: India, where one-fifth of parliamentary seats are set aside for scheduled tribes and castes, is a well-known example. Amongst our country cases, reserved seats for representatives of 'overseas' Chinese in Taiwan, or non-indigenous minorities in Samoa, are exemplars of this approach.[63] In contrast to specifically communal representation, however, such seats are usually elected by all voters in much the same manner as other members of parliament.

Although it retains a foothold in parts of Asia and the Pacific through such instruments, communalism has faded in popularity since its heyday under colonial rule, when such schemes were often introduced in early representative bodies. There are several reasons for this disenchantment with communalism. A core problem is that communal schemes inevitably require some official recognition and determination of group identity. As well as creating real moral dilemmas, this official designation of ethnicity assumes that ethnic identities are immutable and enduring, an assumption that can contribute to the solidification of ethnic politics rather than its breakdown. Because of this, communal systems tend to suffer from a distinct lack of flexibility: changes in the proportions of ethnic groups in the community over time are not reflected in the larger political system, which are effectively frozen in place from whenever the original determinations of group proportions were made. Finally, communalism by its nature mitigates against political integration: it is exceptionally difficult to establish national political parties, for example, under a system of communal representation.

[62] Lijphart, 'Self-determination Versus Pre-determination'.
[63] See Ben Reilly and Andrew Reynolds, *Electoral Systems and Conflict in Divided Societies* (Washington DC: National Research Council, 1999), 41.

Despite these problems, several Asian and Pacific countries continue to maintain some form of communal representation in their political arrangements, with voters from separate groups having their own electoral roll and a guaranteed number of seats in parliament. In addition to its overseas Chinese seats, for example, Taiwan also reserves six seats for its small aboriginal population, who (like Maori voters in New Zealand) have their own separate electoral roll. In the Pacific, two post-colonial states—Fiji and Samoa—also maintain elements of communalism. In Fiji since 1997, two-thirds of all parliamentary seats (a reduction from previous years) are reserved for members of the country's three main ethnic communities (Fijians have 23 seats, Indo-Fijians 19, there are 3 seats for 'general electors' and 1 for the distant island of Rotuma). In Samoa, participation in elections was reserved for members of the *matai*, the country's traditional leaders, at independence. In 1991, the suffrage was broadened to include all citizens, but candidature is still restricted to the *matai* alone. Thus in both cases, while communalism remains important, there has been a dilution of communal institutions over time. However, these examples are few and far between. The contemporary trend in the Asia-Pacific, as around the world, is clearly away from communalism as a viable model of democracy.

In terms of the broader political engineering debates, communal approaches are more consistent with consociationalism than they are with centripetalism. Communally based parties and electoral systems, for instance, are incompatible with centripetalism, as they require a formal identification of ethnicity and can thus contribute to the consolidation of ethnic politics rather than its breakdown. By contrast, as long as communal seats are distributed proportionately, communal rolls and other devices which explicitly recognize ethnic identity are, as Lijphart has noted, entirely consistent with consociational approaches.[64]

Conclusion

Over the past decade, political reformers in various Asian and Pacific democracies have sought to change their political

---

[64] See Arend Lijphart, *Power Sharing in South Africa* (Berkeley, CA: Policy Papers in International Affairs No. 24, Institute of International Studies, University of California, 1985), 25fn.

architecture via consociational, centripetal, and communal approaches to institutional reform. This trend is noteworthy in itself: in most democracies, political institutions are 'sticky' and tend to remain unchanged for long periods—both because of the procedural difficulty in enacting large-scale reform and the political difficulties of convincing incumbent legislators to change the rules of the game that placed them in power. Because of this, reform is often precipitated by macro-level political events, such as a transition from authoritarian rule or a crisis of confidence in the economic or political system. While this pattern has been broadly followed in Asia—with major constitutional and electoral reforms in Indonesia, Korea, the Philippines, and Thailand resulting in part from the perceived failure of their governance arrangements to manage internal regime challenges and external shocks like the Asian economic crisis—there has also been a renaissance of institutional design across the region more generally, as Asian and Pacific governments have tried to transform the way their political systems operate.

In practice, the three political engineering models of consociationalism, centripetalism, and communalism should probably be seen more as ideal types rather than coherent, all-encompassing prescriptions. Indeed, some countries use combinations of each approach. Fiji's contemporary political architecture, for example, combines elements of all three: the 1997 constitution contains a formal power-sharing requirement for a consociational grand coalition government, divides the majority of seats along communal lines, and provides for a centripetal electoral system, the alternative vote. The result is an unusual and sometimes incoherent mixture of consociational, communal, and centripetal approaches to political engineering in one document.

Despite the differences between advocates of consociationalism, centripetalism, and communalism regarding the best institutional arrangements for divided societies, there is nonetheless agreement on some broader issues. One is a general consensus on the capacity of political institutions to change political outcomes, and hence on the utility of political engineering. Another is the central role ascribed to political parties and electoral systems as key institutional variables influencing the reduction—or escalation—of communal tensions in ethnically diverse societies. A third is the need to deal with the political effects of ethnicity directly rather than wishing them away. At a minimum, this means some type of government arrangement that gives all significant groups access to power, either directly

TABLE 4.1. *Consociational, centripetal, and communal institutions*

	Consociationalism	Centripetalism	Communalism
Elections	List PR large districts to maximize proportional outcomes	Vote-pooling to make politicians dependent on communities other than their own	Communal electoral rolls; ethnic division of parliament
Parties	Ethnic parties each representing their own group	Non-ethnic or multi-ethnic parties or party coalitions	Ethnic parties for communal element of elections
Cabinets	Grand coalition governments; minority veto on important issues	Multi-ethnic coalition governments; no minority vetoes	Formal power-sharing according to vote or seat share
Devolution	Segmental autonomy and ethnic federalism	Non-ethnic federalism or autonomy	Partition

or indirectly. For instance, multi-ethnic coalitions are favoured by both consociationalists and centripetalists as a desirable form of power-sharing for divided societies.[65] Table 4.1 sets out the key recommendation of each approach regarding elections, parties, cabinets, and devolution.

In the remainder of this book, I turn my attention from the general to the particular, and examine how Asia-Pacific countries have approached political engineering in these specific fields. Chapter 5 looks at the reform of electoral processes across the region, and the extent to which Asian and Pacific governments have utilized particular models of electoral system design. In Chapter 6, I examine the divergent ways in which Asian and

[65] In a useful insight, Sisk argues that consociationalism and centripetalism are *both* forms of power-sharing, as each seek the same outcomes—democratic stability in a situation of ethnic pluralism—through divergent means. As he notes, while 'many policymakers and scholars alike believe that broadly inclusive government, or power sharing, is essential to successful conflict management in societies beset by severe ethnic conflicts', they differ over whether the consociational approach 'in which groups are represented as groups (usually through ethnically exclusive political parties), in essence as building blocks of a common society' leads to better outcomes than the centripetal approach, 'in which practices seek to transcend ethnic group differences'. See Sisk, *Power Sharing*, 6.

Pacific states have attempted to shape the development of their political parties and party systems, and the extent to which they have encouraged aggregative or multi-ethnic party structures to develop. Chapter 7 takes up the issue of power-sharing via patterns of executive formation—that is, the structure of governing coalitions and cabinets—and also looks at schemes for territorial devolution across the region.

Each chapter attempts to shed some light on the key question of which approaches to political engineering have been tried and under what circumstances they succeed or fail. One conclusion that will become readily apparent is that in recent years Asia-Pacific governments have moved away from consociational and communal approaches, and have more often attempted political reforms which follow explicitly majoritarian and centripetal strategies of institutional design. In particular, Asia-Pacific governments have, for both self-serving and national-interest reasons, consistently sought to foster aggregative and centrist political parties and broad-based coalition governments, while actively discouraging sectional or minority groups from forging their own parties. As we shall see, the support for centripetal techniques to be found in the broader scholarly literature thus increasingly reflects the actual institutional choices of the Asia-Pacific's new democracies.

5

Representative Institutions: Elections and Electoral Systems

Electoral reform to change the relationship between voters and legislators, alter established patterns of political behaviour, and strengthen political parties and party systems has been the most prevalent form of political engineering in the Asia-Pacific. Because electoral systems determine how votes cast in an election are translated into seats won in parliament, they are the central 'rule of the game' determining who governs. The constituent elements of any electoral system—such as the formula for translating votes into seats, the way electoral districts are drawn, the structure of the ballot, and the extent to which voting is candidate or party-centred—all exert an independent influence on the behavioural incentives facing political actors, and hence on the development of political parties and the kinds of campaign strategies used by them.

The formative role of elections in shaping broader norms of political behaviour means that they are also 'the most specific manipulable instrument of politics',[1] and are thus—perhaps more than any other political institution—amenable to being engineered in order to achieve specific objectives and outcomes. For instance, many years of comparative electoral research have clearly identified PR as being the foremost institutional variable encouraging party multiplicity in general and the representation of smaller parties in particular.[2] Because of this, the choice of electoral system almost inevitably influences political development in transitional democracies: Lijphart reflects the prevailing

---

[1] Sartori, 'Political Development and Political Engineering', 273.
[2] See Douglas W. Rae, *The Political Consequences of Electoral Laws* (New Haven, CT: Yale University Press, 1967).

wisdom when he writes that 'if one wants to change the nature of a particular democracy, the electoral system is likely to be the most suitable and effective instrument for doing so'.[3]

In examining the relationship between political reform and the redesign of Asia-Pacific electoral systems, this chapter argues that many of the political reforms undertaken across the region in recent years have, at their heart, the objective of promoting the development of more aggregative, centrist, and stable politics by encouraging cohesive political parties and limiting party fragmentation. It also highlights several distinctive patterns of electoral reform across the region, including the increasing prevalence of 'mixed member' systems in Asia; the spread of alternative vote systems in the Pacific Islands; the distinctively majoritarian nature of these reform trends; and the increasing willingness of many Asian and Pacific states to borrow from each other in the search for appropriate models of electoral system design.

Trends in Electoral System Choice

A striking aspect of institutional reform in recent years is the convergence by different Asian and Pacific states on similar electoral system designs. Despite their considerable differences in forms of government, political culture, and democratic consolidation, congruent reform patterns are evident across almost all the East Asian democracies, with Japan, Korea, Taiwan, the Philippines, and Thailand adopting increasingly correspondent electoral models over the past decade.[4] At the same time, there has also been a convergence in reform patterns in the South Pacific, although towards quite different institutional models. These analogous trends in the design, implementation, and

[3] Arend Lijphart, 'Electoral Systems', in Lipset, *The Encyclopedia of Democracy*, 412.

[4] For excellent recent surveys of Asian electoral systems, see Aurel Croissant, Gabriele Bruns, and Marei John (eds.), *Electoral Politics in Southeast and East Asia* (Singapore: Friedrich Ebert Stiftung, 2002); and Allen Hicken and Yuko Kasuya, 'A Guide to the Constitutional Structures and Electoral Systems of East, South and Southeast Asia', *Electoral Studies*, 22 (2003), 121–51. The most comprehensive single collection on the subject is Dieter Nohlen, Florian Grotz, and Christof Hartmann (eds.), *Elections in Asia and the Pacific: A Data Handbook*, 2 vols. (Oxford: Oxford University Press, 2001).

impact of electoral reforms across both Asia and the Pacific are evident in both the technical characteristics and political consequences of the new institutional arrangements.

A particularly clear trend has been the adoption of 'mixed-member' models of electoral system design, in which both proportional and district-based elections are run side-by-side, in parallel. Under such systems, part of the legislature is elected, usually at a national level, by proportional representation, and the rest from local districts. While mixed systems have become common around the world over the past decade, they have been a particularly popular choice in Asia's new democracies—perhaps because they appear to combine the benefits of proportional outcomes with the accountability of district representation.[5] But in sharp contrast to similar reforms in other parts of the world, most of the mixed-member systems adopted in the Asia-Pacific region have also been highly *majoritarian* in both design and practice, leading to quite distinctive outcomes compared to other regions.

This turn towards mixed-member systems has occurred in two different contexts. In Northeast Asia, mixed systems have mostly been introduced as a replacement for or supplement to the single non-transferable vote (SNTV) previously used in Japan, Korea, and Taiwan. In Southeast Asia, by contrast, mixed systems have more often been introduced as a replacement for plurality or plurality-like systems such as the block vote, as in Thailand and the Philippines. While both SNTV and block vote systems were once widespread throughout Asia and the Pacific, today only Vanuatu continues to use SNTV for its parliamentary elections, while Laos is the only remaining example of the block vote in the region (SNTV has, however, been adopted for the new upper chambers in Thailand and Indonesia, while the Philippines' Senate is still elected by the block vote).

Both SNTV and block vote systems share a common drawback: because they encourage parties to put forward multiple candidates for election in the same district, both systems encourage *intra-party* competition. Under SNTV each elector has one vote,

---

[5] For more on mixed-member systems, see Andrew Reynolds, Ben Reilly, and Andrew Ellis, *Electoral System Design: The New International IDEA Handbook* (Stockholm: International Institute for Democracy and Electoral Assistance, 2005).

there are several seats to be elected in the district, and the candidates with the highest number of votes fill these positions. This means that the number of candidates a party nominates in each district is critical: too few, and parties miss out on valuable chances to win additional seats; too many, and they risk splitting their vote and losing winnable seats. Despite being structurally majoritarian, SNTV can thus advantage well-organized smaller parties, and often delivers relatively proportional election outcomes.

Under the block vote, by contrast, electors have as many votes as there are seats to be elected, and can use all their votes for the same party if they so desire. As a result, outcomes tend to be highly lopsided, greatly advantaging whichever party gains a plurality of the vote.

A key design flaw is that by forcing candidates from the same party to compete against each other for the same pool of voters, both systems emphasize personal attributes over and above those of the party. The resulting candidate-centred, intra-party competition has been widely identified as a cause of factionalism, corruption, and clientelism. SNTV's abandonment in Japan, for example, was fuelled by a series of corruption scandals linked to factional competition which damaged confidence in the political system.[6] Likewise, in Thailand, reformers blamed the block vote for contributing to vote-buying and money politics: because it was difficult for candidates to campaign effectively across the whole of a multi-seat district, particularly in rural areas, politicians tended to rely heavily on local canvassers to deliver votes from particular villages or districts in return for financial rewards. In the Philippines, the combination of candidate-centred elections with oligarchic family dynasties, enduring patron-client links, and weak political parties was widely seen as having subverted party system development and undermined coherent public policy, paving the way for Marcos's assumption of power in 1972.[7]

In each case, reformers hoped that the introduction of mixed-member electoral system models would undermine the institutional foundations of patronage politics by moving away

[6] See Steven R. Reed, 'Democracy and the Personal Vote: A Cautionary Tale from Japan', *Electoral Studies*, 13/1 (1994), 17–28.
[7] See R. Velasco, 'Philippine Democracy: Promise and Performance' in Laothamatas, *Democratization in Southeast and East Asia*.

from a situation where members from the same party competed with each other and personal relationships predominated, to a new environment in which genuine party allegiances and programmatic strategies could emerge. In Thailand, for instance, it was hoped that a shift to mostly single-member districts would undercut the prevalence of 'money politics', as local candidates would not have to rely on local agents to the same extent as they had in multi-member electorates. Reform advocates therefore argued that a change to a single-member system would reduce the impacts of vote-buying, pork-barrel politics, and corruption.[8] In Japan, similarly, reformers hoped that changing the electoral reform would foster the development of a two-party system and competition over policy rather than patronage.[9]

Across Asia, the rejection of SNTV and block vote systems led directly to the introduction of mixed systems combining plurality and proportional systems. Korea, which adopted a parallel mixed-member system in 1963, should probably be seen as the instigator of this movement, although it was not until 2004 that the allocation of list seats became truly proportional.[10] The Philippines adopted a mixed-member model as part of its 1987 Constitution, although the first elections under the system were not held until 1998. Taiwan was the next to introduce the mixed-member option, moving to a SNTV–PR combination in 1992, followed by Japan in 1994. Since then, Thailand and East Timor have also followed suit. By contrast, the countries of the island Pacific appear to have followed a separate reform strategy in recent years, with the 2 largest states, Fiji and Papua New Guinea, both adopting versions of a quite different system, the alternative vote. The remainder of this chapter discusses these divergent experiences of electoral engineering across Asia and the Pacific.

---

[8] Maisrikrod, 'Political Reform and the New Thai Electoral System', 196.

[9] See Takayuki Sakamoto, 'Explaining Electoral Reform: Japan versus Italy and New Zealand', *Party Politics*, 5/4 (1999), 419–38.

[10] Korea thus has some claims to having invented this model, *contra* the claim that non-compensatory mixed systems were 'invented' in Eastern Europe before being taken up by other states like Japan and Taiwan. See Sarah Birch, *Electoral Systems and Political Transformation in Post-Communist Europe* (Hampshire and New York: Palgrave Macmillan, 2003), 32.

Electoral Reform in Asia

Japan is the best-known example of electoral reform in Asia, and the Japanese case highlights some broader political concerns felt across the region. Electoral reform was primarily intended to re-orient Japanese politics away from special interests and foster a two-party system which would be more responsive to the interests of the median voter. In 1994, after a long debate about the political impacts of its electoral arrangements, Japan replaced SNTV with an overtly majoritarian form of mixed system, with three-fifths of all seats chosen from single-member districts. As the region's only stable long-term democracy, the Japanese reforms were stimulated not just by the collapse of public confidence in SNTV, but also by a deliberate effort to change the conduct of national politics by manipulating the electoral system. Opportunism also played a part: following a protracted factional struggle, Japan's long-ruling Liberal Democratic Party (LDP) government had split in June 1993, handing power to a seven-party coalition held together primarily by a shared commitment to electoral reform. A last-minute intervention by the LDP saw the introduction of a parallel mixed-member system, with 300 seats elected from single-member constituencies, and the remaining 200 seats (reduced to 180 in early 2000) chosen from a regional PR list in 11 multi-member districts. Unlike the mixed systems used elsewhere in Asia, the Japanese system allows candidates to transfer between tiers— a provision which enables so-called 'zombie' candidates who have lost their district seat to 'rise from the dead' on the party list.[11]

Recent reforms in Taiwan have followed a similar pattern. Taiwan first adopted a mixed system for its Legislative Yuan elections in 1992, but continued to use SNTV rules to elect most of the legislature. However, the same problems of personalized and factionalized party politics that plagued Japan under SNTV also afflicted Taiwanese politics.[12] In 2002, Taiwanese President Chen Shui-bian advanced a similar scheme to the Japanese reforms, proposing that two-thirds of Taiwan's parliament be elected by plurality rules and the remainder from a national

[11] Ellis S. Krauss and Robert Pekkanen, 'Explaining Party Adaptation to Electoral Reform: the Discreet Charm of the LDP?', *Journal of Japanese Studies*, 30/1 (2004), 7.
[12] John Fuh-sheng Hsieh, 'The SNTV System and Its Political Implications', in Hung-Mao Tien (ed.), *Taiwan's Electoral Politics and Democratic Transition: Riding the Third Wave* (Armonk, NY: M.E. Sharpe, 1996).

list, with electors having a separate vote for each (previously, list seats were simply allocated to parties polling more than 5 per cent of the total vote in proportion to their vote share at the district level). Under this new model, which was eventually approved in 2005, the parliament was halved in size to 113 seats, two-thirds of which are elected in single-member districts, with the remaining 34 chosen from a national PR list and six seats reserved for aboriginal voters. This new mixed-member plurality-PR model will be used for the first time at parliamentary elections scheduled for 2007, and has brought Taiwan's electoral arrangements squarely into line with other East Asian democracies.[13]

The Korean experience of mixed systems has, until recently, represented a third approach to electoral reform in the region. Over the years, Korea has experimented with different combinations of local districts and national lists, all of them strongly majoritarian in practice. Since March 2004, of the Korean National Assembly's 299 seats (restored after a cut to 273 seats at the 2000 elections as a cost-saving response to the Asian economic crisis), 243 are elected from single-member constituencies by a plurality formula, while the remaining 56 are allocated from a national constituency by proportional representation. Whereas previously voters received one ballot only, they now receive separate votes for the district and list seats. As the two components continue to be completely unlinked, this has only a marginal impact upon proportionality, although it does mean that smaller parties with a dispersed vote share are likely to receive some seats. Prior to 1996, by contrast, national list seats were given to parties on the basis of their *seat* share at district elections, meaning that the list allocation exacerbated any disproportionality arising from the local contests.[14]

Thus, divergent approaches to electoral reform have resulted in highly congruent electoral reforms in these three Northeast Asian cases. A similar conclusion applies to the Southeast Asian democracies of the Philippines and Thailand, which also implemented major electoral reforms during the 1990s. Under

---

[13] See Jih-wen Lin, 'Party Realignment and the Demise of SNTV in East Asia', unpublished paper, Institute of Political Science, Academia Sinica, Taiwan (2005).

[14] For a discussion see David Brady and Jongryn Mo, 'Electoral Systems and Institutional Choice: A Case Study of the 1988 Korean Elections', *Comparative Political Studies*, 24/4 (1992), 405–29.

its 1987 Constitution, the Philippines was the first Asian democracy to adopt a mixed-member system, with up to 52 seats (20 per cent of the legislature) chosen from a national list. Uniquely, however, list seats in the Philippines are not open to established parties but are instead designed to represent 'sectoral interests' and marginalized groups such as youth, labour, the urban poor, farmers, fishermen, and women. First implemented in 1998, the party-list regulations restrict each groups' representation to a maximum of three seats only. This restriction hampers the development of parties based around social cleavages. While cleavage-based parties are encouraged to run on the party list, the institutional framework provides a strong disincentive for their expansion, because garnering more support does not translate into more seats. Thus, while the Philippines' party list system may initially seem an exception, in practice it is another example of how new Asia-Pacific democracies have sought to avoid enfranchising ethnic or regional minorities.

The effect of these rules appears to have been widespread confusion, and the list seats have been dogged by problems, with less than half the winning list candidates taking up their seats after the 1998 and 2001 elections.[15] The new system has, however, resulted in more diversity within parliament than previously. Steven Rood argues that despite its problems, the party list experiment has 'injected a little more ideology into government processes', with list MPs playing an increasingly prominent role in the media and on legislative committees.[16] Other observers argue that the only way to promote genuine party development and accountability in the Philippines may be to allocate a much larger portion of all seats to party lists, eliminate the provision capping the number of seats that can be won, and allow all parties to compete freely for them.[17]

Like the Philippines, Thailand also moved to a mixed-member majoritarian system in 1997, with 400 of the parliament's 500 seats elected from single-member districts by plurality rules, and the remainder chosen by PR from a national list. Although established parties can compete for these seats (unlike in the Philippines), the effect of this reform has been the creation of

---

[15] R. J. May, 'Elections in the Philippines, May 2001', *Electoral Studies*, 21/4 (2002), 673–80.

[16] Rood, 'Elections as Important and Complicated Events', 152.

[17] Gabriella R. Montinola, 'Parties and Accountability in the Philippines', *Journal of Democracy*, 10/1 (1999), 126–40.

two classes of Thai politicians with radically divergent career incentives. The constituency MPs represent local districts and need to bring development opportunities to them; while the list MPs are supposed to concentrate their energies on issues of national, not local, importance, and are also expected to provide a wellspring of ministerial aspirants. Unlike Japan, cross-over between the two groups is not permitted, further emphasizing their mutual distinctiveness. As a result, elected members of the Thai cabinet are drawn disproportionately from this relatively small group of national list MPs rather than district representatives. Cabinet members are further insulated from constituency demands by the rule that they must resign from parliament upon taking up their ministries. Together with the oversight bodies provided in the 1997 constitution, these measures were designed to radically change the conduct of democratic governance in Thailand.[18] As Allen Hicken explains:

The drafters hoped that adding a national party list tier and doing away with intra-party competition would encourage voters and candidates to focus more on party policy positions regarding national issues. This in fact began to occur in the 2001 election. For the first time in recent Thai electoral history, political parties, led chiefly by the Thai Rak Thai (TRT) party, put significant effort into developing coordinated party-centred electoral strategies. Parties began to differentiate themselves in terms of their policy platforms and in some cases made those differences an important campaign issue.[19]

One example of this move towards programmatic campaigning was the TRT's campaign success in promising almost-free health care, forgiveness of rural debt, establishment of village borrowing funds, and other popular policies. By sidelining the previously dominant rural vote brokers and appealing directly to the electorate for support, these inducements proved highly popular: the newly-formed TRT won almost half of all seats at the 2001 elections, and gained a clear majority four years later. As Hicken argues, Thailand's electoral reforms were instrumental in this transformation.

Three other cases of recent democratization in Asia—Indonesia, Cambodia, and East Timor—also demonstrate some

---

[18] See Murray, 'Thailand's Recent Electoral Reforms'.
[19] Allen Hicken, 'Thailand' in Reynolds, Reilly and Ellis, *Electoral System Design*, 107.

of the underlying issues driving electoral reform across the region. While both Indonesia and Cambodia continue to use straight party-list PR systems, demands for the introduction of a mixed or district-based system as a means of stimulating greater political accountability have been articulated across the political spectrum in both countries. In Indonesia, the seven-member team of government officials and academics set up in 1998 to examine alternative electoral models, *Tim Tujuh*, proposed a mixed-member model very much like those elsewhere in Asia.[20] Under their proposed 'district plus' system, 76 per cent of seats would have been allocated to single-member districts, with the remaining 24 per cent elected by proportional representation. While popular with reformists, this proposal was opposed by Indonesia's main political parties, who succeeded in establishing instead an unusual hybrid system for Indonesia's 1999 elections. This comprised a unique combination of party-list PR with 'personal vote' characteristics, whereby the votes parties gained in particular municipalities (*kapupatem*) within each multi-member district would be used to determine which particular candidates would be elected. In theory, popular local candidates who attracted an above-average proportion of votes in a particular *kapupatem* would thus increase their chances of gaining a list seat. In practice, however, this provision proved almost impossible to administer, and was widely ignored by the electoral authorities.

In the run-up to Indonesia's 2004 elections, a more conventional model of 'open list' proportional representation was adopted. This time, all candidates were chosen from party lists, but voters were able to influence the composition of these lists by voting directly for a chosen candidate. Again, the motivation for this reform—common in Europe, but unique in the Asia-Pacific—was to give voters more influence over which candidates from a given party list would be elected, thus in theory strengthening the link between voters and politicians. As in 1999, however, this provision had a negligible influence on election outcomes: only 2 seats out of 550 were chosen this way, as an exceptionally large number of personal votes were needed to alter a candidate's position on the party list. In some ways this may have been fortunate, given that the broader thrust of electoral reform in

---

[20] For a good account of *Tim Tujuh*'s work, see John McBeth, 'Dawn of a New Age', *Far Eastern Economic Review*, 12 September 1998.

Indonesia aimed to encourage party cohesion by centralizing control of party organizations—an objective incompatible with open list voting, which 'allows entrants to free-ride on the party label while simultaneously encouraging them to curry a personal reputation for the provision of particularistic goods'.[21]

Nonetheless, demand for some form of district-based system remains strong in Indonesia, fuelled in part by the expectation that democratic prospects would be enhanced if the power of party elites was reduced and politics brought politics closer to the masses.[22] In response to these widely-expressed sentiments, one reform that did get implemented was a drastic reduction in 'district magnitude'—that is, the number of members elected from each electoral district. In contrast to previous years, where provincial units delineated constituency boundaries, Indonesia's 2004 elections were conducted using much smaller constituencies, capped at a maximum of twelve members per district. This raised the threshold for electoral success and made it much more difficult for smaller parties to win seats than at previous elections.[23] The overall effect—as in the other Asian cases—was to make Indonesia's 2004 electoral arrangements considerably more *majoritarian* than previously.

In Cambodia too, a series of reforms to the United Nations-inherited electoral system has led to greater majoritarianism. Prior to Cambodia's 1998 elections, the electoral formula was changed so that seats were allocated according to the 'highest average' method at the provincial level rather than the nation-wide 'largest remainder' system used in 1993—a change which discriminated against smaller parties. In response to calls for greater local accountability, district boundaries were adjusted and a number of new districts created, with the result that over one-third of all Cambodian parliamentarians now represent single-member districts.[24] As in Indonesia, the net effect of these

[21] Stephan Haggard, 'Democratic Institutions, Economic Policy, and Development', in Christopher Clague (ed.), *Institutions and Economic Development* (Baltimore, MD and London: Johns Hopkins University Press, 1997), 140.

[22] See Andrew Ellis, 'The Politics of Electoral Systems in Transition: The 1999 Elections in Indonesia and Beyond', *Representation*, 37 (2000), 241–8.

[23] Stephen Sherlock, 'Consolidation and Change: The Indonesian Parliament After the 2004 Elections' (Canberra: Centre for Democratic Institutions, 2004), 4.

[24] At the time of writing there were eight single-member constituencies in Cambodia, up from six in 1993.

changes has been the elimination of many small political parties, to the advantage of the larger incumbents. The increase in single-member districts and the change in electoral formula for the 1998 election meant that several smaller parties which would have gained seats if one national constituency had been used fell short, while the two major parties—the Cambodian People's Party (CPP) and FUNCINPEC—both gained 'seat bonuses'. Overall, the CPP gained five additional seats on the basis of the change in allocation formula, giving it a slim parliamentary majority. Calculations suggest that ten additional parties would have gained representation had the 1998 election been held under the 1993 electoral laws.[25]

The most recent example of democratization in Asia, East Timor, also used a mixed-member system for its foundation elections in 2001. However, the East Timorese model stands apart from the region's other mixed systems by allocating most seats to the party list rather than to districts. For the August 2001 constituent assembly elections, seventy-five seats were elected on a nationwide basis by proportional representation, and only thirteen seats (one for each district) by plurality rules. These elections were won in a landslide by the Revolutionary Front for an Independent East Timor (Fretilin) which captured fifty-five of the eighty-eight Assembly seats, winning forty-three of the seventy-five national seats and all of the available district seats. The Assembly then transformed itself into a legislature and passed a new constitution for the country which specifies that future elections must be held under proportional representation for a much smaller parliament.

Finally, the electoral arrangements of Asia's two resilient semi-democracies, Malaysia and Singapore, can be covered briefly. While the core features of the electoral system have remained unchanged since independence in both states, a succession of apparently technical changes have tilted the playing field increasingly in favour of incumbents. Malaysia uses a standard Westminster system with plurality elections, but constituency boundaries are gerrymandered to favour rural communities, and the electoral commission is a compliant servant of the government. The government has never lost an election and, with the exception of the 1969 elections, has always won the two-thirds majority required to amend the constitution. At the 2004 elections, the ruling *Barisan Nasional* coalition won

[25] My thanks to Michael Maley for the data on this point.

over 90 per cent of seats on 63 per cent of the vote. The situation is even more advantageous to the ruling party in Singapore, which has never come remotely close to a change of government. There, however, most MPs are elected from multi-member 'Group Representation Constituencies' each returning between four and six members; voters choose between competing party lists rather than candidates; and the highest-polling party wins all seats in the district. Combined with heavy restraints on opposition movement and a compliant pro-government press, this 'party block' system has hugely benefited Singapore's ruling People's Action Party (PAP), which regularly wins over 90 per cent of seats in parliament. At the 2001 elections, for example, the PAP won 82 out of 84 parliamentary seats with 74 per cent of the vote.

Table 5.1 sets out the changes in electoral systems across Asia since 1990.

As will now be clear, several patterns of electoral reform in Asia stand out when examined from a comparative perspective. First, in almost all cases, Asia's mixed-member systems are heavily weighted in favour of the majoritarian element of the system, and against the PR list. In Korea, Thailand, and the Philippines, roughly 20 per cent of seats are elected from the national list. In Japan, the figure is 38 per cent; in Taiwan's new system it is 30 per cent. In all cases, the bulk of seats in the legislature are chosen from local districts rather than the

TABLE 5.1. *Electoral systems changes in Asia since 1990*

Country	Former electoral system	New electoral system
Cambodia	Closed-list PR (largest remainder method)	Closed-list PR (highest average method) (1998)
East Timor	—	Mixed plurality-PR (2001)
Indonesia	Closed-list PR	Open list PR (2004)
Japan	SNTV	Mixed plurality-PR (1994)
Philippines	Plurality-block	Mixed plurality-PR (1998)
Korea	Modified plurality*	Mixed plurality-PR (1996/2003)
Taiwan	Mixed SNTV-PR	Mixed plurality-PR (2005)
Thailand	Block vote	Mixed plurality-PR (1997)

Key: PR = Proportional Representation; SNTV = Single Non-Transferable Vote.

* Korea's 1988 system delivered list seats to the party that won the most seats in the district contest, ensuring it an overall majority in the assembly. This was changed in 1996 to allocate list seats on the basis of each party's vote (rather than seat) share at the district level. In 2003, a standard mixed-member model, with separate votes for each tier, was adopted.

national list. As Table 5.2 shows, all the East Asian mixed systems (with the exception of East Timor) are clearly majoritarian in their overall structure. This stands in direct contrast to the international norm, where well-known examples of mixed systems, such as Germany and New Zealand, feature an equal or near-equal split between the district and list components. Asian states have also rejected the kind of compensatory mechanisms used by these countries, in which list seats are allocated in such a way as to produce proportional outcomes overall. While such 'mixed member proportional' (MMP) systems are used in a number of European and Latin American countries, none have been adopted in Asia. Rather, every Asian mixed-member system runs the list component of elections in parallel with the district contest, but with no interchange between the two.[26]

The limited number of proportional representation seats in most Asian cases compared to other regions can be explained in part by the desire of incumbents to minimize the threat of political fragmentation by restricting the electoral prospects of minor opposition parties. While smaller parties can legitimately hope to gain some representation from the list seats, overall levels of proportionality in such systems are in most cases more like those of a plurality system than a proportional one. The combination of the lack of any compensatory mechanism and the relatively small number of proportional seats on offer reinforces the majoritarian tendencies described earlier.

TABLE 5.2. *Mixed-member electoral systems in Asia*

Country	District seats	District system	List seats	List System	Total seats
Japan	300	Plurality	180	List PR	480
Korea	243	Plurality	56	List PR	299
Taiwan	73	Plurality	34	List PR	113*
Thailand	400	Plurality	100	List PR	500
Philippines	209	Plurality	up to 53	List PR, with 3 seat limit	262
East Timor	13	Plurality	75	List PR	88

*includes six additional seats reserved for aboriginal minorities.

[26] Although some scholars incorrectly classify the Philippines as a compensatory system. See Louis Massicote and André Blais, 'Mixed Electoral Systems: A Conceptual and Empirical Survey', *Electoral Studies*, 18/3 (1999), 353.

Asia's mixed-member electoral systems are thus extreme examples of what Matthew Shugart and Martin Wattenberg, in the most comprehensive evaluation of mixed systems to date, call 'mixed-member majoritarian' (MMM) systems.[27] The Asian versions are 'extreme' forms of this system type because as well as having no compensatory mechanisms, with one exception they all elect a majority of seats from districts, not lists—making them distinctive in comparative terms.[28] As Shugart and Wattenberg note, around the world 'most MMM systems have a nearly even split between tiers, such that around half of the seats are allocated proportionately'.[29] By contrast, for the five Asian cases of Japan, Korea, the Philippines, Taiwan, and Thailand, the average proportion of list seats is just 25 per cent. In other words, Asian MMM systems are, in structural terms, twice as majoritarian as those in other parts of the world.

The reasons advanced for introducing mixed systems underline these differences. Outside Asia, the introduction of mixed systems was most often motivated by a desire on the part of electoral reformers to maintain single-member electorates while still presenting minor parties with opportunities for relatively equitable representation.[30] In Asia, by contrast, the motivation for the introduction of party lists in mixed-member systems appears to have more to do with a desire to promote

[27] See Matthew S. Shugart and Martin P. Wattenberg (eds.), *Mixed-Member Electoral Systems: the Best of Both Worlds?* (New York: Oxford University Press, 2001). Although they do not focus on Asian cases beyond Japan, Shugart and Wattenberg's discussion of how MMM systems were chosen may also have relevance for the Asia-Pacific. Specifically, they find that in most cases the adoption of MMM systems was the result of a compromise between incumbent and newly emerging political parties with strongly divergent preferences (Hungary, Italy, Japan, and Mexico are all examples of this).

[28] The Asian cases also highlight some of the problems in the way Shugart and Wattenberg define MMM as any unlinked mixed-member system, regardless of its distribution of seats between districts and list. In Asia, this would include not just Japan, Korea, Taiwan, Thailand, and the Philippines, but also East Timor, in which 85 per cent of all seats are chosen by proportional representation. This makes little sense; I therefore prefer to reserve the MMM term for unlinked systems which elect a *majority* of seats from districts.

[29] Matthew S. Shugart and Martin P. Wattenberg, 'Mixed-Member Electoral Systems: A Definition and Typology', in Shugart and Wattenberg, *Mixed-Member Electoral Systems*, 19.

[30] Matthew S. Shugart and Martin P. Wattenberg, 'Introduction: the Electoral Reform of the 21st Century?', in Shugart and Wattenberg, *Mixed-Member Electoral Systems*, 1–6.

national political parties and enhance the role of the established party organizations while ensuring some (limited) representation of minorities.[31] Compounding this, electoral thresholds to encourage political aggregation and prevent small parties being elected are also common. In both Thailand and Taiwan, for example, parties competing for party-list seats must attain at least 5 per cent of the vote—a provision which discriminates against minor parties. In Korea, the rules are more complex: although a 3 per cent threshold also applies to the party list, this is disregarded for parties that win at least five district seats. The Philippines also applies a 2 per cent threshold to the party list, and a three-seat cap on the number of seats each party list can win.

Across the region, the impact of these restrictions has been to limit the growth of parties representing social cleavages or ethnic minorities. While the fact that most legislators continue to be elected from districts creates incentives for politicians to cultivate 'personal' rather than party-based support, the broader institutional framework makes it difficult for small parties with a dispersed vote share to win any district seats.[32] Along with the majoritarian structure of the region's electoral systems, the increasing use of thresholds and other restrictions on cleavage-based parties represent a significant hurdle for minority groups seeking political representation.

Shugart and Wattenberg conclude that MMM systems are more likely than most alternatives to produce 'two-block' party systems, and more likely than any others to simultaneously generate local accountability and a nationally-oriented party system.[33] The Asian experience largely supports these findings: in most cases, the introduction of MMM systems has advantaged existing large, nationally-focused political parties, hampered smaller or regionally based parties, and led to a consolidation in the party system. As will be discussed in more detail in Chapter 6, party numbers have fallen since the introduction of

[31] See, for example, the discussion of the party list in the Philippines in Julio Teehankee, 'Electoral Politics in the Philippines' in Croissant, Bruns, and John, *Electoral Politics*, 149–202.

[32] See John M. Carey and Matthew S. Shugart, 'Incentives to Cultivate a Personal Vote: A Rank Ordering of Electoral Formulas', *Electoral Studies*, 14/4 (1995), 441–60.

[33] Matthew S. Shugart and Martin P. Wattenberg, 'Conclusion: Are Mixed-Member Systems the Best of Both Worlds?', in Shugart and Wattenberg, *Mixed-Member Electoral Systems*, 591.

reforms in most cases, and parties in countries like Japan and Thailand have had to become more responsive to centrist policy demands rather than sectional interests.[34] In this respect, at least, the Asian experience is consistent with other world regions.

Despite this, mixed-member systems also have a number of clear disadvantages. By privileging local districts over national lists, they continue to generate structural incentives favouring personal rather than party-based support. By dividing seats between the district and list tiers, they create two classes of representatives—one group with districts to look after who are beholden to their local electorate, and a second group chosen from the party lists, without formal constituency ties, who are primarily beholden to their party leaders. Most importantly, the failure of the region's mixed systems to guarantee proportionality means that some parties can be shut out of representation despite winning substantial numbers of votes. When combined with vote thresholds and seat caps on the party list, this further limits the representation of minorities.

To illustrate the extent to which Asian states have become more majoritarian as a result of these reforms, Table 5.3 displays the change in the proportionality of election results between pre-reform and post-reform elections across the region, using Lijphart's measure of the average seat–vote deviation for the two largest parties at each election.[35] As the table shows, in almost all cases disproportionality following the introduction of electoral reforms was considerably higher than in the pre-reform period. As Aurel Croissant notes of the Southeast Asian cases: 'The change in vote–seat deviation in the wake of electoral reforms is remarkable. Ironically, this is the case for Thailand's segmented system where the degree of electoral disproportionality rose significantly *after* components of proportional representation were introduced. The same is true for the Philippines's party-list system, used for the first time in 1998 and again in 2001.'[36] Only Indonesia bucks this trend—somewhat surprisingly given the marked reduction in average district magnitude there.

---

[34] Hicken, 'Thailand'; Krauss and Pekkanen, 'Explaining Party Adaptation', 2.
[35] Lijphart, *Electoral Systems and Party Systems*.
[36] Aurel Croissant, 'Electoral Politics in Southeast and East Asia: A Comparative Perspective' in Croissant, Bruns, and John, *Electoral Politics*, 329.

TABLE 5.3. *Electoral disproportionality in pre-and post-reform elections*

Country	Disproportionality average all elections	Disproportionality latest election
Cambodia	5.42 (1993–8)	6.10 (2003)
Indonesia	1.87 (1999)	1.50 (2004)
Japan	4.80 (1947–2000)	7.10 (2004)
Korea	7.00 (1988–2000)	7.52 (2004)
Taiwan*	3.52 (1992–2004)	NA (2007)
Thailand	2.70 (1992–2001)	6.04 (2001)
Philippines	4.46 (1987–98)	6.55 (2004)**

* Legislative Yuan elections.
**Party list seats only.
Source: Croissant, 'Electoral Politics', 329; author's calculations.

Electoral Reform in the Pacific

What about the Pacific countries? In contrast to Asia, Papua New Guinea and the Pacific Islands have shown little interest in mixed-member systems. Rather, the most influential electoral reform in recent years has been the replacement of plurality elections with variants of the alternative vote, which requires successful candidates to gain not just a plurality but an absolute majority of votes. Under this system, voters rank-order candidates on the ballot paper in order of their choice, by marking a '1' for their most favoured candidate, a '2' for their second choice, '3' for their third choice, and so on. Any candidate who gains an absolute majority of first-preference votes is immediately elected. If no-one has a majority, the candidate with the lowest vote total is 'eliminated' from the count and his or her ballots re-examined for their second preferences, which are assigned to the remaining candidates as marked on the ballot. This process is repeated until one candidate has an absolute majority or until there are no votes left in the count.[37]

[37] A close variant of the alternative vote is also used in Nauru, one of the world's smallest democracies with a population of just 12,000. Under Nauru's system, each preference marked on the ballot paper is assigned a value: a first preference is worth '1', a second preference is one-half a vote, a third preference one-third, and so on. When votes are tallied, the total preference scores for each candidate are calculated, and the candidate(s) with the highest score(s) wins the seat. This system has some unusual theoretical properties, and bears a strong relationship to the method of election proposed by the eighteenth-century French mathematician Jean-Charles de Borda as an optimum decision-making procedure for

As discussed in Chapter 4, some scholars recommend the alternative vote as being particularly appropriate for ethnically divided societies, on the basis that it encourages vote-seeking politicians to campaign for 'second-choice' votes, thus encouraging cross-ethnic politics in the context of election campaigns. Where a significant moderate sentiment exists in the electorate, ethnic candidates may have an incentive to move to the centre on policy issues to attract these voters, or to accommodate fringe issues into their broader policy. Under either scenario, the possibility of reciprocal vote transfers between rival parties and candidates can create important 'arenas of bargaining', increasing the prospects of vote transfers flowing from ethnic parties to non-ethnic ones, and strengthening the 'moderate middle'. This explains the enthusiasm with which advocates of centripetalism often view such systems.[38]

The two largest Pacific Island countries, Fiji and Papua New Guinea, have both adopted alternative vote elections in recent years. The most comprehensive—and controversial—attempt at electoral engineering has taken place in Fiji, where politics has long been characterized by an uneasy co-existence between two main communities: indigenous Fijians of Melanesian and Polynesian heritage and Indo-Fijians descended from indentured labourers brought to Fiji in the nineteenth century. Fiji's modern political history has been dominated by attempts to find a stable political formula that satisfies both groups. In 1986, a military coup brought down an elected government seen as overly close to the Indo-Fijian community. In 1997, after ten years of economic stagnation and increasing international isolation, Fiji adopted a new constitution and a package of political reforms designed to move the country 'gradually but decisively' towards multiethnic politics. One of these reforms was the introduction of the alternative vote which, it was hoped, could promote reciprocal vote-pooling and hence political accommodation between the two main communities.[39]

assemblies and committees. See Benjamin Reilly, 'Social Choice in the South Seas: Electoral Innovation and the Borda Count in the Pacific Island Countries', *International Political Science Review*, 23/4 (2002), 355–72.

[38] See Horowitz, *Ethnic Groups in Conflict* and *A Democratic South Africa?*; Reilly, *Democracy in Divided Societies*.

[39] See Fiji Constitution Review Commission, *The Fiji Islands: Towards a United Future* (Suva: Parliament of Fiji, 1996).

At the first elections under these new arrangements in 1999, an unexpectedly strong vote for the Indo-Fijian supported Fiji Labour Party, combined with a fragmentation of the indigenous Fijian vote, resulted in a landslide victory for Labour and its leader Mahendra Chaudhry, who became Fiji's first Indo-Fijian prime minister. But almost a year to the day after the election, in May 2000, a group of gunmen headed by a part-Fijian businessman, George Speight, took the new government hostage, claiming a need to restore indigenous paramountcy to the political system. By the time the hostages were released and Speight and his supporters arrested, Fiji had returned to military rule. Some commentators ascribed this unhappy outcome to the new electoral system, arguing that the alternative vote as implemented in Fiji 'proved extraordinarily complex, the results ambiguous in important respects, and its merits as a tool for generating inter-ethnic accommodation highly questionable'.[40] In August 2001, Fiji went back to the polls under the same electoral rules, but with quite different results as the incumbent government of military-appointed indigenous Fijian Prime Minister Laisenia Qarase emerged victorious. Both the 1999 and 2001 elections were highly disproportional, in part because of the effects of a 'ticket vote' option which had been added to the ballot paper, allowing parties to determine the direction of preference flows.[41] As a result, the alternative vote has continued to be criticized by some observers of Fijian politics.[42]

Papua New Guinea, which used the alternative vote from 1964 to 1972 and again since 2002, provides a very different insight into the system's utility in ethnically diverse societies. There, the possibility of reciprocal vote transfers between clan groups encouraged cooperation and accommodation in the context of Papua New Guinea's notoriously fragmented society by allowing candidates with limited 'home' support to campaign for second-preference support amongst rival groups. Utilizing traditional tribal allies and allegiances to create majority victors, this encouraged a considerable level of cross-ethnic cooperation at the three pre-independence elections held under the system.

[40] Fraenkel, 'The Alternative Vote System in Fiji', 9.
[41] Benjamin Reilly, 'Evaluating the Effect of the Electoral System in Post-Coup Fiji', *Pacific Economic Bulletin*, 16/1 (2001), 142–9.
[42] Fraenkel, 'The Alternative Vote'; Fraenkel and Grofman, 'A Neo-Downsian model', cf. Donald L. Horowitz, 'The Alternative Vote and Interethnic Moderation: A Reply to Fraenkel and Grofman', *Public Choice*, 121 (2004), 507–16.

However, these accommodative patterns disappeared with the change to a plurality system in 1975, which undercut incentives for inter-ethnic cooperation and turned elections into a zero-sum contest between rival tribal groups in which candidates could win election with miniscule vote shares, leading to large-scale electoral violence and an increasingly unrepresentative national legislature.[43]

In an attempt to combat this downward spiral, in 2002 the alternative vote was reintroduced for future elections, with voters limited to a maximum of three preferences. As well as ensuring that winning candidates would have to gain a much greater share of votes to get elected, it was hoped that this new 'limited preferential' system would reduce electoral violence and encourage candidates to cooperate with each other during election campaigns—both features distinctively absent under plurality elections. In 2004, these hopes were put to the test at six by-elections held under the new system in different regions of the country. These elections largely replicated the pre-independence experience with the alternative vote: all featured much higher support levels for winning candidates, more cooperative campaign tactics, and much lower levels of electoral violence than those held in the same regions just two years earlier under plurality rules.[44] In contrast to Fiji's experience, then, the Papua New Guinea case lends support to arguments in favour of the alternative vote as a means of promoting ethnic accommodation in divided societies.

Why has AV succeeded in Papua New Guinea but not in Fiji? First and foremost, there is the question of social structure. Papua New Guinea's uniquely fragmented society means that most electorates are themselves highly heterogeneous in ethnic terms, making some cross-ethnic vote pooling almost inevitable. Fiji, by contrast, is more polarized than fragmented, with high levels of residential self-segregation between the two main communities, limiting opportunities for inter-ethnic vote-pooling at the constituency level. Fiji's constitutional design only exacerbates this problem: of the twenty-five open electorates which enable multi-ethnic competition, less than half are reasonably balanced in their mixture of indigenous Fijian and Indo-Fijian

---

[43] For a detailed discussion see Reilly, *Democracy in Divided Societies*, chapter 4.

[44] See Bill Standish, 'Limited Preferential Voting: Some Early Lessons', Paper presented at conference on Overcoming Constraints in Papua New Guinea, Lowy Institute for International Policy, Sydney, 18 January 2005.

118   *Elections and Electoral Systems*

voters. Most electorates are dominated by one community or the other, offering little incentive for genuine inter-ethnic vote-pooling. Finally, different ballot formats elicit different behaviour in each case. In Papua New Guinea, electors have to mark at least three preferences, meaning that they have to look outside their tribal grouping to effect a valid vote. In Fiji, by contrast, the ticket option on the ballot paper hands control of preference allocation to the party elites, with sometimes bizarre consequences.[45]

Elsewhere in the Pacific, continuity rather than change has been the predominant pattern in terms of electoral system choice. Colonially-inherited plurality systems persist in the independent states of Solomon Islands, Samoa, Tonga, Tuvalu, and most of Micronesia (with the exception of Nauru and Kiribati, where a run-off is used). Vanuatu, uniquely, continues to use SNTV, the result of a constitutional requirement that the electoral system should 'ensure fair representation of different political groups and opinions'.[46] Overall, while the Pacific clearly evidences quite different institutional choices to those of Asia, those reforms that have occurred are, like Asia, clearly pushing politics in the direction of more aggregative and majoritarian outcomes.

Conclusion

As will now be apparent, several distinctive patterns of electoral reform, such as the predominance of mixed-member systems in Asia and the growing interest in alternative voting in the Pacific, stand out when surveying the Asia-Pacific region as a whole. It is important to emphasize that these patterns are not limited to the Asia-Pacific region: over the past decade, both mixed-member systems and, to a lesser extend, the alternative vote have become increasingly popular electoral reform choices around the world.[47] However, the specific experience of electoral reform in

[45] At the 1999 elections, for instance, the Fiji Labour Party directed their preferences away from their main rival for Indo-Fijian votes and towards ultra-nationalist Fijian parties—a tactically rewarding but reputationally damaging strategy which clearly would not have been followed by most Indo-Fijian voters.
[46] Constitution of the Republic of Vanuatu, Art. 17(11).
[47] See Shugart and Wattenberg, *Mixed-Member Electoral Systems*; Benjamin Reilly, 'The Global Spread of Preferential Voting: Australian Institutional Imperialism?', *Australian Journal of Political Science*, 39/2 (2004), 253–66.

Asia and the Pacific has been unusual by international standards in a number of ways.

Overwhelmingly, Asia-Pacific democracies have adopted electoral reforms that are strongly majoritarian in both design and outcome. Structurally, this preference for majoritarianism is apparent in the 'parallel' nature of the mixed-member systems chosen, their weighting in favour of the district rather than the list component, and the use of technical devices such as vote thresholds (in Taiwan, Thailand, and Korea), reduction in district magnitude (Indonesia), increasing use of single-member districts (Cambodia), and restrictions on competition for party list seats (the Philippines). All of these measures push electoral politics in the same broad direction. Writing about the process of electoral reform in Korea, Croissant noted that the 'debate on electoral reforms focuses very much on the question of how to improve the majority generating function of the electoral system—i.e. its capability to produce single party majorities in parliament'.[48] This statement could well be applied across the Asia-Pacific more generally.

Nonetheless, it is important to emphasize the different motivations which lay behind these reforms. In Thailand, the party list seats are supposed to produce high-quality candidates who may not be suited to the cut and thrust of electoral campaigning, but may provide a pool of potential ministers. In Japan, the motive was to lower the value of the heavily weighted rural seats that unduly encouraged pork-barrel politics, and encourage a move towards two-party politics. The reasoning in Korea and Taiwan was similar to Japan's, but with one important addition. Regionalism is a problem in both countries, and is particularly acute in Korea, so their party list is elected on a nationwide basis, encouraging parties to pitch their policy messages to a national audience rather than concentrate on a regional one. In the Philippines, the core problem has long been the domination of politics by traditional elites, and the party list system is therefore only open to disadvantaged groups. Despite the similarity of the institutions chosen, political engineers in all five countries were responding to quite specific political problems and crafting innovative institutional responses.[49]

---

[48] Aurel Croissant, 'Electoral Politics in South Korea', in Croissant, Bruns, and John, *Electoral Politics*, 257.

[49] See Roland Rich, 'Designing Democracy Along the Pacific Rim', *Democracy at Large*, 2/1 (2006), 2.

While the promotion of cohesive parties and stable governments were also important in the Pacific Islands, electoral reforms there have evidenced different patterns. Unlike the Asian preference for mixed models, the most popular reform in the Pacific Islands region has been the replacement of plurality systems with the alternative vote. However, despite these very different institutional configurations, the deeper motivations driving electoral reform in the Pacific appear broadly similar to those evident in Asia. In Fiji and Papua New Guinea, for example, a key objective was to alter the conduct of competitive politics by changing the incentives facing politicians in their quest for electoral victory. In Papua New Guinea, arguments in favour of the re-introduction of the alternative vote centred on the need for majority victors and inter-tribal accommodation; in Fiji, the objective was to engineer multi-ethnic politics via cross-ethnic preference swapping. Strengthening political parties was also an overt aim in both countries.

In both Asia and the Pacific, then, reformers sought to encourage cohesive political parties while limiting ethnic or minority movements. As we have seen, both majoritarian mixed-member models (in Asia) and alternative vote systems (in the Pacific) tend to favour broad-based parties and aggregative politics. These reform trends become even clearer when the many and varied attempts made by Asian and Pacific government to shape the development of their party systems are examined. In addition to using electoral system design to try to change the way political parties function, many Asian and Pacific states have also attempted to reform their party systems more directly, through overt engineering of the rules governing the formation, organization, and behaviour of political parties. This is the subject of the following chapter.

....
6
....

Mediating Institutions: Political Parties and Party Systems

The sustained focus on reshaping political parties and party systems has been perhaps the most distinctive single feature of political engineering in the Asia-Pacific. Scholars of democracy have long considered political parties to play a crucial role not just in representing interests, aggregating preferences, and forming governments, but also in managing conflict and promoting stable politics. Because they are the key vehicle for translating diverse public opinion into coherent public policy, strong parties are a vital component of efficient governance and hence development. Consolidated party systems are especially important in new democracies, where the negative consequences of weak parties are often most apparent. Writing in the late 1980s at the beginning of Asia's democratization wave, Larry Diamond observed that:

With the emergence of new democratic opportunities (dramatically in South Korea, more subtly and gradually in Thailand), the construction of broad-based, coherent parties—mobilizing and incorporating popular interests, organized effectively down to the local level, and penetrating particularly through the countryside—looms as one of the preeminent challenges of democratization.[1]

Despite their acknowledged importance, parties have traditionally been viewed as social phenomena beyond the scope of deliberate institutional engineering. In recent years, however, political reformers in a diverse array of Asian and Pacific states including Thailand, Indonesia, Fiji, and Papua New Guinea

[1] Larry Diamond, 'Introduction', in Diamond, Linz, and Lipset, *Democracy in Developing Countries: Asia*, 29.

have tried to shape the development of their party systems by strengthening party organizations, promoting cross-regional party structures, countering the rise of ethnic parties, and generally encouraging the growth of cohesive party organisations. While not yet the subject of much attention, these political experiments are likely to have important consequences for governance in the region. This chapter examines these various attempts across the Asia-Pacific to engineer the development of political parties and party systems.

The Importance of Parties

Political parties perform a number of essential functions in a democracy: ideally, they represent political constituencies and interests, recruit and socialize new candidates for office, craft policy alternatives, set policymaking agendas, form governments, and integrate disparate groups and individuals into the democratic process.[2] These linking, mediating and representational functions mean that parties are one of the primary channels for building accountable and responsive government in new democracies. As Atul Kohli argues, in fragile democracies where political communities are not well established the need for functioning parties of competing orientations becomes that much greater. Well-organized parties are one of the few available political instruments that can both represent interests and concentrate them at the top, enabling party leaders, if they win majority support, to pursue development democratically. Crafting well-organized parties thus remains an important long-term goal of political engineering in the Third World.[3]

This stylized depiction of the contribution parties make to democratic consolidation can, however, be undermined by the reality of special-interest, pork-barrel politics. Because most democracies are based on the idea of the parliamentary member representing a particular territorial as well as a policy space, representatives are supposed to act simultaneously

---

[2] See Larry Diamond, 'Introduction: In Search of Consolidation', in Larry Diamond, Marc F. Plattner, Yun-han Chu, and Hung-mao Tien (eds.), *Consolidating the Third Wave Democracies: Themes and Perspectives* (Baltimore, MD and London: Johns Hopkins University Press, 1997), xxiii.

[3] Atul Kohli, 'Centralization and Powerlessness: India's Democracy in a Comparative Perspective', in Joel S. Migdal, Atul Kohli, and Vivian Shue (eds.), *State Power and Social Forces: Domination and Transformation in the Third World* (Cambridge: Cambridge University Press, 1994).

as the principal for the interests of their supporters *and* make policy decisions that are in the interests of the country at large. If parties are unable to coordinate their candidates' positions effectively, there will often be an inherent tension between the interests of individual legislators (who will benefit by catering to demands for clientelism and patronage) and those of parties (which need to establish coordinated positions on policy issues to function effectively).

Thus in Thailand's fragmented pre-reform party system, for instance, 'coordination problems centered on the struggle for pork. With multiple contenders and weak party organizations, there were few constraints on politicians in the competition for patronage and pork-barrel expenditures and limited incentives to cooperate around reforms that provide public goods.'[4] In the same vein, elections in the Philippines have been characterized by weakly organized parties dependent on patron–client ties. Utilizing traditional kinship networks, Filipino politicians have for many decades appealed for votes not on the basis of policy or ideology, but rather by distributing material goods to their supporters in exchange for electoral support and loyalty.[5] As a consequence, 'the logic of patronage politics remains central to understanding Filipino politics, and political parties remain weak, ill-defined, and poorly institutionalized'.[6] The presence of such clientelistic, patronage-based parties in both Thailand and the Philippines resulted in a large group of individual legislators who remained tied to local patrons and vote mobilizers in their constituencies, and were often unwilling or unable to act collectively in parliament (mass switching of parties after every election was the norm in both countries).[7]

Problems of weak, patronage-based parties are also evident in some of the Asia-Pacific's more developed states such as Korea, where electoral competition 'revolves around personality-dominated, clientelistic parties build on the basis of vast networks of patron–client relations'.[8] Korean commentators have consistently identified party weakness as a threat to their

---

[4] Stephan Haggard, 'Democratic Institutions, Economic Policy, and Development', 136.

[5] See Landé, *Leaders, Factions and Parties.*

[6] Hutchcroft and Rocamora, 'Strong Demands and Weak Institutions', 281.

[7] Steven Rood, 'Elections as Complicated and Important Events in the Philippines', in Hsieh and Newman, *How Asia Votes*, 157.

[8] Aurel Croissant, 'South Korea', in Nohlen, Grotz, and Hartmann, *Elections in Asia and the Pacific*, 414.

country's democratic consolidation. Byung-Kook Kim, for instance, argues that Korea remains hobbled by its incoherent and unstable party system: 'Since 1987, Korean political parties have encountered profound difficulty in developing a discourse which could aggregate diverse societal demands and interests into coherent programmes, with clear priorities and consistent internal logic.' If this 'deviant path of political development' is not corrected, he warns, 'the entire project of political democratization could fall into bankruptcy'.[9]

The capacity of parties to generate programmatic policy offerings and ensure disciplined, predictable collective action on the part of their members is thus a crucial element of effective governance. These goals are enhanced by the extent to which parties are *institutionalized* and can maintain allegiance and discipline on policy issues.[10] In the most comprehensive work on the subject to date, Scott Mainwaring and Timothy Scully assert that the level of party institutionalization depends on four factors: the regularity of party competition, the depth and stability of party roots in society, the popular acceptance of party and electoral competition as the means of determining who governs, and the extent to which parties are organized internally. While well-institutionalized parties can typically maintain internal discipline and present a consistent policy platform to voters, in under-institutionalized systems 'party organizations are generally weak, electoral volatility is high, party roots in society are weak, and individual personalities dominate parties and campaigns'.[11]

While this focus on party institutionalization is relatively recent, the broader scholarly literature has displayed a strong normative bias in favour of well-rooted, organizationally developed political parties for decades. In his classic work on political change, for example, Huntington argued that strong parties are 'the prerequisite for political stability in modernizing countries'.[12] Three leading scholars of democracy have bluntly

[9] Byung-Kook Kim, 'Party Politics in South Korea's Democracy: the Crisis of Success', in Larry Diamond and Byung-Kook Kim (eds.), *Consolidating Democracy in South Korea* (Boulder and London: Lynne Rienner Publishers, 2000), 58, 80.

[10] See John Aldrich, *Why Parties?* (Chicago, IL: University of Chicago Press, 1995).

[11] Scott Mainwaring and Timothy Scully, 'Introduction', in Mainwaring and Scully (eds.), *Building Democratic Institutions*, 20.

[12] Huntington, *Political Order*, 412.

stated that 'without effective parties that command at least somewhat stable bases of support, democracies cannot have effective governance'.[13] More recently, in one of his final publications, Seymour Martin Lipset extolled the 'indispensability of political parties' for the survival of both transitional and established democracies.[14] In sum, political scientists coming from a range of theoretical and regional perspectives consistently cite the virtues of stable and programmatic political parties for effective governance in emerging and consolidated democracies alike. However, they offer little advice as to how such party systems may be encouraged or promoted.

Political Parties and Social Diversity

The institutionalized, aggregative, and cohesive party organizations advocated in much of the scholarly literature on democratization can be contrasted with parties whose support base stems primarily from narrow sectoral or communal ties. Outside the consociational literature, few scholars endorse parties which cater to and explicitly represent ethnic cleavages. As Gunther and Diamond write, 'The electoral logic of the ethnic party is to harden and mobilize its ethnic base with exclusive, often polarizing appeals to ethnic group opportunity and threat...the ethnic party's particularistic, exclusivist, and often polarizing political appeals make its overall contribution to society divisive and even disintegrative.'[15] At the margins, the presence of such parties can lead to what Sartori dubbed 'polarized pluralism', where the ideological distance between the parties expands, to the detriment of the political centre.[16] Indeed, in Western democracies, the presence of parties with extremely divergent policies and preferences has historically been one of the single most important predictors of

---

[13] Larry Diamond, Juan Linz, and Seymour Martin Lipset, 'Introduction: What Makes for Democracy?', in Diamond, Linz, and Lipset, *Politics in Developing Countries*, 34.

[14] Seymour Martin Lipset, 'The Indispensability of Political Parties', *Journal of Democracy*, 11/1 (2000), 48–55.

[15] Richard Gunther and Larry Diamond, 'Types and Functions of Parties', in Larry Diamond and Richard Gunther (eds.), *Political Parties and Democracy* (Baltimore, MD and London: Johns Hopkins University Press, 2001), 23–4.

[16] Giovanni Sartori, *Parties and Party Systems: A Framework for Analysis* (New York: Cambridge University Press, 1976), 137–9.

political instability.[17] By contrast, in more aggregative and centripetal party systems, elections tend to be fought out between a small number of cohesive parties, and most politicians 'crowd the center' in their quest for the median voter and avoid sharp differentiation with their competitors. As a result, 'they tend to have a moderating influence on the way interests are aggregated'.[18] This suggests that ideally, a small number of programmatic parties capable of translating diverse public preferences into coherent policy is probably the optimum party system model. Diamond, for instance, argues that the optimum conditions for democratic consolidation included a 'settled and aggregative' party system in which 'one or two broadly based, centrist parties fight for the middle ground'.[19]

But simply focusing on the number of parties tells us little about the size or relative importance of different parties. Political scientists have therefore developed a measure of the 'effective number of parties' (ENP), which takes both the number and size of parties into account in order to give a more accurate depiction of a particular party system.[20] The ENP index is the inverse of the sum of the squared proportions of each party's share of the vote (or the seats). Thus, for n parties with p_i representing the proportion of seats won by party i,

$$\text{ENP} = \frac{1}{\sum^n p_i^2}$$

So, for a party system with two parties each holding 50 per cent of the seats, the calculation is $1/(.25 + .25)$, giving an ENP of 2.00—as we would expect. If the seat shares shift so that one of the two parties holds 70 per cent of all seats, then the ENP calculation is $1/(.49 + .09)$, i.e. 1.72, reflecting the likely reality that this is now closer to a one-party dominant system than a true two-party system. Similarly, in a system with three parties, one with 40 per cent of all seats and two with 30 per cent, then the ENP calculation becomes $1/(.16 + .09 + .09)$, i.e. 2.94—again in line with our intuitive expectations.

Using this generic measure of party fragmentation, Figure 6.1 shows the relationship between the effective number of political

[17] Taylor and Herman, 'Party Systems', 35–6.
[18] Haggard, 'Democratic Institutions', 137.
[19] Diamond, 'Toward Democratic Consolidation', 239.
[20] See Markku Laakso and Rein Taagepera, 'Effective Number of Parties: A Measure with Application to Western Europe', *Comparative Political Studies*, 12 (1979), 3–27.

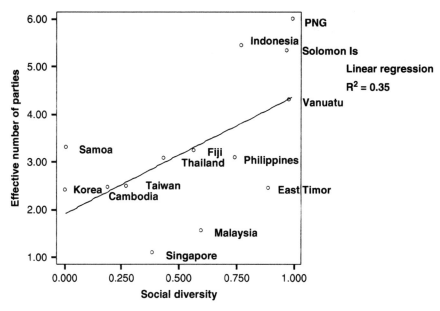

Fɪɢ. 6.1. *Party numbers and social diversity in the Asia-Pacific*

parties and social diversity across all Asia-Pacific democracies in 2000—a year which marked a symbolic end of the 'democratization decade' of the 1990s and the political reforms of that era.[21] As the figure shows, there is considerable variation in party numbers and party systems across the Asia-Pacific. At one end, diverse societies such as Indonesia, Papua New Guinea, and the Solomon Islands all featured highly fragmented party systems. This is no surprise: because political parties in theory represent the political expression of underlying societal cleavages, we would expect more fragmented societies to have more fragmented party systems too.[22]

[21] Independents are counted as small one-person parties. Source data from Nohlen, Grotz, and Hartmann, *Elections in Asia and the Pacific*; Hsieh and Newman, *How Asia Votes*; LeDuc, Niemi, and Norris, *Comparing Democracies 2*; author's calculations.

[22] Seymour Martin Lipset and Stein Rokkan, 'Cleavage Structures, Party Systems, and Voter Alignments: An Introduction', in Lipset and Rokkan (eds.), *Party Systems and Voter Alignments: Cross-National Perspectives* (New York: Free Press, 1967).

According to the regression coefficient accompanying Figure 6.1, over one-third of the variation in party numbers across the Asia-Pacific region can be explained by differences in ethno-linguistic fragmentation.[23] The expectations of the comparative literature—that more diverse societies should produce more fragmented party systems—thus appear substantially borne out. However, the countries with the smallest number of effective parties were not the most socially homogeneous states like Japan or Korea, but rather the semi-democracies of Singapore and Malaysia, both of which feature one-party dominant systems sustained by a range of restrictions on opposition parties.[24] While the relationship between party numbers and social diversity is strong, it is clearly mediated by many other factors.

Because of this, some scholars have suggested that ethnic diversity may not operate independently as much as *interactively* with the electoral system to influence the number of parties. Several recent studies of party systems in Europe and Africa, for example, have found that an interactive measure of electoral institutions and ethno-linguistic fragmentation is a better explanator of party numbers than either variable operating independently.[25] To test if this is also the case in the Asia-Pacific, I combined the social diversity and electoral systems measures from earlier chapters into one multiplicative variable—ELF × MDM, the product of ethno-linguistic fragmentation and median district magnitude in each country. However, this new variable had no significant association with party multiplicity. Unlike the established democracies of the West, or the new democracies of Africa, party pluralism in the Asia-Pacific

[23] The Pearson correlation is .59, significance <.05.

[24] This is partly an artefact of the way party numbers are calculated: in Malaysia, for example, the ruling alliance is counted as one party, in line with electoral statistics, rather than as the fourteen-party coalition which contested the 1999 elections. Similarly in Papua New Guinea, where nearly all the thirty-three independents elected at the 1997 election had joined parties by 2000, the ENP figure clearly understates the real level of political fragmentation. Nonetheless, the overall relationship is clear: more diverse societies typically have more diverse party systems too.

[25] See Peter Ordeshook and Olga Shvetsova, 'Ethnic Heterogeneity, District Magnitude and the Number of Parties', *American Journal of Political Science*, 38 (1994), 100–23; Gary Cox, *Making Votes Count: Strategic Coordination in the World's Electoral Systems* (Cambridge: Cambridge University Press, 1997); Shaheen Mozaffar, James R. Scarritt, and Glen Galaich, 'Electoral Institutions, Ethnopolitical Cleavages and Party Systems in Africa's Emerging Democracies', *American Political Science Review*, 97/3 (2003), 379–90.

does not seem to be a consequence of the interaction between ethnic fractionalization and district size. Rather, social diversity itself provides a better and more direct explanation of party fragmentation than the interactive measure—a conclusion in line with earlier studies of this phenomena, which found that higher levels of societal diversity in democracies tends to produce higher number of political parties.[26]

Political Parties and Governance

As we have seen, these variations in effective party numbers across the region should have a direct impact on government performance—in part because of the different electoral incentives facing politicians under different party systems. In one-party dominant or two-party systems, parties must cultivate and maintain support across a range of social groups, and therefore need to provide benefits to society at large in order to maximize their chances of re-election. In multiparty systems, by contrast, parties may need only a small plurality of votes to win office, and can thus focus on providing sectoral benefits to their supporters rather than public goods to the electorate as a whole. As state resources are diverted towards rewarding the few rather than the many, politicians in such systems are increasingly pushed to deliver more private goods than would be either necessary or possible under a more consolidated party system. At an extreme, such private goods can include the fruits of nepotism, cronyism, and corruption—all long-standing problems in Indonesia, the Philippines, Thailand, and a number of other Asia-Pacific states.

There is increasing empirical evidence that variations in governance depend in part on the nature of the party system. For instance, cross-national studies have found that an increase in the number of parties represented in the legislature leads to higher government spending on subsidies and transfers but lower spending on public goods.[27] In India, for instance, states with multiple parties in government had higher personnel expenditures, lower developmental expenditures, and poorer

---

[26] See Powell, *Contemporary Democracies*, 84.

[27] Bumba Mukherjee, 'Political Parties and the Size of Government in Multiparty Legislatures: Examining Cross-Country and Panel Data Evidence', *Comparative Political Studies*, 36/6 (2003), 699–728.

provision of public goods than those with two-party systems.[28] In general, because of their central role in aggregating preferences and mobilizing consent, there are sound theoretical and empirical reasons to believe that variation in political party systems do have a direct impact on public welfare, and that two-party systems are more likely than multiparty systems to provide collective goods to the median voter.[29]

Studies have also emphasized the benefits of such 'moderate multipartism' for the survival of new democracies. Powell's work on democratic durability suggests that the most favourable party system comprises a limited number of cohesive and broad-based parties rather than many small, fragmented, personalized, or ethnically-based parties.[30] Diamond, Linz, and Lipset's multi-volume comparison of democracy in developing countries concluded that 'a system of two or a few parties, with broad social and ideological bases, may be conducive to stable democracy'.[31] In the same vein, Myron Weiner and Ergun Özbudun found that the one common factor amongst the small number of stable third-world democracies was the presence of a broad-based party system, prompting them to conclude that 'the success of democratic politics in developing societies is strongly associated with the presence of broadly based, heterogeneous, catch-all parties with no strong links to the cleavage structure of society'.[32]

If we know that they are desirable, the next question must surely be how such stable and aggregative parties and party

[28] See Pradeep Chhibber and Irfan Nooruddin, 'Do Party Systems Count? The Number of Parties and Government Performance in the Indian States', *Comparative Political Studies*, 37/2 (2004), 152–87.

[29] Several studies of democratic transitions have identified party systems as the key institutional determinant affecting the distributive impacts of economic reform. Haggard and Kaufman, for instance, found that economic reforms 'are more likely to be sustained where elite supporters within the policy and business communities could mobilize broader bases of electoral and interest-group support'. For this reason, they 'placed special emphasis on the way party systems aggregated the preferences of competing economic interests', noting that while moderate catch-all party systems appeared to facilitate preference aggregation, fragmented and polarized party systems constituted a particular barrier to reform. See Haggard and Kaufman, *The Political Economy of Democratic Transitions*, 265.

[30] Powell, *Contemporary Democracies*, 99–108.

[31] Diamond, Linz, and Lipset, 'Introduction: What Makes for Democracy?', in *Politics in Developing Countries*, 35.

[32] Ergun Özbudun, 'Institutionalizing Competitive Elections in Developing Countries', in Myron Weiner and Ergun Özbudun (eds.), *Competitive Elections in Developing Countries* (Durham, NC: Duke University Press, 1987), 405.

systems can be encouraged to develop. While forging a cohesive party system in societies riven by deep communal cleavages is easier said than done, recent reforms in Indonesia, Papua New Guinea, the Philippines, and Thailand have attempted to encourage the development of broad-based parties and party systems. In the following section, I look at these attempts to strengthen parties and remodel party systems through various institutional incentives and constraints. In doing so, I identify three distinct strategies of 'party engineering' that have emerged from compromises between self-interested ruling parties: those which seek to promote the development of national party systems and hamper the growth of regional, local, or secessionist parties; those which attempt to control, influence, or restrict the number of parties; and finally, those which try to strengthen party organizations by building stable party structures from the top-down. The remainder of this chapter looks at each of these strategies in turn.

Building National Political Parties

The most direct means of fostering broad-based political parties with a truly nationwide policy focus is to ensure that parties themselves are elected on a national basis and draw support from different regions of the country and segments of the electorate. However, this is easier said than done. In presidential systems—that is, Indonesia, Korea, Taiwan, and the Philippines, as well as the semi-presidential systems of East Timor and Taiwan—candidates for president are indeed elected nationally and thus need to appeal to a nationwide constituency. In the Philippines, senators are also elected on an at-large basis from one national constituency, making them more responsive to geographically dispersed interests and less focused on particularistic policy than their counterparts in the House of Representatives.[33]

However, the constraints of geography, the desire for accountability, and the practicalities of election system design make direct national election of all seats impractical in most countries.

---

[33] See Kent Eaton, *Politicians and Economic Reform in New Democracies: Argentina and the Philippines in the 1990s* (University Park, PA: The State University of Pennsylvania Press, 2002).

Many states therefore employ more indirect approaches to the promotion of nationally oriented politics, such as requiring parties to take account of regional, ethnic, and religious balance when putting forward candidates for election. Thailand, for example, has since 1981 required registered parties to establish membership and branch networks in each of the country's four main regions, while for the ostensibly non-party Senate elections the regions must be 'equitably represented' among candidate lists.[34] The Philippines places similar cross-national thresholds on party formation: by law, political parties must have regional offices in at least nine of the sixteen regions of the country, and must gain support in more than half of the cities and provinces where their candidates run.[35]

The country that has taken the engineering of party systems the furthest, however, has been Indonesia. While only three officially sanctioned and controlled national parties were allowed under Suharto's New Order regime, its collapse in 1998 saw over 100 new parties emerge in a matter of months, many with extremely limited support bases. This mushrooming of new parties provoked widespread fears that Indonesia's emerging party system could be too fragmented, with too many parties, for democracy to function effectively.[36] At the same time, there were overriding concerns, particularly with the breakaway of East Timor in 1999, of secessionism in provinces such as Aceh and Papua, and the very real fear of the country breaking up under separatist pressures. With Indonesian politics in flux, a widely-held view was that the country needed nationally-focused parties which could gain the support of voters from across the archipelago and form legitimate, stable governments. Indeed, the development of such a national party system was seen as an essential step in countering secessionist sentiment and building a viable democracy.

To achieve these twin goals—promoting broad-based parties while resisting separatist ones—Indonesia's political reformers introduced a complex collection of incentives and restraints on party system development. On the one hand, all parties were required to demonstrate a national support base as a pre-

---

[34] Constitution of the Kingdom of Thailand, Art. 99 and Electoral Law, Art. 35.

[35] Christof Hartmann, Graham Hassall, and Soliman M. Santos, Jr, 'Philippines', in Nohlen, Grotz, and Hartmann, *Elections in Asia and the Pacific*, 195.

[36] Paige Johnson Tan, 'Anti-Party Reaction in Indonesia: Causes and Implications', *Contemporary Southeast Asia*, 24/3 (2002), 484–508.

condition for them to compete in the transitional 1999 elections. Under the new rules, each party was required to establish branches in one-third of Indonesia's (then) twenty-seven provinces, as well as offices in more than half the districts or municipalities within these provinces, before they could contest the election. As King notes, 'where previously the number of election contestants was stipulated by law, permitting only three, now they were limited on the basis of insufficient geographical coverage and depth of penetration of their organizations'.[37] The bias in favour of national parties was so strong that regional parties were even banned from competing in elections to the regional assemblies, where again only national parties were permitted.

These new rules had an immediate impact on party numbers: of 141 parties that applied to contest the 1999 elections, only forty-eight gained approval to run, and of these only five attained significant representation at the election itself: the Indonesian Democratic Party (PDI) led by then President Megawati Sukarnoputri; GOLKAR, the party machine created by Suharto; and three Islamic parties, the National Mandate Party (PAN), the Development Unity Party (PPP), and the National Awakening Party (PKB) of Megawati's predecessor, Abdurrahman Wahid.[38] For the next elections in 2004, the party laws went even further: new parties had to establish branches in two-thirds of all provinces and in two-thirds of the municipalities within those provinces, while each local party unit had to demonstrate that it had at least 1,000 members (or at least one-thousandth of the population in smaller regions) before being permitted to compete in the elections. This led to a further drop in party numbers, with only twenty-four parties qualifying for the 2004 elections: the six top parties from 1999, plus eighteen new parties that met the new membership requirements.

At the April 2004 parliamentary elections, most of these major parties were able to attract a significant spread of votes across western, central, and eastern Indonesia. While there were clear regional strongholds (the Islamic parties dominated in Sumatra, PDI did best in Java/Bali, while GOLKAR remained strong in eastern Indonesia), in contrast to 1999 all major parties gained

---

[37] Dwight Y. King, *Half-Hearted Reform: Electoral Institutions and the Struggle for Democracy in Indonesia* (Westport, CT and London: Praeger, 2003), 51.

[38] Leo Suryadinata, *Elections and Politics in Indonesia* (Singapore: Institute of Southeast Asian Studies, 2002), 90–2.

seats across the archipelago. Whereas the 1999 assembly was dominated by the 'big five', Indonesia's 2004 parliament featured the 'big seven': the five main parties from 1999, plus two new entrants: the Justice and Welfare Party and the Democrat Party.[39] Of these, GOLKAR and PDI together controlled around 40 per cent of seats, and five others each between 8 and 10 per cent. While King argues that Indonesia's post-Suharto elections broadly replicated the societal and religious cleavages present in 1955, the fact that the major parties were able to command such cross-regional support is actually a significant difference.[40] As well as being important for Indonesia's longer-term democratic prospects, this also had implications for electoral violence: as parties and candidates needed to have cross-regional appeal, election-related conflicts were for the most part 'limited in number and local in scope'.[41]

Indonesia also held its first direct national election for president and vice-president in 2004. Like the new party laws, the presidential voting system contained several measures designed to ensure that only broadly-supported, nationally-oriented candidates could be elected to office. First, only parties winning at least 5 per cent of the vote or 3 per cent of seats in the parliamentary elections were able to nominate candidates for the presidency, sidelining smaller parties. Second, presidential and vice-presidential candidates had to run together as a team; as a result, it was assumed that major parties would choose a combination of Javanese and outer islands candidates in order to maximize their appeal. Third, the election was conducted over two rounds of voting; to avoid the second round, first-round winners had to gain an absolute majority of votes nationwide as well as at least 20 per cent in half of all provinces.[42] This latter provision—known in the scholarly literature as a 'distribution requirement'—was borrowed from Nigeria, another large and ethnically diverse country. Again, the aim was to ensure that the winning candidate not only commanded support from a majority of voters, but also from different parts of the country. In this respect, the presidential electoral system shares with the

[39] See Sherlock, 'Consolidation and Change'.

[40] King, *Half-Hearted Reform*, chapter 7.

[41] Donald K. Emmerson, 'A Year of Voting Dangerously?', *Journal of Democracy*, 15/1 (2004), 100.

[42] The second round of voting entailed a straight run-off between the two leading candidate teams, with no distribution requirements.

party formation laws a common centripetal logic, in that it aims to push politics towards the centre by advantaging parties with a cross-regional support base.

How did these provisions work in practice? At the July 2004 presidential elections, no candidate gained a majority of votes in the first round of elections, necessitating a second round run-off in October which was won convincingly by Susilo Bambang Yudhoyono of the new Democrat Party, a secular and relatively progressive Javanese ex-general who teamed up with GOLKAR stalwart Jusef Kalla from Sulawesi as his vice-presidential running mate to sweep the field, carrying twenty-eight of Indonesia's thirty-two provinces. Yudhoyono's opponent, incumbent President Megawati Sukarnoputri, won only the predominantly Hindu island of Bali (a traditional PDI stronghold) and a few smaller provinces in eastern Indonesia. Thus, while not put directly to the test, the overall outcome of Indonesia's first direct presidential election did result in the election of a candidate with broad cross-regional support, in line with the aspirations of the constitutional drafters.

Compare this with corresponding presidential elections in Korea and Taiwan, both of them held under a simple plurality system with no regional distribution requirements. At Korea's December 2002 presidential elections, Roh Moon-Hyun of the Millennium Democratic Party (MDP) won a slender victory on a reformist platform which pledged, among other things, to combat the crippling regionalism that has long affected both legislative and presidential elections. However, his own election—like that of Kim Dae-Jung before him—was heavily dependent on regional voting blocks, particularly in the country's southwest, where he won a massive 93.4 per cent of votes cast. By contrast, he polled only 26.5 per cent in the southeast, a situation which only deepened Korea's seemingly endemic problem of regionalism.[43] In Taiwan, where the breakthrough election in 2000 of an opposition candidate, Chen Shui-bian, radically altered the political landscape, the election outcome was also contentious. Like Roh in Korea, Chen's victory was extremely narrow, with only a 2.5 per cent margin separating him from the second-placed candidate, James Soong. Subsequent analysis suggested that Soong, not Chen, was probably the most popular candidate overall, and the likely winner in a

---

[43] Scott Walker and Kyung-Tae Kang, 'The Presidential Election in South Korea, December 2002', *Electoral Studies*, 23/4 (2004), 844.

run-off.[44] In both Korea and Taiwan, then, the mechanics of the presidential electoral system not only played a decisive role in determining the actual result, but served to undermine the kind of broad-based political outcome that was achieved in Indonesia

Restricting the Number of Parties

As the Indonesian case illustrates, new democracies frequently experience an explosion in party numbers once the dead hand of authoritarian government has been lifted and parties are able to organize and mobilize openly. As a result, party proliferation is a common feature of transitions from authoritarian to democratic rule. A second approach to political engineering in Asia and the Pacific has therefore been to try to influence the number of parties that can establish themselves and compete in elections, and hence to shape the development of the party system.

There are several means of doing this. One is to establish and enforce rules governing political party formation, registration, and funding. The Indonesian case described above is the clearest example of this approach. As well as restricting regional parties, Indonesia's new party laws also attempt to limit party numbers by introducing systemic pressures for smaller parties to amalgamate with each other. Following the 1999 election, parties which failed to gain more than 2 per cent of seats in the lower house of parliament or 3 per cent of seats in regional assemblies had to merge with other parties to surmount these thresholds in order to contest future elections—a provision which resulted in a number of smaller parties amalgamating prior to the 2004 elections.

A similar trend has been evident in Thailand, which has a long history of fragmented party politics leading to ineffectual coalition governments and, often, military coups. As well as the cross-regional membership requirements, new parties now must also show they have at least 5,000 members within six months of being registered. The Thai authorities have taken an activist approach to the enforcement of these new laws, disallowing parties that do not meet the membership criteria.[45] In Korea,

[44] E. Niou and P. Paolino, 'The Rise of the Opposition Party in Taiwan: Explaining Chen Shui-bian's Victory in the 2000 Presidential Election', *Electoral Studies*, 22/4 (2003), 721–40.
[45] Personal communication, Allen Hicken, 15 November 2004.

similarly, local party organizations must prove they have a minimum number of party members in a specified number of electorates across the country, a requirement which 'favours big parties above minor parties [and] also contributes to political stability by preventing extreme pluralism (that is, very small parties with limited public support) from emerging'.[46] Such schemes thus echo the Indonesian reforms, even though they are aimed at restricting political fragmentation more generally rather than separatist parties in particular.

Vote-pooling electoral systems such as the alternative vote described in Chapter 5 can also encourage cross-party cooperation and aggregation. Because they make politicians from different parties reciprocally dependent upon vote transfers from their rivals, elections held under alternative vote rules can encourage party aggregation by rewarding joint campaigns, pre-election coalitions, and other forms of inter-party collaboration with increased prospects of electoral success. For instance, in pre-independence Papua New Guinea aspiring candidates could form mutual alliances, campaigning together and urging voters to cast reciprocal preferences for one or the other, precisely because the electoral system rewarded such behaviour. These alliances provided an early stimulus to the development of political parties in Papua New Guinea.[47] In 1999, a similar system was introduced in Fiji and also considered (but ultimately not implemented) in Indonesia. In each case, encouraging the development of a more aggregative party system was an important goal.

Electoral and party system reforms were aimed specifically at reducing the number of parties in two of our cases, Indonesia and Thailand, as well as in Japan. How did these various attempts to limit party fragmentation work in practice? In both Thailand and Indonesia, the introduction of the new party rules led to a 50 per cent fall in total party numbers between pre-reform and post-reform parliaments. In Thailand, for instance, the effective number of parties declined from an average of 7.2 in the 10-year period from 1986–96 to 3.8 at the first post-reform elections in April 2001. In Indonesia, the absolute number of parties competing in the elections dropped from 48 parties contesting

---

[46] Dai-Kwon Choi, 'The Choosing of Representatives in Korea', in Graham Hassall and Cheryl Saunders (eds.), *The People's Representatives: Electoral Systems in the Asia-Pacific Region* (Sydney: Allen & Unwin, 1997), 83.

[47] See Reilly, *Democracy in Divided Societies*, 58–94.

the 1999 election to 24 parties for the 2004 poll—again, a 50 per cent decline over one parliamentary term—and a similar but less extreme decline in the number of parties in parliament, from 21 in 1999 to 17 in 2004—although the effective number of parties in parliament actually rose, from 5.4 in 1999 to 8.3 in 2004, as votes which went to the smaller parties in 1999 were spread more evenly across the established larger parties. In Japan, electoral reforms also led to a steady drop in effective party numbers—from an average of 3.7 effective parties over the entire post-war period to an average of 2.9 parties since the 1994 reforms—a 20 per cent decline over 9 years.

Compare this with the experience of the Philippines, whose 1987 constitution was also based on the desire for a more inclusive and responsive political system, but which included no constraints upon party fragmentation. There, party numbers have steadily increased since the return to democracy in 1986, especially compared with the experience of the pre-Marcos demo-cratic period from 1946–69.[48] As Jungug Choi has shown, part of the reason for this was the introduction of term limits for both legislators and the president in the 1986 constitution. A response to the disastrous Marcos period of authoritarian rule, term limits were also aimed at undercutting the entrenched wealthy family dynasties that have long been a feature of Filipino politics. In the process, however, term limits had the unintended effect of weak-ening the power of incumbents, lowering barriers for new en-trants, and drastically undermining incentives for presidents and legislators to invest in longer-term party-building. The re-sult since 1986 has been an increase in party fragmentation to more than double the level that applied in the 1946–69 demo-cratic period—an ironic outcome, as an underlying aim of the 1986 constitution was to improve political stability.[49] Following her election in May 2004, Philippines President Gloria Macapa-gal Arroyo outlined new plans to strengthen the party system by restricting party-switching and providing public funding to major parties. She also voiced qualified support for the 'Charter Change' campaign which advocates a parliamentary and federal

[48] See Allen Hicken, 'From Province to Parliament: Party Aggregation in Developing Democracies', Paper presented to the annual meeting of the Ameri-can Political Science Association, Philadelphia (2003).

[49] Jungug Choi, 'Philippine Democracies Old and New: Elections, Term Limits, and Party Systems', *Asian Survey*, 41/3 (2001), 488–501.

system of government as the key to transforming the Philippines' deep-seated political pathologies.[50]

Strengthening Parties in Government

A third approach to party engineering in the Asia-Pacific has been to try to strengthen internal party organizations by privileging party interests within the structure of government. In both Indonesia and Thailand, for example, all lower house candidates must now represent a political party, and are not permitted to stand as independents. In Indonesia, the systemic and educative role of parties is also emphasized in new legislation governing party registration, and party leaders are given significant power in terms of candidate selection and replacement. In 1999, for the first time, public funding was also introduced.[51] In Korea, both main parties introduced major changes to their own internal governance arrangements in 2001. American-style primary elections were initiated as the parties sought to transform themselves into more open organizations with a mass-membership base. The new nomination system of open and closed party primaries had an immediate impact, with the nomination of Roh Moon-Hyun, a relative outsider, as the MDP's candidate for president. Roh's rapid rise in popularity, particularly amongst younger voters, and his subsequent victory at the 2002 presidential elections, greatly strengthened the new 'people's primary' and internal party governance measures, spurring the rival Grand National Party to announce similar reforms. Whether these changes will be sufficient to transform Korea's weak, regionalized, and personality-dominated party system into one based around true mass parties with a national reach, however, remains to be seen.[52]

Another means of engineering stability is to try to encourage party cohesion within parliament. Such provisions aim to strengthen parties' internal control over their members in order to maintain greater organizational cohesiveness and stability.

[50] See Jose Veloso Abueva, *Charter Change for the Philippines: Towards a Federal Republic of the Philippines with a Parliamentary Government* (Manila: Citizens' Movement for a Federal Philippines and KC Institute of Federal-Parliamentary Democracy, 2005).

[51] King, *Half-Hearted Reform*, 52.

[52] See Im, 'Faltering Democratic Consolidation in South Korea'.

One way of doing this is to restrict the capacity of parliamentarians to change parties once elected. Practices of 'party hopping', or turncoatism—once widespread in many Asian countries—have been curtailed by the introduction of anti-switching provisions in states such as Fiji, Malaysia, Thailand, Samoa, and Papua New Guinea. These measures aim to make it difficult or impossible for a politician elected under one party label to switch to another party in exchange for a ministerial appointment or similar inducement. In Thailand, for example, the 1997 constitution mandates that candidates must be members of a political party for at least ninety days prior to an election—double the standard interval between the end of a parliamentary term and the election that follows. As a result, politicians who switch parties to help bring down a government usually cannot legally contest the forthcoming election.[53]

However, these kinds of restrictions have little sway over party defections which take place outside the parliamentary arena or in periods between elections. They also do little to combat the related problem of multiple endorsement, where the same candidate may be nominated by several parties, or where parties endorse multiple different candidates in the same electorate—a common occurrence in the Philippines, Papua New Guinea, and some Pacific Island states, where parties are weak and often irrelevant. In Papua New Guinea, for example, as many electors vote for their local clan candidate rather than for political parties, independents with no party affiliation have been a major political force in parliament. This has created severe political instability, as parliamentary majorities shift from issue to issue and vote to vote. At the 1997 and 2002 elections, independent members of parliament were the largest single 'party' at the first sitting of parliament in terms of numbers, holding more than one-third of seats on both occasions, although many subsequently assumed a party affiliation.

Partly in response to the increasing atrophy of its party system, in 2001 the government of Papua New Guinea introduced an ambitious package of political reforms aimed at stabilizing executive government and building a coherent party system from the top down. Under the new rules, all parties are supposed to have fee-paying members, a party constitution, and allow internal competition for party leadership before they can be

[53] Hicken, 'From Province to Parliament'.

registered and compete in elections. In an attempt to address the chronic under-representation of women in Papua New Guinean politics, parties that put forward female candidates for election are now able to recover most of their election expenses if they win over 10 per cent of the vote. The provision for party registration was tied to a new system of party funding, under which each registered party will receive 10,000 kina (about $US 3,000 dollars) per MP per year. The intention of these reforms was to move parties away from being purely vehicles for personal advancement, and to encourage intending candidates to stand for election under a party banner rather than as independents.

To stabilize the country's unruly executive government, new restrictions have also been placed on the freedom of MPs to change their allegiances once elected. Politicians elected with party endorsement must now vote in accordance with their party position on key parliamentary decisions such as a vote of confidence in the prime minister, or face a possible by-election. As *every* Papua New Guinea government elected prior to 2002 has fallen prematurely between elections as a result of post-election party hopping, these reforms represent a major challenge to established political practice, especially for independents (whose allegiances have often shifted in return for a ministerial position or similar inducement). In combination with the change of electoral system described in Chapter 5, Papua New Guinea's new rules of the game thus represent one of the most far-reaching attempts to engineer the party system anywhere in the Asia-Pacific region.[54] They also had an immediate and highly consequential political impact: the first post-reform government is the longest-lasting since independence, and looks set to be the first ever to serve out a full five-year term.

The longer-term effects of Papua New Guinea's revised political arrangements will not be evident for some time. Initial trends have been somewhat contradictory: while party numbers rose immediately after the reforms, with forty-three parties meeting the registration requirements, this was in part the result of the incentives for party formation inherent in the new laws, which had the effect of encouraging candidates who would formerly have stood as independents to do so under a party banner instead. As a result, the number of parties represented

[54] See Benjamin Reilly, 'Political Engineering and Party Politics in Papua New Guinea', *Party Politics*, 8/6 (2002), 701–18.

in parliament initially also rose, from seventeen political parties in the 1997 parliament to twenty-two at the first sitting of the 2002 parliament. However, there was a sharp decline in the number of independent candidates, from thirty-six in the 1997 parliament to seventeen in 2002—again, largely as a result of the incentives for independent members to join political parties in parliament. By 2004, the number of parliamentary parties had declined to fifteen as a result of inter-party mergers, at least some of which appeared to be reactions to the incentives for party aggregation inherent in the new laws.[55]

Conclusion

How will these various experiments in political engineering affect the development of Asia-Pacific party systems over time? In most cases, the jury is still out, given that many of the reforms have not yet been tested in action. However, some clear trends are emerging.

First, attempts to engineer party systems appear to have succeeded in many cases, although not always in the way intended. Indonesia, for example, initially experienced a sharp reduction in party numbers following the introduction of new party laws. While hundreds of new parties appeared in the lead-up to the 1999 elections, only six achieved any significant representation, and the Indonesian political system quickly became dominated by a few large parties. However, the 'effective' number of parties at the 2004 elections actually increased, as several new entrants established themselves as significant players. In contrast to previous years, many larger parties were able to attract a regional spread of voter support across western, central, and eastern Indonesia—no small achievement, given Indonesia's modern history and the dangers of acute fragmentation that it faces. As a result, while Indonesia's parliament remained politically fragmented, the new institutional arrangements did appear to meet their core aim of promoting the development of a more coherent party system with broad support across the country.

But party engineering has costs as well as benefits. As evidenced by the 50 per cent reduction in party numbers between

---

[55] See Louise Baker, 'Political Integrity in Papua New Guinea and the Search for Stability', *Pacific Economic Bulletin*, 20/1 (2005), 108.

1999 and 2004, Indonesia's electoral laws benefit incumbent parties by restricting the level of political competition and placing barriers on potential new entrants into the political marketplace. As a result, there is a real danger of overkill inherent in the new party provisions, especially given that plans for future elections include raising the barriers to smaller parties and new entrants even higher. Under existing legislation, most parties elected at the 2004 elections will be barred from competing at the next elections in 2009, because they failed to win more than 3 per cent of seats. These parties will be encouraged to amalgamate with others in order to reach this support marker. Even more severe restrictions will be placed on future candidates for the presidency: under current plans, only parties that win at least 20 per cent of the vote at the 2009 parliamentary elections, or at least 15 per cent of seats, will be entitled to enter candidates for the presidential and vice-presidential race. All of this not only discriminates against smaller parties, but tilts the electoral playing field markedly in favour of incumbents and established parties more generally.

A similar conclusion applies to Thailand, where the 1997 constitutional reforms aimed at combating political instability and fractionalization contain so many incentives favouring strong parties that they may have unbalanced Thai politics. In particular, the electoral and party reforms appear to have facilitated the rapid emergence of Thaksin Shinawatra's TRT party as the dominant political force. Already in a commanding position following the 2001 elections, Thaksin initiated a series of post-election mergers and coalition deals with other parties which led to the TRT controlling 365 of the 500 parliamentary seats. As a result, it was able to legislate virtually unopposed, winning the 2005 elections by a massive margin and becoming the first government in Thailand's democratic history to win an election outright. In a paradoxical twist, however, some of the political reforms that helped create the current moderate multiparty system, such as a strong independent electoral commission, have been rolled back. As his political dominance increased, commentators increasingly compared Thaksin to Malaysia's Mahathir, whose extended prime ministership concentrated personal power and undermined democracy.[56]

---

[56] See 'Thailand Politics: Thaksin as Mahathir?', *The Economist Intelligence Unit—Business Asia*, 30 June 2003.

Finally, many of the party system reforms investigated in this chapter have profound impacts on the political expression of ethnicity, and thus on the potential for ethnic politics. In some cases this has been an unanticipated by-product of the party reforms, but in others it was a primary impetus from the beginning. For example, a major factor behind the new Indonesian party laws was to make monoethnic, regionalist, or separatist parties unviable. In this, they appear to have succeeded. It is virtually impossible for a party to get its name on the ballot in Indonesia today unless it can demonstrate a level of national support that is likely to be beyond the reach of even the most well-organized regional movement. The new presidential electoral laws only strengthen this approach.

However, whether this in itself is enough to change the way party competition works and forge more durable and stable democratic politics remains to be seen. In Indonesia, the new laws have been criticized for locking minorities out of power, and for placing unreasonably high hurdles in front of potential new parties. As one observer has noted, if the laws requiring parties to prove minimum membership numbers all the way down to the local district level are strictly enforced, 'parties may, instead of collecting dues from members, be paying them to sign up in future'.[57] Similarly, Papua New Guinea's reforms have, at their heart, the aim of reducing the instability created by that country's exceptional degree of social diversity. But while the new party laws may have helped stabilize government and introduced some much-needed incentives for party system development, they have not yet altered fundamentally established political practices. Party splits, for example, remain common and provide one means of circumventing the new laws.

In general, then, the kind of overt interventions in political party development examined in this chapter entail costs as well as benefits. Restrictions on party fragmentation can easily become restrictions on democracy itself. A lighter touch may well be more desirable for new democracies. In Indonesia, for example, the 2003 party laws place such high thresholds on party support that they clearly represent a restriction upon new entrants into the political system. Exceptions have already been made. For instance, as part of the 2005 peace deal which appears to have ended the long-running civil war in Aceh, the rebel

---

[57] Tan, 'Anti-Party Reaction in Indonesia', 488.

Free Aceh Movement (GAM) was explicitly granted the right to compete in future local and national elections. As a result, there appears to be a direct—and, at the time of writing, unresolved—contradiction between the provisions of the peace deal and Indonesia's national party law. Similarly, the Thai reforms, while sharply reducing fragmentation, have also excessively centralized government power and fostered single-party domination, raising the possibility that they may undermine, rather than strengthen, democratic consolidation.[58] Heavy-handed reforms are likely to produce some unusual and often unintended side effects, a subject I will return to in the final chapter.

Whether Asia-Pacific governments succeed in building sustainable, aggregative, and cohesive party systems through political engineering thus remains to be seen. For the region's more pluralistic societies, the extent to which minorities are integrated into the major parties and can gain political influence if not direct political representation will be a key test. For instance, if Indonesia's restrictions on regional parties end up encouraging extra-constitutional action by aggrieved minorities, they will have exacerbated the very problems they are designed to prevent. If, on the other hand, minorities and majorities alike can be integrated into a few large catch-all parties with broad mandates and centrist policies, then these reforms could encourage the development of more cross-cutting affiliations, leading to more stable politics and a reduction in communal tensions. Evaluating the record of political engineering in such cases thus depends in part on what criteria for success is adopted. What can be said with confidence is that most of the direct interventions across the region clearly aim the same way, towards more institutionalized, aggregative, and consolidated party systems.

[58] Duncan McCargo, 'Democracy Under Stress in Thaksin's Thailand', *Journal of Democracy*, 13/4 (2002), 112–26.

Power-Sharing Institutions: Executive Formation and Federalism

We saw in Chapter 4 that proposals for the sharing or dividing of political power lie at the heart of many political engineering models. Demands for the apportionment of government offices between all significant social groups are frequently invoked in countries making the transition to democracy or emerging from periods of violent conflict, as in post-war Iraq and Afghanistan. Similarly, calls for the devolution or division of political power on a territorial basis are commonly heard during democratic transitions, especially in large, regionally diverse societies. As a result, parliamentary or regionally-based power-sharing has become an increasingly widespread prescription for new democracies around the world, particularly those with deep social divisions. Sisk summarizes the conventional wisdom when he observes that power-sharing, 'if broadly defined to encompass a wide range of practices that promote meaningful inclusivity and balanced influence for all major groups in a multi-ethnic society, is a potential answer to ethnic conflict management in many contemporary situations'.[1]

Such power-sharing can take a variety of forms. At the executive level, for instance, processes of cabinet formation can be based on either formal or informal practices of inclusion. *Formal* power-sharing in this context refers to legally mandated provisions designed to include members of particular political parties or social groups in government, such as constitutional requirements that ministerial positions be allocated in proportion to a party's overall seat or vote share (as in Fiji), or that reserve key positions for members of specified communities (as in Lebanon).

---

[1] Sisk, *Power Sharing*, 9.

Alternately, governments can rely on *informal* power-sharing practices, whereby representatives of different parties or groups are routinely included in cabinet as part of established political practice, but not in response to a legal requirement. The precise application of such informal power-sharing also ranges widely, from the inclusion of symbolic ethnic or regional representatives in more-or-less token ministerial positions all the way through to 'grand coalition' cabinets in which all parties are simultaneously included in a national unity government. Unlike the executive coalitions arising from formal power-sharing rules, however, these kinds of inclusive cabinets are the result of political calculation rather than constitutional fiat.

Both in the Asia-Pacific and around the world, informal approaches to executive power-sharing are practised far more widely than formal alternatives. One reason for this is that formal power-sharing provisions are by their nature unusual and exceptional, tending to be applied in times of war or national emergency, or in countries threatened by or emerging from civil conflict. For example, Fiji's 1997 constitution, which was explicitly designed to return the country to stable democracy by promoting the development of multi-ethnic politics, contains the most comprehensive example of a formal power-sharing requirement in the Asia-Pacific region: all parties winning at least 10 per cent of seats in parliament are entitled to cabinet positions in proportion to their seat share. Another example of formal power-sharing arising from civil conflict is the 'super-majority' requirement for government formation adopted in Cambodia's 1993 constitution, which requires that all new governments be approved by a two-thirds vote of the National Assembly—a provision that makes some form of cross-party governing coalition almost inevitable. As discussed later in this chapter, in both Fiji and Cambodia these provisions have proved difficult to implement in practice, and the experience of government formation has been highly contentious in both countries.

Far more widespread than such formal power-sharing rules, however, are informal routines of regional, religious, and ethnic inclusion in cabinet governments. Of the many examples of such practices, the Malaysian case stands out as perhaps the Asia-Pacific's most enduring example of informal ethnic power-sharing. Since independence in 1957, Malaysia has been governed by a broad umbrella coalition comprising the major Malay party, the United Malays National Organisation (UMNO), and parties representing the main minority communities, notably the Malaysian Chinese Association (MCA) and the Malaysian Indian Congress (MIC). Along with a range of smaller parties, these parties form the main pillars of the *Barisan Nasional* that has ruled Malaysia unchallenged since 1974 (prior to this a similar coalition, the Alliance, held sway). Despite being dominated by UMNO, the fact that all Malaysian governments have maintained representation of the country's three major ethnic groups via this informal power-sharing deal has provided a form of credible commitment that their interests will be protected. However, the *Barisan*'s institutionalization in government has also come at a considerable cost to Malaysian democracy, as the separate identity of the party and the state have become increasingly blurred. Along with the benefits of rapid economic growth and the control of potential social conflict has come the flagrant gerrymandering of constituency boundaries, malapportionment in favour of rural areas, suppression of opposition movements, restrictions on basic freedoms and intimidation of political opponents, all aimed at ensuring the ruling coalition's continuation in power.[2]

Informal executive power-sharing takes place in a less structured way in a number of other Asia-Pacific countries. Many governments make an effort to include a range of representatives from different regions of the country in the governing executive in order to provide some kind of balanced representation. In the Philippines, for instance, the practice of executive formation requires each new president 'to take into consideration the regional, linguistic, ethnic, and religious divisions of the country'.[3] As a result, presidential cabinets habitually consist of representatives drawn from multiple ethnic, regional, and religious communities.[4] In Papua New Guinea, due to the combination of a fragmented society and weak parties, multi-ethnic power-sharing coalitions are the norm, with ministries allocated at least partly on the basis of regional considerations and the need to strike the right balance of Papuans, New Guineans, Highlanders, and Islanders.[5] Elsewhere, power-sharing executives are the

[2] See James Ung-Ho Chin, 'Malaysia: The Barisan National Supremacy', in Hsieh and Newman, *How Asia Votes*, 210–33.

[3] Jürgen Rüland, 'Constitutional Debates in the Philippines: From Presidentialism to Parliamentarism?', *Asian Survey*, 43/3 (2003), 468.

[4] Harold Crouch and James W. Morely, 'The Dynamics of Political Change', in Morley, *Driven by Growth*, 335.

[5] See Sean Dorney, *Papua New Guinea: People, Politics and History Since 1975*, rev. edn. (Sydney: ABC Books, 2000), 39–72.

result of more overtly political calculations. The entrenchment of the TRT in Thailand, for instance, was girded by Prime Minister Thaksin's strategy of bringing additional coalition partners into cabinet in order to provide a buffer against future defections.[6] Perhaps the most extreme example of this strategy has been Indonesia, where the 'national unity' cabinets of post-Suharto presidents Abdurrahman Wahid and Megawati Sukarnoputri co-opted virtually all significant parties into expansive governing cartels which essentially swallowed all potential political opposition.[7]

The formation of governing executives thus represents one means of sharing political power. Another is to constitutionally divide or devolve the core tasks of government. This kind of power-sharing—or, more accurately, 'power dividing'—can be manifested in both 'horizontal' and 'vertical' forms.[8] For instance, the separation-of-powers political system common to presidential models divides power horizontally, creating multiple concurrent majorities to ensure systemic checks and balances. Alternately, territorial arrangements can divide powers vertically by measures such as federalism, regional autonomy, or decentralization of state authority. Thus, in the Asia-Pacific, Korea, Indonesia, and the Philippines are unitary states but all feature clear separation-of-powers presidential systems; Malaysia and Papua New Guinea are federal or quasi-federal polities, with states or provinces given explicit governing powers in addition to the national government; autonomy has been offered to aggrieved regions such as Bougainville in Papua New Guinea, Mindanao and the Cordilleras in the Philippines, and Aceh and Papua in Indonesia; and a number of states (again, most prominently, Indonesia) have embarked on major exercises in political and administrative decentralization. All of these are cases of not so much the sharing as the *division* of governing powers.

In this chapter, I examine the theory and practice of these various approaches to the sharing and dividing of governing power in the Asia-Pacific. I look first at the broad issues of

[6] See James Ockey, 'Change and Continuity in the Thai Political Party System', *Asian Survey*, 43/4 (2003), 663–80.

[7] See Dan Slater, 'Indonesia's Accountability Trap: Party Cartels and Presidential Power After Democratic Transition', *Indonesia*, 78 (October 2004), 61–92.

[8] See Philip G. Roeder, 'Power Dividing as an Alternative to Ethnic Power Sharing', in Roeder and Rothchild, *Sustainable Peace*, 51–82.

executive structure and the distinction between presidential and parliamentary systems across the region, at the divergent approaches taken by Asian and Pacific states to both formal and informal practices of executive inclusion, and at the empirical relationship between these variables and broader goals of political stability. Following this, I construct an 'index of power-sharing' to compare the horizontal sharing of powers over time. Finally, I look at the experience of vertical power-sharing via measures such as federalism, devolution, and autonomy. Overall, the evidence from these cases suggests that while informal executive power-sharing practices have been relatively successful, formal requirements for inclusive cabinets have been dogged by problems. In the same vein, while political decentralization has been a common theme of demands for vertical power-sharing, the actual application of federalism and regional autonomy has been limited. I therefore conclude by examining the disparity between the various theories of political engineering and power-sharing, and the evidence gleaned from the Asia-Pacific region.

Political Engineering and Political Stability

In order to evaluate the success of executive formation practices as a form of political engineering, we need a means of assessing their performance. One way of doing this is to examine how *stable* governments have been under different kinds of institutional architecture. After all, power-sharing (as with most of the political reforms examined in this book) is advocated in part because it is thought to lead to greater 'stability' of government and politics. There are several meanings inherent in this oft-stated objective. First, political stability is sometimes used to refer to the maintenance of formal democracy, or the avoidance of civil strife. However, this broad definition tends to muddy the conceptual waters, confusing stability with other analytically distinct phenomena such as regime type or conflict management. A more precise and more limited definition of political stability relates to the tenure and composition of executive governments.[9] Under this interpretation, political and policy continuity depends significantly on the durability of cabinets. Thus, politics is more 'stable' when governing executives are durable in terms of both longevity and personnel; conversely, executives are

[9] Taylor and Herman, 'Party Systems'.

'unstable' if their composition alters frequently, particularly if governments change between elections due to no-confidence votes, impeachment, party swaps, or similar events. It is widely presumed that short-lived executives will struggle to develop sound public policies and maintain a consistent policy position; conversely, a high level of executive durability is often taken as a sign of a government's capacity to maintain power and implement its policy agenda credibly and predictably.[10]

Broader systemic differences between parliamentary and presidential forms of government also have an important influence on political stability. Advocates of presidentialism, in which state powers are divided horizontally between the executive, legislative, and judicial branches, often point to the durability of office provided by a truly independent executive, and hence the continuity in terms of public policy that a presidential system can bring. Unlike parliamentary governments, which can shift and change on the floor of the house between elections without recourse to the electorate, the tenure of a president and his or her administration is usually relatively secure, as cabinets are not dependent on the support of the legislature for their continuation in office. This leads, in theory at least, to more decisive decision-making, making presidentialism a potentially attractive choice for new democracies, particularly those afflicted by weak parties or shifting parliamentary coalitions.[11] Matthew Shugart, for instance, has argued that new democracies with weak party systems may gravitate towards presidential designs when cohesive national parties (and hence stable parliamentarism) are lacking.[12] More generally, claims that presidential systems deliver greater executive stability than parliamentary ones remain widespread: for instance, in their survey of East and Southeast Asia, Blondel and Inoguchi claim that presidentialism 'has one strongly positive value, which is to ensure the stability of the executive in countries in which parties tend to be "naturally" internally divided, for instance on a geographical basis; or in

---

[10] See Lijphart, *Patterns of Democracy*, 129.

[11] See, for example, Donald L. Horowitz, 'Comparing Democratic Systems', *Journal of Democracy*, 1 (1990), 73–9; Shugart and Carey, *Presidents and Assemblies*; Scott Mainwaring and Matthew Shugart, 'Introduction', in Mainwaring and Shugart, *Presidentialism and Democracy in Latin America*.

[12] Matthew Shugart, 'Presidentialism, Parliamentarism, and the Provision of Collective Goods in Less-Developed Countries', *Constitutional Political Economy*, 10 (1999), 53–88.

which the party system is highly fragmented'.[13] By contrast, critics of presidentialism such as Juan Linz argue that because of its structural rigidity, lack of opposition, and competing bases of legitimacy, 'presidentialism seems to invoke greater risk for stable democratic politics than contemporary parliamentarism'.[14]

While much of this debate has been focused on Latin America and Southern Europe, these claims invite empirical testing in the Asia-Pacific region. There are today three clearly presidential democracies in the region—Indonesia, Korea, and the Philippines—each of which has also experienced extended periods of non-democratic government. Of these the Philippines, which modelled its constitutional arrangements on those of the United States, has the longest experience with presidentialism, having first introduced a presidential constitution in the 1930s. More recently, reforms in formerly authoritarian Korea and Indonesia resulted in their transformation to full presidential democracies, via the direct election of their previously non-elected executive presidents in 1987 and 2004, respectively. In addition, two other new democracies—Taiwan and East Timor—have adopted semi-presidential systems of government, with executive power split between a directly elected president and a prime minister, both of whom have their own separate arenas of authority. All the other cases examined in this book—Fiji, Malaysia, Papua New Guinea, Samoa, Singapore, Solomon Islands, Thailand, and Vanuatu—are parliamentary systems.

If the scholars quoted above are correct, these different systemic choices should impact directly on political stability. To assess whether this is the case, we need to examine the relative durability of executive governments across both types of regime. Table 7.1 shows the historical average tenure (in months) of cabinet governments across both presidential and parliamentary systems in Asia and the Pacific. Following Lijphart's criterion, a new cabinet is determined by one of three events: the holding of general elections, a change in the head of

---

[13] Jean Blondel and Takashi Inoguchi, 'Parties, Bureaucracies, and the Search for an Equilibrium Between Democracy and Economic Development' in Marsh, Blondel, and Inoguchi, *Democracy, Governance and Economic Performance*, 101.

[14] Juan Linz, 'Presidential or Parliamentary Democracy: Does it Make a Difference?', in Linz and Valenzuela, *The Failure of Presidential Democracy*, 70.

TABLE 7.1. *Cabinet stability and executive type in Asia and the Pacific*

Country and democratic period	Average cabinet duration (months)	Executive type
Cambodia 1993–2003	41	Parliamentary
Fiji 1970–87	60	Parliamentary
Indonesia 10/1999–7/2002	21	Presidential
Korea 3/1988–3/2000	26	Presidential
Malaysia 8/1957–12/2001	38	Parliamentary
Philippines 1946–69, 1986–2000	51	Presidential
PNG 1977–2002	18	Parliamentary
Samoa 1991–2001	35	Parliamentary
Singapore 9/1968–12/2001	46	Parliamentary
Solomon Islands 1978–2001	31	Parliamentary
Thailand 9/92–3/2000	10	Parliamentary
Vanuatu 1979–2001	18	Parliamentary
Average parliamentary systems	**33**	—
Average presidential systems	**33**	—
Average all cases	**33**	—

Note: Semi-presidential systems (East Timor and Taiwan) excluded. Data for Malaysia exclude the period 09/70–09/74.
Source: Aurel Croissant, 'Electoral Politics', 340; author's calculations.

government, and (for parliamentary cabinets only) a change in the party composition of the cabinet. This final provision means that the stability measure is inherently biased in favour of presidential systems, in which cabinet is selected by the president alone and has no necessary partisan component. Nonetheless, even using this relatively narrow definition of cabinet durability, there is—surprisingly—no difference between presidential and parliamentary systems. As Table 7.1 shows, historically parliamentary and presidential systems have exactly the same average cabinet duration: thirty-three months in both cases.

Thus, in the Asia-Pacific, the distinction between presidential and parliamentary government does not itself appear to be a determinant of cabinet durability. This is something of a surprise, given expectations for the superior stability of presidential systems. But what about the impact of other institutional variables? After all, in a number of the cases examined in this book, political engineering was aimed specifically at improving the stability of executive government. Indeed, in at least six states—Cambodia, Fiji, Indonesia, Thailand, Papua New Guinea, and the Philippines—changes to party laws, electoral systems, and cabinet formation rules were advocated in part by reference to the need for greater political stability. How have they fared?

One way to answer this question is to examine the average duration of governments in the period after political reforms were enacted, and to compare this with the historical average from the pre-reform period. Table 7.2 therefore compares the longevity of pre- and post-reform governments up until the end of 2004 in Indonesia, Papua New Guinea, the Philippines, and Thailand, each of which undertook major constitutional reforms aimed among other things at enhancing political stability (the two other countries which also attempted such reforms, Cambodia and Fiji, are excluded due to the violent extra-constitutional dissolution of their power-sharing cabinets discussed later in this chapter).

As the table shows, the longevity of executive governments did indeed improve after reforms were introduced. Cabinet durability increased markedly in Indonesia, Thailand, and Papua New Guinea, and more modestly in the Philippines. The most striking increase in political stability occurred in Thailand, which went from an average government lifespan of just ten months in the decade prior to the 2001 elections (the first to be held under the new constitutional arrangements), to over three years since then. In the Philippines, the longevity of cabinets elected under the 1987 constitution has also improved, although only marginally, compared to the pre-Marcos democratic period. In Indonesia, the longevity of each post-Suharto president has increased incrementally. Habibie's transitional administration lasted just seventeen months and initiated fundamental reforms to civil and political rights, including new electoral and decentralization laws, but lacked popular support because of his long-

TABLE 7.2. *Durability of pre- and post-reform governments, in months*

Country	Average government duration	
	pre-reform	post-reform
Indonesia	17 (Habibie, 1999–2001)	29 (Wahid, Megawati, 2001–4)
Philippines	47 (various, 1946–69)	56 (Aquino, Ramos, Estrada, Arroyo, 1986–2004)
Thailand	10 (various, 1992–7)	41 (Chuan, Thaksin, 1997–2004)
PNG	18 (various, 1975–2002)	60 (Somare, 2002–7)

Source: Croissant, 'Electoral Politics', 340; author's calculations.

standing association with Suharto. His successor, Abdurrahman Wahid, the first president chosen under the new political arrangements, continued with the democratization process by forming an unstable grand coalition government before being impeached after twenty-one months in office. Wahid was replaced by his vice-president, Megawati Sukarnoputri, who lasted for thirty-eight months before losing the 2004 elections to Susilo Bambang Yudhoyono, who appears set to become the first democratically chosen Indonesian president to govern for a full term of office. Finally, in Papua New Guinea, the introduction in 2001 of reforms aimed at promoting more stable executive government led to a sharp increase in cabinet durability, with Michael Somare the first prime minister to avoid being overthrown on the floor of parliament. In each case, political reforms appear to have enhanced stability, at least according to this limited indicator of cabinet durability.

However, durability is only one measure of political stability, and a relatively crude one at that. A more encompassing measure of stability could also be interpreted as referring not just to the duration but also to the breadth of representation of executive governments. Here the main criterion is not just the longevity of cabinets, but the extent to which they are inclusive of the broader composition of a country's social and political forces. 'Oversized' cabinets which include additional parties in government beyond those required to secure majority government—and which thus maximize the sharing rather than the concentration of executive power—should in theory engender greater stability under this criterion than 'minimal winning' cabinets in which only those parties required to secure a governing majority, and no more, are included. 'Grand coalition' cabinets, which represent an additional step beyond oversized executives by including *all* significant political actors and groups in cabinet, should provide the strongest guarantee of inclusivity available via the executive formation process.

Again, these different approaches to executive formation invite empirical testing. One way of analysing the relationship between executive governance and political stability across the region is to examine the relative impact of minimal winning, oversized and grand coalition cabinets, as these effectively represent gradations of power-sharing, moving from low to high. The following discussion looks at the experience of each of these three cabinet types amongst our cases.

Oversized Cabinets

Oversized cabinets are by far the most common model of government formation in the Asia-Pacific. Without exception, oversized coalition governments have been the rule in Malaysia, Thailand, Indonesia, Papua New Guinea, and the Solomon Islands, and have been common in Fiji and Vanuatu as well. In Malaysia, as discussed already, a multiparty alliance representing the three main ethnic groups has been the foundation of all governments since 1955. With no formal power-sharing requirements, the *Barisan Nasional* relies on the willingness of its three main constituent ethnic parties—UMNO, the MCA, and the MIC—to 'pool votes' across communal lines. The component parties divide up the electoral map so as to avoid competing with one another on a constituency level, and campaign under the *Barisan* label rather than as separate parties. These arrangements are products of a long history of the *Barisan* (and before it, the Alliance) endorsing an ethnic mixture of candidates across the country and operating as a multi-ethnic coalition. This arrangement proved crucial to the *Barisan*'s victory at the 1999 elections, when the collapse of Malay support for UMNO forced Mahathir to shift his electoral base to Chinese and Indian constituencies.[15]

Oversized multiparty coalitions have also been common in other Southeast Asian countries. In Thailand, for example, all governments from the resumption of democracy in 1992 until the end of 2004 comprised broad, oversized coalitions designed to ensure cross-regional representation and, more importantly, provide a buffer against possible defections. Thus, following his victory in the 2001 elections, new Prime Minister Thaksin Shinawatra sought out a range of additional coalition partners in order to insulate his government from defectors and limit the ability of factional players to undermine cabinet stability. Despite his TRT party having a near majority of seats, the *Seritham* (Liberal Democrat) party was persuaded to merge with it after the election, its 14 seats giving Thaksin an absolute parliamentary majority of 262 seats. Additional cabinet representation was also given to coalition partners New Aspiration and Chart Thai—their 36 and 41 seats, respectively, giving the new government a comfortable majority in the House of Representatives.[16]

---

[15] For an account of these elections, see William Case, 'New Uncertainties for an Old Pseudo-Democracy: The Case of Malaysia', *Comparative Politics*, 37/1 (October 2004), 83–104.

[16] Ockey, 'Change and Continuity'.

Similar practices are also common in the island Pacific. In post-independence Papua New Guinea, different constellations of six main parties, plus a host of independents, have formed the core of successive oversized parliamentary coalitions—again, in large part to provide a buffer against defections and ensure a degree of cabinet stability. In Vanuatu, single-party cabinets were maintained from independence in 1980 until 1991, when the ruling Vanua'aku Pati split in two; all cabinets since then have been oversized coalitions. In Fiji, despite the failure of the 'grand coalition' provisions of the 1997 constitution, cabinets both prior to and since the 2000 coup have also been slightly oversized in practice, with governments including ministerial representatives of other parties in order to maintain some nominal degree of multi-ethnic representation. In the Solomon Islands, similarly, almost all post-independence governments have comprised multiparty coalitions, a practice which has become more common in recent years as the party system has atrophied.

A final example of oversized executive formation comes from the Asia-Pacific's newest democracy, East Timor. Following the transitional 2001 elections which marked the end of United Nations' administration there, East Timor's constituent assembly adopted a semi-presidential form of government, with power divided between the president (Xanana Gusmão, elected separately in April 2002) and a prime minister and cabinet chosen from the new legislature. Assuming a non-partisan president such as Gusmão, such a constitutional model effectively makes some sharing of power between the president and the legislature mandatory. The first government formed under the new constitution comprised ten Fretilin representatives and four independents. Given that Fretilin alone held a substantial parliamentary majority, this made East Timor's first independent government an oversized coalition also, although most of the independents remain associated with Fretilin in some form.[17]

Grand Coalitions

In forming coalition governments, it is possible to go further than an oversized coalition in terms of executive inclusivity by

[17] Dennis Shoesmith, 'Timor-Leste: Divided Leadership in a Semi-Presidential System', *Asian Survey*, 43/2 (2003), 231–52.

ensuring the representation of *all* significant political forces in cabinet. The Asia-Pacific region provides three examples of such grand coalitions. The first was the transitional government formed in Cambodia after the 1993 election, in which the incumbent Cambodian People's Party (CPP) gained fewer seats than the royalist opposition, FUNCINPEC, but no party won a working majority. Amid threats of renewed civil war from the CPP if it was excluded from government, a deal brokered by the United Nations saw a power-sharing coalition featuring 'co-prime ministers' from the two parties installed, which proved highly unstable in practice. Another example of a grand coalition comes from Indonesia, where Abdurrahman Wahid forged a series of all-party cabinets over the course of his presidency from 1999 to 2001. A third, technical example is the formal power-sharing provisions of Fiji's 1997 constitution—which exist in law but, prior to 2006, had never been put into practice. All three cases illustrate the difficulties of the grand coalition model, which while attractive in theory has often proved unworkable in practice.

Cambodia's grand coalition, which came about primarily because of the unwillingness of the CPP to relinquish power after the 1993 elections, demonstrates the difficulties of maintaining power-sharing agreements in the absence of an accommodatory political culture. Since it reflected neither the election outcome nor common policy ground between the two parties, the co-prime ministerial arrangement never functioned well: the CPP remained in effective control of most of the armed forces, the bureaucracy and the judiciary, while FUNCINPEC's attempt to gain a greater share of real power paralysed the executive branch and the National Assembly. After a series of political crises, the coalition fell apart completely in 1997 when the CPP forces of the 'second Prime Minister', Hun Sen, attacked those of FUNCINPEC and the 'first Prime Minister', Prince Ranariddh, and claimed power alone.[18] The CPP-FUNCINPEC coalition was revived for a second time after the 1998 elections—not through any rapprochement between the party leaders, but solely due to the two-thirds requirement for government formation that had earlier been inscribed, at the CPP's insistence, into the constitution. Again, however, Hun Sen became sole prime minister, while Ranariddh and other members of the opposition

---

[18] Jeffrey Gallup, 'Cambodia's Electoral System: A Window of Opportunity for Reform' in Croissant, Bruns and John, *Electoral Politics*, 33.

(such as the new Sam Rainsey Party) were either co-opted or sidelined. Following the 2003 election, the two-thirds majority requirement again led to a stand-off between the two major parties over the formation of a national government, with observers branding the power-sharing rule 'a significant obstacle to forming elected government and to political stability'.[19]

In Indonesia, the grand coalition experiment was similarly troubled. President Wahid came to power in October 1999 via a complex process of political bargaining within the newly enshrined legislature, following Indonesia's first democratic elections in over forty years. None of the leading parties had the numbers to govern alone, and Wahid's National Awakening Party was one of many small parties jostling for power. Amidst frantic cross-party negotiations, Wahid's supporters forged a broad but unstable coalition of Islamic and secular parties, resulting in his surprise ascension to the presidency. He proceeded to form a grand coalition government encompassing a broad spectrum of Indonesian society including party, religious, and regional representatives. However, this 'National Unity Cabinet' proved highly unstable in practice, with a bewildering array of ministers appointed and then removed over the twenty-two months of Wahid's presidency. Following a protracted power struggle the Indonesian legislature—the only directly elected organ of state in existence at the time—began to assert its growing strength vis-à-vis the president, and in August 2001 Wahid was effectively impeached and replaced by his vice-president, Megawati. While continuing the practice of oversized coalitions, she did not attempt to replicate the grand coalition model directly. Instead, harking back to the politics of her father, former President Sukarno, she described her first cabinet as a *Gotong Royong* (mutual cooperation) government—in political science terms, an oversized cabinet but not a grand coalition. This approach was continued by her successor, Yudhoyono, who formed what he called an 'Indonesian unity' oversized cabinet following his election in 2004.

Finally, in Fiji, the constitutional provision that all parties winning at least 10 per cent of seats in parliament be proportionately represented in the cabinet has so far proved unworkable— due to the unwillingness of some parties to abide by the power-sharing rules entrenched in the 1997 Constitution. Following the

---

[19] Albritton, 'Cambodia in 2003', 102. See also Gallup, 'Cambodia's Electoral System', 39.

election in 1999 of Fiji's first Indo-Fijian Prime Minister, Mahendra Chaudhry, the major Fijian opposition party rejected the option of taking up their share of cabinet seats—an option open to them only because the openly worded power-sharing provisions of the constitution made participation in the national unity government optional, not mandatory. Chaudhry's government was overthrown in an ethnic coup a year later. The power-sharing issue was revisited at the 2001 elections, when the victorious Fijian prime minister, Laisenia Qarase, refused to invite Labour members to take up the cabinet positions due to them. Qarase defended his decision by claiming that a grand coalition would not contribute to a stable and workable government or the promotion of national unity. It was not until April 2006, following Qarase's re-election, that a power-sharing cabinet was finally sworn in, with nine ministries allocated to the Fiji Labour Party. However, this grand coalition was not to last. In December 2006, a military coup overthrew the government, ending—perhaps permanently—democracy in Fiji.

Minimal Winning Cabinets

At the other end of the spectrum from grand coalitions are 'minimal winning' cabinets, in which only those parties needed to ensure a bare legislative majority, and no more, are included in government. In most but not all cases, this means a one-party cabinet. Two models of minimal-winning cabinets are evident in the Asia-Pacific. The first occurs in those countries with dominant single-party systems. Executive government in Singapore, for example, has been completely monopolized by the People's Action Party, and hence by minimal-winning one-party cabinets, since independence. The same applies to Samoa, where the Human Rights Protection Party has been in power continuously—and mostly alone—since 1982. In such cases, sharing of power between political elites takes place predominantly *within* the dominant party. A second example of minimal winning cabinet formation practices comes from the region's pure presidential systems, which must be categorized as examples of minimal winning cabinets almost by definition, as the president wins 'all' seats available for election—that is, one—and does not require the confidence of the legislature to remain in office except in usual circumstances.[20] Thus presidential systems such as Korea or the Philippines are usually considered to have minimal winning cabinets, even though their party composition is often opaque.

There are two exceptions to this classification for our cases. One is Indonesia: despite being widely regarded as a presidential system, prior to 2004 the Indonesian president was—as we have seen—chosen by the parliament rather than being directly elected, and thus had to take much greater account of the balance of forces in the assembly than would usually be the case in a normal presidential system. This fact, along with the exceptional nature of their freely elected governments (the first of the post-Suharto era) and the minority status of their parties, helps to explain the oversized *kabinet pelangi* (rainbow cabinets) which were a feature of both Abdurrahman Wahid's and Megawati Sukarnoputri's presidencies.

Another special case is Taiwan. Until May 2000, all Taiwanese elections had delivered majority government to the KMT party, and this one-party dominance was reflected in a succession of single-party cabinets. In 1996, however, Taiwan switched to a semi-presidential form of government, and in early 2000 opposition candidate Chen Shui-bian was elected president. The magnitude of this first-ever change of government, the narrow margin of Chen's victory, and the ongoing domination by the KMT of Taiwan's parliament, the Legislative Yuan, all contributed to Chen forming an unusual broad-based cabinet which initially included thirteen KMT representatives and only eleven ministers from his own party. Despite ongoing problems with this arrangement (the KMT had threatened to expel any of its members who accepted posts in Chen's cabinet) the co-opting of KMT officials continued, in less dramatic fashion, through to Chen's re-election in 2004. Taiwan's cabinet type can thus be classified as minimal-winning until May 2000, and oversized after that.

To try to make sense of these different executive formation practices, Table 7.3 depicts the long-term record of the three cabinet forms—oversized, grand coalition, and minimal winning—for each of our country cases over time. As the table shows, most countries have consistently employed oversized

[20] For a fuller discussion of this issue, see Lijphart, *Patterns of Democracy*, 105, 161.

TABLE 7.3. *Executive formation in the Asia-Pacific*

Executive type	Cases
Minimal winning	Philippines
	Samoa
	Singapore
	Korea
	Taiwan, 1992–2000
	Vanuatu, 1980–91
Oversized	Cambodia, 1998–2004
	East Timor
	Fiji*
	Indonesia, 2001–4
	Malaysia
	Papua New Guinea
	Solomon Islands
	Taiwan, 2000–4
	Thailand
	Vanuatu, 1991–2004
Grand coalition	Cambodia, 1993–7
	Indonesia, 1999–2001

Note: * While grand coalition executives are a formal requirement of Fiji's 1997 Constitution, until 2006 no grand coalition government had been formed. In practice, cabinets have been moderately oversized coalitions, as detailed in the text.

cabinets. While a number of states featured different cabinet types during periods of authoritarian rule than has been the practice under democratic regimes (under Suharto in Indonesia, or military rule in Fiji, for example), of the region's genuine democracies only Taiwan and Vanuatu have changed significantly over the period of this study—in both cases, moving from minimal winning to oversized cabinets, largely as a result of changes in their party systems in recent years. Most other states have exhibited high degrees of continuity in cabinet formation over time.

Measuring Power-Sharing

Using this broad three-way classification of minimal-winning, oversized, and grand coalition cabinet types, we are now in a position to construct an index which aggregates the key components of government formation in order to measure the extent of executive power-sharing across the Asia-Pacific region.

The two most salient components of executive power-sharing are the number of parties included, and the extent to which governments comprise single-party majorities or multiparty coalitions. Lijphart has argued that 'the difference between one-party majority governments and broad multiparty coalitions epitomizes the contrast between the majoritarian principle of concentrating power in the hands of the majority and the consensus principle of broad power-sharing'.[21] Following this reasoning, one measure of power-sharing is to look at the number of effective political parties represented in parliament and the extent to which oversized rather than minimal winning cabinet formations are employed. A combined index of this information provides an (admittedly crude) means of comparing the sharing of executive power across different countries.

Table 7.4 presents one such attempt to measure the relative degree of executive power-sharing in the Asia-Pacific on a long-term basis. The index captures a combination of two key elements of executive power-sharing: *representation*, reflected by the effective number of parliamentary parties, and *inclusion*, reflecting the extent to which oversized cabinet types were employed. The index was created by standardizing the mean scores on both measures over the entire democratic period of each country (or, in the semi-democracies of Cambodia, Singapore, and Malaysia, over all elections), and then averaging the sum of these two standardized variables to arrive at an aggregate Index of Power-Sharing for every country. The table displays the aggregate ranking of all countries on this power-sharing index, listed in descending order.

As the table shows, the extent of executive power-sharing varies widely across the Asia-Pacific. At one end, Papua New Guinea, Indonesia, and Thailand have all featured very high levels of power-sharing on this measure. By contrast, sharing of executive power has been minimal in Samoa, Korea, and Singapore. How do we explain this discrepancy of outcomes?

One readily apparent explanation here, as in other areas examined in this book, is the influence of social diversity upon political practice. Across the region, greater levels of societal diversity are strongly correlated with higher levels of power-sharing. In general, socially fragmented states such as Papua New Guinea, Indonesia, Solomon Islands, and Fiji tend also to have above-average levels of power-sharing according to this

---

[21] Lijphart, *Patterns of Democracy*, 90.

TABLE 7.4. *An index of power-sharing for the Asia-Pacific*

Country	Mean effective number of parliamentary parties	Mean proportion of oversized cabinets	Index of power-sharing (standardized)
PNG 1977–2004	9.16	1.00	1.68
Indonesia 1999–2004	6.85	1.00	1.15
Thailand 1992–2004	5.03	1.00	0.73
Solomon Is 1978–2004	4.12	.82	0.31
Fiji 1999–2004	3.06	1.00	0.27
East Timor 2001–4	2.42	1.00	0.13
Cambodia 1993–2004	2.36	.90	0.00
Malaysia 1957–2004	1.57	1.00	−0.07
Vanuatu 1979–2004	3.48	.54	−0.15
Philippines 1986–2004	4.90	.00	−0.44
Taiwan 1992–2004	2.56	.33	−0.60
Samoa 1991–2004	3.04	.09	−0.77
Korea 1988–2004	2.83	.00	−0.92
Singapore 1968–2004	1.03	.00	−1.33

Source: Croissant, 'Electoral Politics', 340; Hsieh and Newman, *How Asia Votes*; Nohlen, Grotz, and Hartmann, *Elections in Asia and the Pacific*; author's calculations.

index. This follows the strong correlation between social diversity and party pluralism observed in Chapter 6. A positive relationship between social diversity and power-sharing is thus not surprisingly, given that one component of the power-sharing index is itself the effective number of parliamentary parties. Indeed, only two of the Asia-Pacific's ethnically plural societies, the Philippines and Singapore, consistently employ minimal-winning cabinets—although as noted above, both have practised informal power-sharing in other ways. In the Philippines, while cabinets have been minimal winning in formal terms, winning coalitions are built by co-opting independents and representatives from other parties, and cabinets habitually include representatives from Luzon, the Visayas, and Mindanao, as well as representatives of the Protestant and Muslim minorities.[22] Similarly, in Singapore, governments are keen to project a multi-ethnic image, and usually ensure Malay and Indian representatives are included in cabinet and in important symbolic positions as well.[23]

[22] Rüland, 'Constitutional Debates in the Philippines', 468.
[23] See Diane K. Mauzy, 'Electoral Innovation and One-Party Dominance in Singapore', in Hsieh and Newman, *How Asia Votes*, 247.

A second, and perhaps more surprising, observation is the negative correlation between power-sharing and cabinet longevity. As the scattergram at Figure 7.1 shows clearly, countries with high levels of power-sharing tend to have *less* stable politics than average. This would appear to be something of a rebuff to those who see power-sharing as the answer to a country's political ills, particularly enthusiasts for consociational solutions such as Nordlinger, McRae, and Lijphart.[24] However, the direction of causality between these two factors is not at all clear. On the one hand, as we have seen, more heterogeneous states tend to have higher levels of power-sharing, and countries facing deep social and political conflicts often adopt power-sharing measures in the hope of stabilizing national politics. On the other hand, actual examples of the most comprehensive forms of power-sharing in the region, such as the use of grand coalition governments in Indonesia, co-prime ministerial arrangements in Cambodia, or mandatory cabinet positions in Fiji, have often

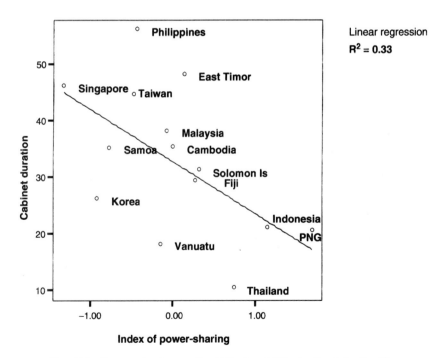

FIG. 7.1. *Power-sharing and political stability in the Asia-Pacific*

[24] See note 17, Chapter 4.

been highly unstable. What can be said with confidence is that higher levels of power-sharing have not resulted in greater political stability, on aggregate.

One final point to note: both the power-sharing and cabinet duration indexes are based on aggregate data from each country's entire democratic history up to 2004. This means that, in some cases, the picture being presented is based more on historical than current practice. For example, the Philippines ranks low on the power-sharing index but has very high levels of cabinet duration—primarily because of its combination of presidentialism with five-year terms. However, in the Philippines case,

cabinet duration gives a completely wrong impression of the degree of executive dominance ... most presidents are caught in endless bargaining processes with individual members of the congress due to the absence of presidential majorities in congress, the weak credibility of congressional majorities, the lack of presidential decree authorities and a highly volatile party system. This leads to institutional or clientelist gridlocks and political frustrations of the executive.[25]

Similarly, in Thailand, the historical pattern of weak and unstable cabinets has in recent years been turned on its head by the rise of the TRT to a position of unchallenged dominance. Finally, the measures of party fragmentation used to construct the index may themselves be deceptive in some cases. In Malaysia, for instance, the official electoral statistics list the *Barisan* coalition as one party rather than a multiparty coalition, meaning that calculations which rely on it (such as my power-sharing index) inevitably understate the true extent of executive power-sharing in Malaysia.

Federalism, Devolution, and Autonomy

So far, this chapter has focused on the horizontal dimension of power-sharing, based around the inclusion of different parties and groups in government. However, as noted in the introduction, power-sharing can also take place on a vertical basis, via the division of powers between national, regional, and local

---

[25] Croissant, 'Electoral Politics', 342.

levels of government, and the territorial devolution of political authority to subnational jurisdictions such as states, provinces, autonomous units, or local governments. Despite a widespread normative bias in favour of unitary states, most of the plural societies in the Asia-Pacific region make some provision to spread, separate, or share powers in this way, ranging from full-scale federalism to wide-ranging decentralization to special autonomy arrangements for particular regions.

Territorial devolution enables groups in different regions and at different levels of government to access and exercise governing authority independently of central control. Unfortunately for comparative purposes, the experience of devolution in the Asia-Pacific is currently rather limited and inconclusive. Of all the countries included in this study, Malaysia is the only unambiguous example of a federal system in which governing power is constitutionally divided between national and state governments—and even there, federalism is weakened by the government's ability to amend the constitution by a two-thirds vote of parliament, as it has done almost annually since independence. Papua New Guinea's provincial government system is semi-federal at best, while unitary systems prevail in all the remaining cases—even in far-flung, spread-out and regionally diverse cases such as Indonesia, where federalism has been a persistent demand for decades. A similar conclusion applies to the subject of devolution of authority to local-level governments. Asia-Pacific governments such as Thailand, the Philippines, Solomon Islands, and Indonesia have embarked on major exercises in regional devolution, transferring a range of powers and revenue-raising responsibilities from central to provincial and in many cases local governments.[26] While these are grand and in some cases radical experiments, again this process is only just beginning. Given the short time span for evaluating most cases and the uncertain future of all of them, all that can be said with confidence is that the impact of both federalism and devolution in the Asia-Pacific remains something of an open question.

There have, however, been special autonomy arrangements for particular regions such as Mindanao and the Cordilleras in the Philippines, Aceh and Papua in Indonesia, and Bougainville in

---

[26] See Mark Turner (ed.), *Central–Local Relations in Asia-Pacific: Convergence or Divergence?* (Hampshire and New York: Palgrave, 1999).

Papua New Guinea, as well as complex arrangements for cultural and economic autonomy in non-democratic environments such as contemporary China.[27] These involve the designation of special status and distinctive governing powers for a defined regional entity under the national authority of the state, and have become an increasingly attractive avenue for policymakers attempting to manage secessionist or self-determination struggles, particularly in Southeast Asia and the South Pacific. Examples of peace agreements in which autonomy have been used as a mechanism for conflict management include the 1976 Tripoli Agreement and its successor, the optimistically titled 'Final Peace Agreement' of 1996 for Muslim Mindanao, as well as the 1986 peace pact in the Cordilleras (both in the Philippines); the Matignon Accords of 1988 and 1998 in New Caledonia (which remains, for the time being, jurisdictionally part of France); the Bougainville Peace Agreement of 2001 which led to the formation of an Autonomous Bougainville Government (in Papua New Guinea); and the 2005 peace deal between Jakarta and representatives of the *Aceh Merdeka* (Free Aceh) movement (in Indonesia).

Again, however, it is simply too early to judge the success or otherwise of most of these experiments for our purposes. Some, such as the Bougainville and New Caledonian agreements, appear to have been integral to the success of peace-making in ending actual or potential violent conflicts, while others such as the autonomy arrangements for Mindanao and the Cordilleras failed to gain sufficient voter support when put to referendum and have been mostly ineffectual in bringing an end to the conflict.[28] In Indonesia, 'special autonomy' laws for Aceh and Papua introduced in 2001, offering both provinces more local control over cultural, political, and economic affairs and a greater portion of the revenue from local natural resource projects, have themselves become the subject of contention, bogged down by debates about implementation. One study of autonomy as a means of managing secessionism concluded that these cases 'confirm a central theme of the comparative literature on autonomy: the fragility of such arrangements and their vulnerability to reversal. Special autonomy arrangements are exceedingly

---

[27] See Ghai, *Autonomy and Ethnicity*.

[28] For an analysis, see R. J. May, 'Ethnicity and Public Policy in the Philippines', in Brown and Ganguly, *Government Policies and Ethnic Relations*, 321–50.

difficult to entrench as national elites almost always resist demands to devolve political authority and are suspicious of any initiative that may set a precedent for other regions. This is particularly the case in large multi-ethnic countries such as Indonesia.' [29]

One clear lesson from these cases is that creating autonomous regions based around ethnically-homogeneous component units of the kind recommended by consociationalists is extremely difficult. Regions such as Aceh, Mindanao, and Papua are all themselves internally multi-ethnic—a factor that has been exacerbated by official transmigration policies in Indonesia, where residents of overpopulated regions have been encouraged to move to peripheral but under-populated outer regions such as Papua. Coming on top of successive earlier waves of migration, this has led to the dispersion and inter-mixture of many different groups: demographic calculations suggest that the Asia-Pacific now has the highest level of ethnic inter-mixture of any region in the world.[30] This makes it likely that most autonomous regions or federal units in the region will themselves contain significant internal minorities rather than comprising one homogeneous nation. Even Malaysia's long-standing federal system, which comprises a combination of former sultanates with colonial administrative units, features state boundaries that cut across, rather than reinforce, pre-existing social divisions. As a result, vertical power-sharing in most Asia-Pacific countries is likely to feature subnational units which are themselves ethnically intermixed—making them, once again, more amenable to centripetal rather than consociational approaches to political engineering.

Conclusion

Overall, the results of this comparative enquiry tend to complement the findings of the earlier chapters. In Chapter 3, we saw that higher levels of social diversity, as measured by the degree of ethno-linguistic fragmentation in each country, had distinctive

---

[29] Rodd McGibbon, 'Secessionist Challenges in Aceh and Papua: Is Special Autonomy the Solution?', *Policy Studies 10* (Washington, DC: East-West Center, 2004), viii.

[30] See Reilly, *Democracy in Divided Societies*, 189–91.

impacts upon development and democracy across the Asia-Pacific. Using the same data-set, in Chapters 5 and 6 we saw that this same measure of social diversity was one of the strongest correlates of party pluralism across the region. Building on these findings, this chapter has shown that increasing societal diversity is also strongly associated with higher levels of executive power-sharing across the Asia-Pacific region. There is thus an accumulation of evidence reinforcing the independent impact of social structures on political outcomes, and strong support for the contention that political practice in the Asia-Pacific has been shaped to a significant extent by the degree of societal diversity from country to country, as suggested in Chapter 1.

These results represent something of a challenge to a number of well-entrenched political science theories. For example, probably the best-established model of government formation in the scholarly literature is the 'minimal winning coalition' theory formulated by William Riker, which predicts the formation of cabinets with the smallest number of parties necessary to maintain government wherever possible, with additional parties included only if they are needed to guarantee a legislative majority.[31] Most of this formal literature on coalitions is drawn from either Western experience or deductive theory-building, and finds little if any support when the empirical record of government formation in the Asia-Pacific is examined.[32] Rather, in most of the new democracies of Asia and the Pacific governments comprise broad multiparty coalitions constructed to deliver balanced ethno-regional representation and provide a buffer against party defections. As a result, most countries, most of the time, employ oversized rather than minimal winning cabinet formations. And, in contrast to the range of predictors of government formation that can be drawn from the formal literature, underlying levels of societal diversity appear to be (again) the strongest predictor of coalition formation, with the highest levels of power-sharing occurring in the most diverse societies.

The other main conclusion of this chapter concerns the implications of the Asian approach to power-sharing for the broader

[31] William Riker, *The Theory of Political Coalitions* (New Haven, CT: Yale University Press, 1962).
[32] See, for example, Michael Laver and Norman Schofield, *Multiparty Government: The Politics of Coalition in Europe* (Oxford: Oxford University Press, 1991).

scholarly debate on political engineering. While the experience of federalism, devolution and autonomy across the region is too limited to reach any firm conclusions at this point, the basic ethnic demography of the Asia-Pacific means that most forms of devolution are likely to result in multi-ethnic component units rather than the ethnically homogeneous jurisdictions recommended in the consociational literature. In terms of executive formation patterns, the trends are much clearer: most Asia-Pacific democracies have rejected the formal executive power-sharing and grand coalition models endorsed by consociationalists in favour of more fluid and informal approaches to executive formation. They have tended to eschew rigid rules mandating the composition of cabinets in favour of more flexible practices of inclusion. The limited use to date of explicit power-sharing requirements, the troubled experiments with grand coalition cabinets in Indonesia and Fiji, and the strong association of such practices with political instability, all underscore this aversion towards consociational measures. By contrast, informal power-sharing approaches, in which political inclusion is a result of deal-making rather than law, appears to have become successfully institutionalized in a number of cases. The concluding chapter to this book, Chapter 8, looks at the implications of these patterns for political engineering in Asia and the Pacific more generally, and examines whether regional patterns of electoral system design, party formation rules, and executive formation practices collectively do indeed constitute a distinctive model of democratic governance.

········

8

········

Conclusion

The time has come to step back from the detailed descriptive accounts of the preceding chapters and look at the bigger picture. By investigating the relationship between political reform and the management of internal cleavages, this book has examined how the Asia-Pacific's fledgling democracies have refashioned their institutional configurations in the hope of creating more stable and sustainable democratic systems. As detailed over the past few chapters, these overt attempts to engineer politics have focused on redesigning the basic institutional components of representative democracy: elections, parties, legislatures, and executive governments. In this final chapter, I discuss the implications of these reform trends for political development in the Asia-Pacific region and for new democracies in other parts of the world.

First, to sum up the combined evidence presented so far: while social compositions vary from the relatively homogeneous states of Northeast Asia to the complex heterogeneity of the South Pacific, important *social and political cleavages* are present in virtually all new Asia-Pacific democracies. These cleavages range from the multiple overlapping cultural, linguistic, religious, and regional schisms that define Indonesia to the bipolar indigenous-versus-immigrant divisions found in Fiji, and from the national identity issue that forms the bedrock political cleavage in Taiwan to the intense regionalism that continues to characterize electoral competition in Korea.

The interplay between these cleavages and the opening of political space that attends democratization can unleash powerful political pressures for segmental politics, presenting aspiring political entrepreneurs with the temptation to exploit ethnopolitical divisions in the quest for electoral success. Especially in the absence of cross-cutting ideological fissures or strong party identification, the introduction of competitive elections in socially diverse environments can thus create strong incentives for vote-seeking politicians to indulge in particularistic and clientelistic electoral strategies in their attempt to win and maintain office.

Compounding these pressures, the pre-existing *institutional configuration* of a number of Asia-Pacific states has also played a role in promoting particularistic politics. Until recently, for instance, even relatively homogeneous societies such as Korea and Thailand featured personalized and candidate-centred elections which encouraged particularistic campaign tactics, and pork-barrel politics. In pre-1997 Thailand, the combination of block vote election laws with a weak and fragmented party system created incentives for vote-buying, patronage, and corruption. In Korea, democratic elections have been dominated by transient, personality-driven parties dependent on regional support bases. In Taiwan, the predominant use of SNTV electoral laws forced candidates from the same party to compete with one another for votes—leading again to personalized and factionalized electoral politics.

In each of these cases, the combination of distinct social cleavages with facilitating political institutions encouraged campaigning politicians to mobilize communal ties or other kinds of clientelistic linkages in their quest for electoral victory. In many countries, the resulting emphasis on particularistic electoral strategies led, unsurprisingly, to public policies which rewarded members of some groups, sectors, or regions more than others. In extreme cases such as Papua New Guinea, the triple whammy of social heterogeneity, party fragmentation and plurality elections resulted in deep pathologies of governance, with political strategies based around the delivery of private or club goods to clan supporters rather than public goods to the electorate as a whole— pathologies which have gravely undermined prospects for development.

In recent years, however, increasing elite awareness of these problems, combined with the inevitable calculations of self-interested actors seeking to advance their own political prospects, has stimulated a search for appropriate changes to the rules of the democratic game. By opening the door to large-scale political reform, democratization acted as both cause and effect, stimulating some damaging pathologies of governance while simultaneously presenting opportunities to respond to these systemic threats via institutional reform. Although always country-specific, attempts to address recurring problems of clientelism, rent-seeking, and ethnic politics led to highly convergent reform strategies in many Asian and Pacific states. Across the region, these reforms typically sought to improve government stability, encourage party aggregation, restrict the enfranchisement of regional or ethnic minorities, and foster majoritarian political outcomes. As Diamond has noted, one paradox of democracy is that in some circumstances 'a political system can be made *more* stably democratic by making it somewhat *less* representative'.[1] This was clearly the strategy pursued by many Asia-Pacific reformers.

Figure 8.1 sets out a simple causal model of this story. Social cleavages, weak party systems, and candidate-centred electoral laws which fostered intra-party competition each played an independent role in promoting clientelistic politics, underprovision of public goods, and unstable governments. As a consequence, most political reforms sought to push outcomes in the other direction, towards programmatic party politics and stable executive governments. Thus, Asia-Pacific governments have tried to engineer aggregative politics through the introduction of a range of electoral reforms, including mixed-member majoritarian electoral systems (in Korea, the Philippines, Taiwan, and Thailand), regional distribution requirements for presidential elections (in Indonesia), minimum-vote thresholds to discourage splinter parties (in Korea, the Philippines, Thailand, and Taiwan), and the introduction of alternative vote electoral systems (in Fiji and Papua New Guinea). In the political party arena, similarly, attempts have been made to restrict regional parties (in Indonesia), present ethnically-mixed candidate lists (Singapore), limit the representation of sectoral parties (the Philippines), and promote party aggregation (Papua New Guinea, Indonesia, and Thailand again). Finally, the construction of oversized, multiparty cabinets has been a common feature of government formation in states as varied as Cambodia, Indonesia, Fiji, Malaysia, Papua New Guinea, Solomon Islands, and Vanuatu.

---

[1] Larry Diamond, 'Three Paradoxes of Democracy', *Journal of Democracy*, 1 (1990), 55 (emphasis in original).

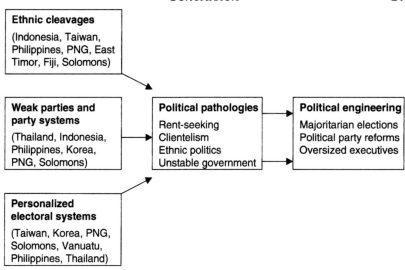

FIG. 8.1. *A causal model of political engineering in the Asia-Pacific*

At least four separate conclusions can be drawn from all of this. First, stability, predictability, and order have been core themes motivating political engineering across the Asia-Pacific region. The fact that these same goals were politically advantageous to incumbent governing parties and coalitions also played a key role, given that virtually all reforms required legislative and sometimes constitutional change. Second, and in contrast to the predictions of much of the scholarly literature, many of these attempts to consciously engineer political outcomes appear to have succeeded in meeting at least some of their goals. However, there have been ongoing problems of coherence and unintended consequences. Third, in terms of the debate over the best approach to building sustainable democracy in divided societies, Asia-Pacific states have shown a clear preference for majoritarian and centripetal approaches to political engineering, and have in most cases eschewed consociational models based on ethnic parties, proportional elections, and formal power-sharing rules. Finally, as a result of this unusual approach to political reform in the region, there appears to be an emerging 'Asia-Pacific model'—or, to be precise, an East Asian model—of electoral democracy. All of this makes the Asia-Pacific distinctive by comparison with other world regions. The remainder of this chapter examines each of these four conclusions in turn.

Trends in Asia-Pacific Reforms

The Asian approach to political engineering illustrates one of the recurring themes animating the choice of political institutions: the trade-off between efficiency and representation. Classically, 'representational' institutions were considered to facilitate the direct translation of popular preferences and cleavages into the political sphere with as little interference as possible, via political parties representing distinct social groups, proportional representation elections, and low barriers to minority enfranchisement. Together, these institutions should ideally lead to the development of a diverse multiparty system in which all significant social groups and interests are separately represented. By contrast, 'efficient' institutions that can deliver clear parliamentary majorities offering distinct policy alternatives are more often associated with majoritarian elections and 'catch-all' political parties that command electoral support across social cleavages. In theory, these make it more likely that minority and majority interests alike will be aggregated into a few large parties which alternate in power over time.

By the terms of this long-running debate, most of the political reforms in the Asia-Pacific over the past decade have clearly come down on the side of efficiency and against representation. It is important to recognize just how distinctive Asia's move towards majoritarianism is in comparison to other world regions. The broader scholarly literature on elections often assumes an implied (or sometimes explicit) teleological progression towards greater proportionality when electoral reforms are adopted. Thus David Farrell argues that globally 'since the early 1990s, the trend has been away from plurality and towards proportional systems'.[2] Perhaps as a result of this, in the established democracies of the West there has been a marked increase in effective party numbers over the past decade.[3] In the Asia-Pacific, however, this trend has been reversed: major electoral reforms in Korea, Indonesia, Taiwan, Thailand, and the Philippines, as well as less dramatic reforms in Cambodia and Indonesia, have all

[2] David Farrell, *Electoral Systems: A Comparative Introduction* (Hampshire and New York: Palgrave, 2001), 19.

[3] See Paul Webb, 'Conclusion: Political Parties and Democratic Control in Advanced Industrial Societies' in Paul Webb, David Farrell and Ian Holliday (eds.), *Political Parties in Advanced Industrial Democracies* (Oxford: Oxford University Press, 2002), 440.

resulted in the introduction of *less* proportional systems than those that preceded them. In the Pacific Islands, similarly, the focus of electoral reform has been on the replacement of plurality rules with true majority systems such as the alternative vote.

To illustrate just how distinctive the Asia-Pacific is, we can engage in some comparisons with other democratizing regions such as Africa, Latin America, and post-communist Europe. In the new democracies of Africa, for example, there has been a strong trend towards the increasing use of list PR electoral systems—and an equally strong preponderance of one-party dominant regimes. Starting with the UN-sponsored democratization of Namibia in 1989, major transitional elections in South Africa (1994), Mozambique (1994), Liberia (1997), Sierra Leone (2002), and Rwanda (2003) were all conducted under PR. Of Africa's more established democracies, only Botswana and Mauritius use plurality systems. The overall trend has clearly been towards greater proportionality, with the island state of the Seychelles the only example of an Asian-style mixed-member majoritarian model in the entire African region.

Similarly, Latin America's new and restored democracies have, virtually without exception, maintained the PR systems that they inherited from their autocratic predecessors.[4] *Every* Latin American state, from Mexico in the north to Argentina in the south, combines a presidential system of government with a congress elected by proportional representation—despite the mixture of presidentialism and PR being blamed for the 'difficult combination' of hamstrung executives with fragmented legislatures across the continent.[5] In addition, the mixed-member systems used in Mexico, Venezuela, and Bolivia are all compensatory in some form, producing broadly proportional outcomes.[6] In the Asia-Pacific, by contrast, only Indonesia and Cambodia use list PR systems, and there are no compensatory mechanisms despite the widespread use of mixed-member models.

[4] The one partial exception to this statement is Chile, which uses an unusual form of PR in two-member districts, thus operating more like a majoritarian system than a proportional one.

[5] See Scott Mainwaring, 'Presidentialism, Multipartism, and Democracy: The Difficult Combination', *Comparative Political Studies*, 26/2 (1993), 198–228.

[6] Mark P. Jones, 'A Guide to the Electoral Systems of the Americas', *Electoral Studies*, 14/1 (1985), 5–21; idem, 'A Guide to the Electoral Systems of the Americas: An Update', *Electoral Studies*, 16/1 (1997), 13–15.

The distinctiveness of the Asia-Pacific approach to institutional design is even more marked when we examine the new democracies of Eastern and Central Europe. There, the tendency has been to follow the example of Western Europe and introduce highly proportional elections, protection for communal and ethnic parties, and strong guarantees of minority rights. As Sarah Birch notes, since 1990, proportional representation has become the modal electoral system for Europe's new democracies: 'Post-communist political transformation was accompanied by a spate of electoral reforms that... installed new systems that were either based entirely on proportional representation or had a strong proportional element.'[7] At the end of communist rule, the twenty new democracies of Eastern and Central Europe all adopted full PR or mixed systems; none chose majoritarian models; and of those with mixed systems only two small states, Albania and Armenia, adopted the majoritarian variant common in the Asia-Pacific. And, in further contrast to the Asia-Pacific experience, recent electoral reforms have all pushed outcomes in the direction of greater proportionality; no states have shifted back towards majoritarianism.

By comparison, as we have seen, the Asia-Pacific focus has been on introducing overtly majoritarian mixed-member electoral arrangements, reducing the proportionality of the PR systems that do exist, and retarding the electoral prospects of smaller political parties. Thus, with the exception of East Timor, all Asian states which today employ mixed-member systems (Japan, Korea, Taiwan, the Philippines, and Thailand) subordinate the proportional party-list element to the majoritarian, district-based part. As discussed in Chapter 5, this makes these systems quite unusual in structural terms: on average, Asian mixed systems elect twice as many seats from single-member districts than those in other parts of the world. Reinforcing this majoritarian shift is the fact that Asian states which have *not* adopted mixed-member systems have nonetheless chosen electoral models which advantage larger national parties and penalize small ones. In Cambodia and Indonesia, successive electoral reforms have sharply reduced district magnitude and hence proportionality. In Singapore and Malaysia, revised district boundaries have further strengthened what were

---

[7] Birch, *Electoral Systems*, 136.

already highly majoritarian electoral systems. In each of these cases, electoral reform had the effect of restricting political fragmentation, penalizing small parties, and promoting the interests of larger incumbents. As a result, in contrast to democratizing states in Europe, the new democracies of the Asia-Pacific have become more 'efficient' but less 'representative' in recent years.

Another area of contrast between the Asia-Pacific and Europe is the differing approach to political parties, particularly those representing ethnic minorities. In Asia, governments have tried to discourage the formation of ethnic parties in a variety of ways, from placing constitutional prohibitions on their formation to introducing subtle barriers upon their participation in elections. This approach stands in sharp contrast to the protection—indeed, encouragement—offered to such parties in Europe. For example, the Organization for Security and Cooperation in Europe (OSCE), which covers Western and Eastern Europe as well as Russia and Central Asia, explicitly affirms the right of ethnic minorities to form their own parties and compete for office on a communal basis. This right has been enshrined in official proclamations such as the 1990 Copenhagen Declaration—which specifies 'the important role of... political parties... in the promotion of tolerance, cultural diversity and the resolution of questions relating to national minorities'[8]—and the 1992 Helsinki Document, which commits participating states 'to ensure the free exercise by persons belonging to national minorities, individually or in community with others, of their human rights and fundamental freedoms, including the right to participate fully... through political parties and associations'.[9] More recently, another OSCE body has affirmed 'the freedom to establish political parties based on communal identities', arguing that in some cases 'such communal parties may be the only hope for effective representation of specific interests and thus, for effective participation'.[10]

The situation in the Asia-Pacific is very different. Instead of supporting communal parties, countries like Indonesia have deliberately attempted to subvert their appearance. So, through

[8] Organization for Security and Cooperation in Europe, *Copenhagen Document of the Conference on the Human Dimension* (1990), paragraph 30.
[9] Organization for Security and Cooperation in Europe, *Helsinki Document* (1992), paragraph 24, part VI.
[10] The Foundation on Inter-Ethnic Relations, *The Lund Recommendations on the Effective Participation of National Minorities in Public Life & Explanatory Note* (1999), 9, 24.

a variety of incentives and constraints on party formation, have Thailand, Singapore and Papua New Guinea. While such constraints would constitute a clear breach of the international treaties which bind European and post-communist states, they have received wide acceptance in the Asia-Pacific region. A similar conclusion applies to the use of electoral thresholds: a number of European countries specifically exempt parties representing ethnic minorities from application of the threshold. In Germany, Denmark, and Poland, for example, exemptions from the 5 per cent threshold apply to parties representing specified 'national minorities'. No such exemptions apply in the Asia-Pacific; indeed, as the preceding discussion makes clear, any such provision would run counter to the general logic which seeks to restrict, rather than assist, minority parties.

Finally, survey research from across the region suggests that Asian public opinion is also less open than that of other regions to minority rights guarantees. Opinion polls in seven East Asian nations reported that respondents displayed significantly higher support for majoritarian democracy over more 'pluralist' models of democracy which gave legal guarantees to minorities. Those countries with the highest support for democracy also had the lowest support for pluralism, prompting the survey's authors to conclude that a distinctive feature of East Asian democracy is the lack of public support for pluralistic values and minority rights instruments.[11] Asia's majoritarian political reforms thus appear to reflect, at some level, the popular attitudes held by a significant number of Asian citizens.

Political Engineering and Political Outcomes

The promise of political engineering continues to attract ambiguous responses from many political scientists. Even enthusiasts such as Horowitz express scepticism about the prospects of appropriate institutional packages being adopted in divided societies.[12] Amongst others, there is outright rejection of the idea that political engineering can facilitate either democratiza-

[11] See Robert Albritton and Thawilwadee Bureekul, 'Social and Cultural Supports for Pluralist Democracy Across Seven Asian Nations', Paper presented to the annual meeting of the International Studies Association, Honolulu (2005).

[12] See Donald L. Horowitz, 'Constitutional Design: Proposals Versus Process' in Reynolds, *The Architecture of Democracy*, 15–36.

tion or the management of internal conflict. Brian Barry, for example, argues that trying to change the nature of a country's party system by institutional redesign is virtually impossible.[13] John McGarry and Brendan O'Leary state that attempts to build broad-based parties in multiethnic societies 'may be well-intentioned ways of regulating ethnic conflict, but they are mostly based on wishful thinking...the belief that one can generate parties with such effects through heroic acts of will or engineering is fundamentally utopian'.[14] Looking at the Pacific, Jon Fraenkel contends that political reforms in Fiji and Papua New Guinea have relied on 'exaggerated claims about the institutional causes of governance failures and naive expectations that juggling with electoral rules will transform political culture'.[15] Such conclusions represent a widespread counsel of scepticism about the efficacy of political engineering.

Examination of the empirical record of reforms in the Asia-Pacific's emerging democracies over the past decade call such claims into question. In each of the three main institutional arenas investigated in this book—electoral systems, political parties, and executive governments—the empirical evidence suggests that attempts to engineer political outcomes have, more often than not, achieved at least some of their stated objectives. Thus, electoral reform in Thailand, which sought to consolidate the party system, resulted in a 50 per cent fall in party numbers between pre- and post-reform elections. In Indonesia, new electoral laws curbed the natural fragmentation one would expect in so diverse an archipelago, encouraging parties and candidates to compete for votes across the archipelago rather than relying on regional support. The same trend is apparent in the political stability measures examined in the previous chapter, with Indonesia, Thailand, and Papua New Guinea all recording significant increases in the durability of their executive governments following the application of constitutional reforms aimed at stabilizing national politics.

[13] Brian Barry, 'Political Accommodation and Consociational Democracy', in *Democracy and Power: Essays in Political Theory 1* (Oxford: Oxford University Press, 1991), 146.
[14] John McGarry and Brendan O'Leary, 'Introduction: The macro-political regulation of ethnic conflict', in John McGarry and Brendan O'Leary (eds.), *The Politics of Ethnic Conflict Regulation: Case Studies of Protracted Ethnic Conflicts* (London and New York: Routledge, 1993), 21–2.
[15] Jon Fraenkel, 'Electoral Engineering in Papua New Guinea: Lessons From Fiji and Elsewhere', *Pacific Economic Bulletin*, 19/1 (2004), 130.

Of course, the fact that political reforms may have met some of their stated objectives does not mean that they are therefore the most desirable or appropriate models. Contradictory incentives and unintended side-effects appear to be a common problem, highlighting what some suggest may be an 'iron law of the perverse consequences of institutional design'.[16] Thus, while Thailand's new constitutional arrangements undoubtedly improved political efficiency, they also led to political power becoming highly concentrated in the hands of Prime Minister Thaksin, one of Thailand's richest men—raising questions about the extent to which democracy is being promoted in the process. Indeed, measures to encourage greater political stability in Thailand appear to have created a raft of unintended consequences, including the delegitimization of the constitutional order.[17]

Inherent tensions in the constituent elements of institutional reform packages is evident in a number of cases examined in this book. Consider the shift towards mixed-member majoritarian systems across the Asia-Pacific. There are sound reasons for believing that the numerical bias in favour of single-member districts over party list seats in Korea, Taiwan, Thailand, and the Philippines will, over time, improve political accountability by forging closer links between individual politicians and voters, just as proponents of this model have claimed. However, this same feature may simultaneously retard another desired aim—the development of more nationally-focused and programmatic political parties—as district-based systems are generally considered to be less effective in promoting nationally cohesive parties than PR. Similarly, the use of open list voting in Indonesia, introduced in 2004 in order to build greater links between individual candidates and the electorate, may over time create side-pressures for party fragmentation—precisely the opposite of the results intended. Likewise, in both Indonesia and Thailand, the overt stimulus for party consolidation at lower house elections may be undercut by the design of the

[16] Sunil Bastian and Robin Luckham, 'Conclusion: the Politics of Institutional Choice', in Sunil Bastian and Robin Luckham (eds.), *Can Democracy be Designed? The Politics of Institutional Choice in Conflict-Torn Societies* (London and New York: Zed Books, 2003), 314.

[17] In September 2006, the military stepped in, removing Thaksin from power, suspending the constitution and installing a puppet government.

new upper houses, where candidature is explicitly restricted to non-party representatives.

Many of the region's reforms thus appear to lack coherence when viewed from a comparative perspective. The Philippines provides a good illustration of this incoherent approach to political engineering. There, numerous aspects of the electoral process—limited public funding, a candidate-centred written ballot, and frequent party switching—have undermined broader goals of political consolidation. In addition, while the reservation of party list seats for marginalized interests has made Philippines politics more representative, 'it has also partially ghettoized those interests. Mainstream political parties and politicians seem largely content to leave programmatic campaigning and the representation of marginalized interests to party list groups.'[18] Combined with a ban on the five strongest parties standing candidates for the party list, and a three-seat limit for each list regardless of their vote share, this has encouraged a proliferation of organizations representing underprivileged groups—and arguably undermined the push for more coherent party politics.

Countervailing incentives arising from multiple concurrent reform objectives are another problem. Again the Philippines provides a clear example, via the one-term limit that applies to the tenure of both the presidency and the congress. Intended to prevent the re-emergence of the political dynasties that dominated in the pre-Marcos period, these term limits have had the unintended effect of sabotaging other institutional measures aimed at building stronger parties, undermining incentives for incumbent politicians to invest time and energy in building party membership and organizational capacity.[19] In Korea too, the one-term limit on the presidency has been blamed for reinforcing the weak party system, and exacerbating the deep-rooted coordination failures which continue to afflict Korean party politics.[20] In Japan, the 'dual candidate' system, which allows defeated district candidates to 'rise from the dead' on the party list, has similarly undermined other broader reform goals such as the

---

[18] Allen Hicken, 'Parties and Elections', in Erik Kuhonta, Dan Slater, and Tuong Vu (eds.), *Southeast Asia in Political Science: Theory, Region, and Method* (Stanford: Stanford University Press), forthcoming.

[19] See Choi, 'Philippine Democracies Old and New', 488–501.

[20] Ibid, 500–1.

creation of less personalistic and more programmatic political parties.[21] In all of these cases, reform aims have been hampered by countervailing, inconsistent, and sometimes incoherent approaches to political engineering.

Consociationalism Versus Centripetalism

The Asia-Pacific experience of political engineering has important implications for the scholarly debate on the optimal models of democratic governance for plural societies. Earlier in this book, Chapter 4 examined the three most prominent approaches to political engineering identified by the scholarly literature: consociationalism, centripetalism, and communalism. While aspects of all three models have been applied at various times, in recent years Asian and Pacific states have shown a clear preference for centripetal reforms rather than those associated with the consociational model. Examples include the introduction of regional vote distribution requirements for presidential elections in Indonesia, cross-ethnic vote pooling in Malaysia, multiethnic group representation constituencies in Singapore, party-list elections for specified non-ethnic sectoral groups in the Philippines, alternative vote elections in Fiji and Papua New Guinea, and efforts to foster consolidated and aggregative political parties in a number of these countries.

Each of these electoral arrangements requires electors to vote on a cross-ethnic basis in some form—meaning that candidates have an incentive to seek electoral support *across* rather than within group lines, while voters must choose between candidates on a basis *other* than ethnicity. By so doing, such devices may, over time, foster the development of broader, cross-cutting cleavages—a vital development if diverse societies are going to make the move away from ethnic politics.

The various attempts to engineer the emerging party system in states such as Papua New Guinea and Indonesia are particularly significant in the context of each country's troubled democratic history. Papua New Guinea's party system has been in a state of steady decay virtually since independence. Similarly, many Indonesians blame the fragmented and polarized party

---

[21] See Margaret McKean and Ethan Scheiner, 'Japan's New Electoral System: la Plus ca Change...', *Electoral Studies*, 19/4 (2000), 447–77.

system of the 1950s for the failure of democracy then and are determined not to see it happen again: opinion polls have found a strong preference for a system of moderate multipartism, rather than party fragmentation.[22] Building a consolidated party system has thus been seen in both countries as an essential step towards building a consolidated democracy. By providing incentives for cross-ethnic accommodation in the context of electoral competition, states like Indonesia and Papua New Guinea are in effect trying to *simultaneously* manage ethnic divisions *and* consolidate democracy—an audacious and potentially influential exercise in large-scale political engineering.

However, the restrictions on political fragmentation and ethnic politics introduced in cases like Indonesia and Papua New Guinea also have clear downsides. While they may improve the prospects for a nationally consolidated party system, the new rules may also undercut the ability of all but a few established parties to form and mobilize support. If ethnic groups are unable to mobilize and compete for political power by democratic means, they will likely seek to achieve their objectives by other ways. A balance therefore needs to be struck between encouraging national parties, which is generally a positive strategy, and restricting regional ones, which can have clear downsides. So far, countries like Indonesia and Papua New Guinea appear to have managed these tensions fairly well. But the danger of overkill—placing so many incentives in favour of party aggregation and against regional or ethnic parties that they form a pattern of systemic discrimination and disempowerment—is clearly present.

Other states have sought to temper the impacts of ethnic politics by less direct means. In Malaysia, the long-standing centripetal practice of vote-pooling across ethnic lines has been a mainstay of national politics for decades, and was a major factor in the *Barisan*'s victory in 1999, at the height of the Asian economic crisis, when the rural Malay vote deserted the coalition. In Singapore, the proportion of multiethnic Group Representation Constituencies has continued to increase— although very much in step with the ongoing dominance of the governing People's Action Party. Finally, in both Fiji and Papua New Guinea, the introduction of alternative vote electoral laws

---

[22] Tan, 'Anti-Party Reaction in Indonesia', 501–2.

aimed to increase cross-ethnic cooperation and promote more broadly-supported candidates. All of these reforms are clearly centripetal in nature. In terms of the core electoral recommendation of consociational theory—proportional representation— the pattern is also clear: reforms in most Asia-Pacific states have made their electoral systems *less* proportional than was the case previously.

Other consociational experiments of earlier decades with communal parties, proportional elections, and mandatory power-sharing have increasingly been rejected in favour of party and electoral reforms that transcend rather than reinforce cleavage boundaries. While broad consociational *practices* of ethnic inclusion and power-sharing continue to resonate across the region, specific consociational *institutions* are now few and far between. Attempts to apply consociational devices in the realm of executive formation, such as formal power-sharing rules or grand coalition governments, have mostly proven difficult or unworkable in practice. Thus in Fiji, a constitutional requirement for a national unity government remained unimplemented for almost a decade due to strident opposition to the idea of coerced cabinet formation. In Cambodia, the supermajority requirement for government investiture has caused ongoing problems, forcing an uneasy marriage between the two main parties which has at times degenerated into outright armed conflict. In Indonesia, the short-lived grand coalition cabinets forged by former president Wahid proved contentious and unstable, and were abjured by his successors. The results of this study thus buttress those of several other comparative investigations which have found empirical support for consociational recommendations lacking.[23]

---

[23] Several recent large-N studies have challenged the empirical evidence for consociationalism. Norris found no support for consociational expectations that greater minority representation would lead to greater support for democracy (*Electoral Engineering*, chap. 5). Similarly, Lane and Ersson report that 'the use of PR election techniques is not systematically related to the occurrence of grand coalitions or oversized coalitions, which is the essence of consociationalism' (*Democracy*, 132). Wilkinson, in *Votes and Violence*, found no support for consociational explanations for the management of ethnic violence in India. Finally, as I have detailed elsewhere, most of the world's ethnically divided long-term democracies use majoritarian elections, not PR. See Benjamin Reilly, 'Does the Choice of Electoral System Promote Democracy? The Gap Between Theory and Practice', in Roeder and Rothchild, *Sustainable Peace*, 159–72.

What accounts for the prevalence of centripetal approaches to institutional design in the Asia-Pacific, especially compared to the importance of consensual or consociational models elsewhere? One answer may lie in the different social structures that prevail in much of the Asia-Pacific compared to regions such as Europe. In contrast to the classic European-inspired conceptions of ethnic struggles, in which a distinct majority confronts a potentially oppressed minority, Asia-Pacific states like Indonesia, Malaysia, and the Philippines instead feature high levels of *intermixture* between groups. In addition, consociationalism assumes the presence of clear ethnic boundaries, strong internal organization on the part of each segment, and relative equality of bargaining power between groups. Few of these assumptions apply in the Asia-Pacific, where ethnic diversity typically does not result in the pillarizing of society apparent in European states such as the Netherlands or Belgium, but more of an ethnic melange. In Indonesia, for instance, overlapping allegiances to culture, region, religion, and language meant that there is typically 'no national pattern of ethnic polarization or rifting deep or consistent enough to override other, cross-cutting identities'.[24] This stands in sharp contrast to classic examples of the consociational model such as Switzerland, where linguistic, religious, and regional cleavages tend to be reinforcing, creating distinct and separate subsocieties. In sum, one reason for the widespread rejection of consociational solutions may be the fact that they are based on assumptions about the nature of social cleavages that simply do not hold in most Asia-Pacific countries.

Beyond these facilitating conditions, this book has also highlighted a number of instances where the effects of social diversity completely overwhelm the predicted response of political institutions suggested by the scholarly literature. For example, despite being one of the most widely accepted axioms generated by modern political science, the predictions of 'Duverger's law'—that plurality electoral rules will generate two-party systems—receive little empirical support from our fifteen country cases.[25] As detailed in Chapter 6, across the Asia-Pacific more diverse societies tend to spawn more diverse party systems, irrespective of whether plurality, majority, mixed, or proportional electoral rules are in place. Exceptional ethnolinguistic

---

[24] Emmerson, 'A Year of Voting Dangerously?', 100.
[25] See Duverger, *Political Parties*. See also Taagepera and Shugart, *Seats and Votes*, 84.

diversity in Pacific states such as Papua New Guinea or Solomon Islands, for instance, has completely outweighed the supposedly reductive effects of their electoral systems, resulting in atomized and fragmented party systems despite several decades of plurality elections.

An Asia-Pacific Model?

This accumulation of evidence for Asia-Pacific exceptionalism brings me to a final key question: to what extent do the reform trends discussed in this book collectively constitute a distinctive regional model of institutional design? One means of gaining traction on this question is to examine the differences between the Asia-Pacific and other world regions on some key measures of institutional performance. Two of the most widely used indicators of electoral and party system characteristics, for example, are the proportionality of electoral outcomes and the effective number of political parties represented in parliament. The relevance of these indicators for cross-country comparison was discussed at some length in Chapters 5 and 6, which examined the record of individual Asia-Pacific countries in terms of both electoral and party system engineering.

To see how the Asia-Pacific compares with other world regions, we need to aggregate long-term trends on both of these measures across all of our cases so as to identify broad cross-regional patterns. Due to their different electoral and party systems, however, there are also important sub-regional differences between the trends evident in Northeast and Southeast Asia compared to the Pacific Islands. Therefore, for this exercise I will focus on the Asian states of Cambodia, East Timor, Indonesia, Korea, Malaysia, the Philippines, Singapore, Thailand and Taiwan, as well as Japan, separately from Papua New Guinea and the Pacific Island states.

Across these ten Asian cases, electoral disproportionality—as measured by the average votes–seats disparity for the two largest parties at all elections since the transition to democracy (or, in the case of the semi-democracies of Cambodia, Malaysia, and Singapore, simply all elections)—is high by world standards, at an average level of 7.3.[26] By contrast, in Western Europe the

---

[26] Calculated from data in Croissant, 'Electoral Politics', 329, updated by the author.

long-term average rate is just 2.9—a testament to the PR electoral systems used everywhere bar France and the United Kingdom.[27] In Eastern and Central Europe, the mean disproportionality figure stands at 5.6 in the 20 new East European democracies from 1992 to 2002.[28] In Latin America, the average disproportionality score for the period 1978–2000 was 5.3, using a more accurate measure, Gallagher's least-squares index.[29] In other words, the rate of disparity between seats and votes in Asia is 50 per cent higher than the long-term average for both Latin America and Eastern Europe, and almost three times that of Western Europe.

By contrast, on the other key indicator of election outcomes examined in this book, the effective number of political parties represented in parliament, Asia is broadly on par with other world regions. The mean aggregate figure of 3.28 parliamentary parties across Asia is similar to long-term patterns in Latin America (3.42)[30] and indeed to all 'established democracies' in the post-war period (3.16).[31] With a few exceptions, the states of these regions are also considerably more homogeneous in social terms than the new democracies of Asia, a fact which underlines the success of the party reduction strategies employed in recent years.[32] The new democracies of Eastern Europe, for example, are less socially diverse but have much more fragmented party systems than Asia, with a mean effective number of parties of 4.12 for the period 1990–2002.[33]

[27] Calculated from data in Lijphart, *Democracies*, 161.

[28] Calculated from data in Birch, *Electoral Systems*, 111–14.

[29] Calculated from data in J. Mark Payne, Daniel Zovatto, Fernando Carrillo Flórez, and Andrés Allamand Zavala, *Democracies in Development: Politics and Reform in Latin America* (Washington, DC: Inter-American Development Bank, 2002), 108.

[30] Ibid. My thanks to Mark Jones for suggesting this reference.

[31] Calculated from data in Lijphart, *Patterns of Democracy*, 74.

[32] At the other extreme, the figures for Africa, with a mean disproportionality score of 9.8 and a mean effective number of parties of 2.5 across 28 states, are highly majoritarian. But the limited number of African democracies, and the prevalence of one-party-dominant regimes in cases like Botswana, Namibia, and South Africa, creates problems for comparative analysis. For this reason, Africa was omitted from the comparative analysis. See Shaheen Mozaffar, 'Electoral Systems and Their Political Effects in Africa: A Preliminary Analysis', *Representation*, 34/3&4 (1997), 148–56.

[33] Birch, *Electoral Systems*, 111.

Figure 8.2 puts these various facts and figures in comparative
context, showing the aggregated disproportionality and party
multiplicity scores for Western Europe, Eastern Europe, Latin
America, Asia, and a fifth non-regional grouping—the 'Anglo-
American' democracies of Australasia (Australia and New Zealand)
and North America (Canada and the United States). Collectively,
these regions include nearly all the major democracies of
the world.[34] The horizontal axis on the figure shows the mean
effective number of parties for each region, while the vertical
axis represents the mean levels of disproportionality. By comparing the scores of the five regions on both indicators, the position of
each world region can thus be shown in relation to all others.

The resulting figure has four quadrants: the top left-hand
quadrant represents high levels of disproportionality and low
numbers of parties, the bottom right-hand quadrant represents

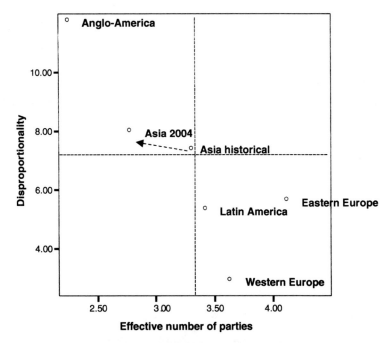

Fɪɢ. 8.2. *Proportionality and party systems in five world regions*

[34] The one major democracy omitted by this regional breakdown is India.
However, including India with the other Asian states makes little difference to
the overall trends reported: the overall disproportionality figure rises to 7.4,
while the mean effective number of parties also rises slightly, to 3.37.

low levels of disproportionality and high numbers of parties. As can be seen, Asia and Anglo-America are both in the upper-left quadrant; while Western Europe, Eastern Europe, and Latin America congregate in the lower-right quadrant. The other two quadrants—representing low party numbers with high proportionality, and high party numbers with low proportionality, respectively—are empty, upholding the scholarly consensus linking electoral proportionality and party numbers across both space and time. Thus the longitudinal trends suggest strongly that electoral systems and party multiplicity remain intimately related across different world regions, despite the great differences in social, economic, and historical conditions.

The figure also emphasizes the common electoral patterns found in those societies with a continental European heritage (i.e. Western and Eastern Europe, and Latin America), which tend to feature proportional elections and multiparty systems, compared to the very different patterns found in the 'Anglo-American' democracies of Australia, Canada, New Zealand, and the United States. Collectively, these Anglo-American democracies are distinguished by the presence of highly majoritarian elections (until 1993, in New Zealand's case) and clear two-party systems (the Anglo-American average is 2.24 parties, with a disproportionality score of 11.75 for the 1945–96 period). Had the United Kingdom—the classic reference model of the two-party system—not been included with Western Europe, these relationships would be even stronger.

Asia sits at the mid-point between these two groups. In general, electoral outcomes in this region are more majoritarian than those of Europe and Latin America, but less majoritarian than in Australasia and North America. This suggests that if there is a distinctive Asian model of democracy, it is one that is located between the winner-take-all, two-party systems of the Anglo-American democracies and the proportional, multiparty European model.

However, it is important to recall that the data presented at Figure 8.2 represents *long-term* averages and that in recent years many Asian states have become significantly more majoritarian on both measures. It therefore also includes a second Asian category, based on the most recent election results as at 2004. On the basis of this data, a number of Asian states appear to be in a process of transformation towards a two-party system—moving ever closer to the long-term democracies of the English-speaking world.

Examination of recent election outcomes provide strong evidence of this shift. In Japan, for example, the effective number of parties has fallen since the introduction of the 1994 electoral reforms, from a long-term average between 1946 and 1994 of 3.7 parties to just 2.4 effective parties following the November 2003 elections. As Steven Reed has argued, if this process continues, 'the dynamics of the electoral system will promote an evolution towards a two-party system'.[35] Similarly, Taiwan's 2004 legislative elections saw the two main party groupings, the 'pan-blue' KMT and the 'pan-green' DPP, garner over 95 per cent of all seats, as voters eschewed smaller parties. As a result, the number of effective parties in Taiwan fell from a mean of 2.69 across all previous elections to just 2.18—the same long-term average as the United Kingdom. Some observers saw this as proof that Taiwan's democracy was 'moving toward a two-party system more quickly than expected'.[36]

In Thailand, as already noted, the 1997 constitutional reforms and the subsequent rise of the Thaksin Shinawatra and the TRT have comprehensively altered the once-fragmented Thai party system—to the point where it has moved beyond a two-party model to become effectively a one-party dominant system, with a dramatic decline in party numbers compared to earlier elections. From an average of 7.2 effective parties prior to 1997, the party numbers after the February 2005 elections—won by the TRT in a landslide of 376 seats, with the Democrat Party the only significant opposition—fell to just 1.65, an outcome interpreted by some commentators as proof of Thailand's 'drift towards a two-party system'.[37]

In Korea also, the long-term trend appears to be in the direction of a consolidation around two large parties. There, effective party numbers fell from an average of 2.95 in 1988–2000 to 2.36 at the 2004 election, in which the new Uri Party of embattled President Rho won a majority of seats in the assembly, while the conservative Grand National Party formed the opposition. Party fragmentation is also down in Cambodia, from an average of 2.39

[35] Steven R. Reed, 'Evaluating Political Reform in Japan: A Mid-Term Report', *Japanese Journal of Political Science*, 3/2 (2002), 260.

[36] See John F. Copper, 'Taiwan's Democracy Takes a New Step', *Far Eastern Economic Review*, 168/1 (2004), 12.

[37] *The Economist*, 'Why They All Love Thaksin', 12 February 2005, 26.

between 1993 and 1999 to 2.29 at the 2003 elections. While neither of these cases could be called two-party systems (particularly Cambodia), in both cases recent changes in the party system have clearly been in the direction of greater consolidation.

The main exceptions to this trend towards two-party politics in Asia are Indonesia and the Philippines—both of which experienced an increase in party numbers following the political openings that accompanied the fall of the Suharto and Marcos regimes, respectively. While Indonesia in particular has introduced various measures to reduce party fragmentation, the outcomes of these have been ambiguous: as discussed in Chapter 6, although the total number of parties in parliament has declined, the effective number of parties has actually increased. A similar trend has been evident in the Philippines. The high levels of social diversity of these two countries, combined with the fact that both have only recently emerged from extended authoritarian periods in which the composition and number of parties were controlled by the authorities, is one explanation for this pattern. Suharto's forced amalgamation of Indonesian politics into three 'official' parties in the mid-1970s was one reason for the mushrooming of new parties when restrictions were lifted in 1998. In the Philippines, similarly, genuine multiparty politics was a central objective of the post-Marcos 1987 constitution's stated aim of promoting 'party multiplicity', in contrast to the one or two-party systems of the past.

These exceptions aside, the shift towards not just majoritarian political *systems* but also increasingly majoritarian *outcomes* provides a striking affirmation of the way that the political architecture of Asia's new democracies has changed in recent years. Asian reformers have often invoked the image of the stable and cohesive two-party systems of the United Kingdom and the United States when advocating political change.[38] The emergence in many Asian countries of embryonic two-party systems in what were previously either one-party autocracies or unstable multiparty democracies is perhaps the most compelling evidence for the success of political engineering in the Asia-Pacific. In effect, we appear to be witnessing both a systematic *convergence* in electoral and party systems across the Asia-Pacific, as well as the region's systematic *divergence* from developing democracies in other parts of the world.

[38] In Japan, for example, former LDP secretary general Ichiro Ozawa argued that a two-party system was necessary for the country's long-term survival. See Sakamoto, 'Explaining Electoral Reform', 419–38.

Conclusion

During the 1990s, the rapid development of many Asia-Pacific economies led to claims for the superiority of a so-called 'Asian model' of democracy as an alternative to the Western liberal model. Emphasizing the strength of Asian culture and values such as family solidarity and community discipline in contrast to the perceived moral turpitude and social decay of the West in general and the United States in particular, the 'Asian model' proponents argued for the virtues of semi-democratic or soft-authoritarian political models which privileged hierarchy and order over individualism and competition.[39] In reality, this was at its heart a model of *non-democracy*—and one which faded from prominence in the wake of the 1997 Asian economic crisis that laid bare the structural weaknesses of the region's political and economic systems.

The evidence of this book suggests that there is indeed an emerging Asian model of democracy—but one that has little relationship with the political restrictions advocated by the region's now-retired autocrats.[40] Rather, in something of a grand irony, the political systems of most new Asia-Pacific democracies are not only becoming more consolidated, but in many cases are actually moving closer to the Anglo-American model of two-party democracy. This movement towards more aggregative and majoritarian political outcomes has been facilitated by deliberate strategies of political engineering in what are, for the most part, competitive electoral democracies. To that extent, the political reform wave that has swept across the Asia-Pacific region over the past decade reflects not so much the vague and rarefied concepts of Asian values or Asian-style democracy, but rather pragmatic attempts to build functioning political systems that can govern effectively, generate development, and have a realistic prospect of survival.

Interpreting the broader implications of this 'two step forwards, one step back' approach to political change in the

[39] For critiques from the region, see Kim Dae-Jung, 'Is Culture Destiny? The Myth of Asia's Anti-Democratic Values', *Foreign Affairs*, 73 (1994), 189–194 and Yung-Myung Kim, '"Asian-Style Democracy": A Critique from East Asia', *Asian Survey*, 37/12 (1997), 1119–34.

[40] See Daniel Bell, David Brown, Kanishka Jayasuriya, and David Martin Jones (eds.), *Towards Illiberal Democracy in Pacific Asia* (London: Macmillan, 1995).

Asia-Pacific region thus remains something of an open question. On the one hand, it may be that the turn towards majoritarian politics heralds a drift away from democratic values towards a new form of illiberal democracy—in effect, a return to Asia's long experience with dictatorial, autocratic, monarchistic, or other forms of non-democratic rule. Certainly the creeping authoritarianism of some of the region's democratically-elected strongmen is cause for concern. But, on balance, I am more optimistic. If Asia-Pacific states can indeed transform their institutional architecture and make the transition from fragmented, personalized, and unstable political systems to cohesive, programmatic, and stable ones—as at least some appear to be doing—their prospects for both democracy and development will be significantly enhanced, as will their ability to manage internal conflicts. While political engineering cannot guarantee the achievement of this goal, it appears to be one means of smoothing and straightening the path.

References

Abueva, Jose Veloso, *Charter Change for the Philippines: Towards a Federal Republic of the Philippines with a Parliamentary Government* (Manila: Citizens' Movement for a Federal Philippines and KC Institute of Federal-Parliamentary Democracy, 2005).

Alagappa, Muthiah, 'Contestation and Crisis', in Muthiah Alagappa (ed.), *Political Legitimacy in Southeast Asia: The Quest for Moral Authority* (Stanford, CA: Stanford University Press, 1995).

Albritton, Robert B., 'Cambodia in 2003: On the Road to Democratic Consolidation', *Asian Survey*, 44/1 (2004), 102–9.

Albritton, Robert, and Thawilwadee Bureekul, 'Social and Cultural Supports for Pluralist Democracy Across Seven Asian Nations', Paper presented to the annual meeting of the International Studies Association, Honolulu, 5 March 2005.

Aldrich, John, *Why Parties?* (Chicago, IL: University of Chicago Press, 1995).

Alesina, Alberto, Reza Baqir, and William Easterly, 'Public Goods and Ethnic Divisions', *Quarterly Journal of Economics*, 114 (1999), 1243–84.

Anderson, Benedict, *Imagined Communities: Reflections on the Origin and Spread of Nationalism* (London: Verso, 1983).

Apter, David E., 'Comparative Politics, Old and New', in Robert E. Goodin and Hans-Dieter Klingemann (eds.), *A New Handbook of Political Science* (Oxford: Oxford University Press, 1996).

Aristotle, *Politics*.

Asian-Pacific Cultural Center, *A Handbook of Asian-Pacific Countries and Regions* (Taipei: Asian-Pacific Cultural Center, 1995).

Aspinall, Edward, *Opposing Suharto: Compromise, Resistance, and Regime Change in Indonesia* (Stanford, CA: Stanford University Press, 2004).

Atlas Narodov Mira (Moscow: The N.N. Miklukho-Maklaya Institute of Ethnography for the Academy of Sciences, Department of Geodesy and Cartography of the State Geological Committee of the USSR, 1964).

Baker, Louise, 'Political Integrity in Papua New Guinea and the Search for Stability', *Pacific Economic Bulletin*, 20/1 (2005), 98–117.

Barkan, Joel D., 'Elections in Agrarian Societies', *Journal of Democracy*, 6/4 (1995), 106–16.

Barry, Brian, 'The Consociational Model and its Dangers', *European Journal of Political Research*, 3 (1975), 393–412.

Barry, Brian, 'Political Accommodation and Consociational Democracy', in *Democracy and Power: Essays in Political Theory 1* (Oxford: Oxford University Press, 1991).

Bastian, Sunil, and Robin Luckham, 'Conclusion: the Politics of Institutional Choice', in Sunil Bastian and Robin Luckham (eds.), *Can Democracy be Designed? The Politics of Institutional Choice in Conflict-Torn Societies* (London and New York: Zed Books, 2003).

Bell, Daniel A., *East Meets West: Human Rights and Democracy in East Asia* (Princeton, NJ: Princeton University Press, 2000).

Bell, Daniel, David Brown, Kanishka Jayasuriya, and David Martin Jones (eds.), *Towards Illiberal Democracy in Pacific Asia* (London: Macmillan, 1995).

Bermeo, Nancy, *Ordinary People in Extraordinary Times: The Citizenry and the Breakdown of Democracy* (Princeton, NJ: Princeton University Press, 2003).

Birch, Sarah, *Electoral Systems and Political Transformation in Post-Communist Europe* (Hampshire, UK and New York: Palgrave Macmillan, 2003).

Blais, André, and Stephanie Dion, 'Electoral Systems and the Consolidation of New Democracies', in D. Ethier (ed.), *Democratic Transition and Consolidation in Southern Europe, Latin America and Southeast Asia* (London: Macmillan, 1990).

Blondel, Jean and Takashi Inoguchi, 'Parties, Bureaucracies, and the Search for an Equilibrium Between Democracy and Economic Development', in Ian Marsh, Jean Blondel and Takashi Inoguchi (eds.), *Democracy, Governance and Economic Performance: East and Southeast Asia* (Tokyo: United Nations University Press, 1999).

Brady, David, and Jongryn Mo, 'Electoral Systems and Institutional Choice: A Case Study of the 1988 Korean Elections', *Comparative Political Studies*, 24/4 (1992), 405–29.

Brass, Paul (ed.), *Ethnic Groups and the State* (London: Croom Helm, 1985).

Bratton, Michael, and Nicolas van de Walle, *Democratic Experiments in Africa* (Cambridge: Cambridge University Press, 1997).

Brown, David, *The State and Ethnic Politics in South-East Asia* (London and New York: Routledge, 1994).

Brown, Michael E., and Šumit Ganguly (eds.), *Government Policies and Ethnic Relations in the Asia-Pacific* (Cambridge, MA and London: MIT Press, 1997).

—— —— (eds.), *Fighting Words: Language Policy and Ethnic Relations in Asia* (Cambridge, MA: MIT Press, 2003).

Bueno de Mesquita, Bruce, James D. Morrow, Randolph Silverson, and Alastair Smith, 'Political Institutions, Political Survival, and Policy Success', in Bruce Bueno de Mesquita and Hilton L. Root (eds.), *Governing for Prosperity* (New Haven, CT: Yale University Press, 2000).

Bueno de Mesquita, Bruce, James D. Morrow, Randolph Silverson, and Alastair Smith, 'Political Competition and Economic Growth', *Journal of Democracy*, 12/1 (2001), 58–72.

Carey, John M., and Matthew S. Shugart, 'Incentives to Cultivate a Personal Vote: A Rank Ordering of Electoral Formulas', *Electoral Studies*, 14/4 (1995), 441–60.

Case, William, *Elites and Regimes in Malaysia: Revisiting a Consociational Democracy* (Monash: Monash Asia Institute, 1996).

—— 'New Uncertainties for an Old Pseudo-Democracy: The Case of Malaysia', *Comparative Politics*, 37/1 (October 2004), 83–104.

Chandra, Kanchan, *Why Ethnic Parties Succeed: Patronage and Ethnic Headcounts in India* (New York: Cambridge University Press, 2004).

Chantornvong, Sombat, 'The 1997 Constitution and the Politics of Electoral Reform', in Duncan McCargo (ed.), *Reforming Thai Politics* (Copenhagen: Nordic Institute of Asian Studies, 2002).

Chhibber, Pradeep, and Irfan Nooruddin, 'Do Party Systems Count? The Number of Parties and Government Performance in the Indian States', *Comparative Political Studies*, 37/2 (2004), 152–87.

Chin, James, 'Politics of Federal Intervention in Malaysia, With Reference to Kelantan, Sarawak and Sabah', *Journal of Commonwealth and Comparative Politics*, 35/2 (1997), 96–120.

Chin, James Ung-Ho, 'Malaysia: The Barisan National Supremacy', in John Fuh-Sheng Hsieh and David Newman (eds.), *How Asia Votes* (New York: Chatham House, 2002).

Choi, Dai-Kwon, 'The Choosing of Representatives in Korea', in Graham Hassall and Cheryl Saunders (eds.), *The People's Representatives: Electoral Systems in the Asia-Pacific Region* (Sydney: Allen & Unwin, 1997).

Choi, Jungug, 'Philippine Democracies Old and New: Elections, Term Limits, and Party Systems', *Asian Survey*, 41/3 (2001), 488–501.

—— 'Ethnic and Regional Politics after the Asian Economic Crisis: A Comparison of Malaysia and South Korea', *Democratization*, 10/1 (2003), 121–34.

Chung-si, Ahn, and Jaung Hoon, 'South Korea', in Ian Marsh, Jean Blondel, and Takashi Inoguchi (eds.), *Democracy, Governance and Economic Performance: East and Southeast Asia* (Tokyo: United Nations University Press, 1999).

Collier, Paul, *The Economics of Civil War* (Washington, DC: World Bank Monograph, 1998).

—— and Anke Hoeffler, 'On Economic Causes of Civil War', *Oxford Economic Papers*, 50/4 (1998), 563–73.

Comparative Politics Section of the American Political Science Association, 'Cumulative Findings in the Study of Ethnic Politics', *APSA-CP Newsletter*, 12/1 (2001).

Connor, Walker, *Ethnonationalism: The Quest for Understanding* (Princeton, NJ: Princeton University Press, 1994).

Copper, John F., 'Taiwan's Democracy Takes a New Step', *Far Eastern Economic Review*, 168/1 (2004), 12–14.

Cox, Gary, *Making Votes Count: Strategic Coordination in the World's Electoral Systems* (Cambridge: Cambridge University Press, 1997).

Croissant, Aurel, 'South Korea', in Dieter Nohlen, Florian Grotz, and Christof Hartmann (eds.), *Elections in Asia and the Pacific: A Data Handbook*, 2 vols. (Oxford: Oxford University Press, 2001).

—— 'Electoral Politics in South Korea', in Aurel Croissant, Gabriele Bruns, and Marei John (eds.), *Electoral Politics in Southeast and East Asia* (Singapore: Friedrich Ebert Stiftung, 2002).

—— 'Electoral Politics in Southeast and East Asia: A Comparative Perspective', in Aurel Croissant, Gabriele Bruns, and Marei John (eds.), *Electoral Politics in Southeast and East Asia* (Singapore: Friedrich Ebert Stiftung, 2002).

—— Gabriele Bruns, and Marei John (eds.), *Electoral Politics in Southeast and East Asia* (Singapore: Friedrich Ebert Stiftung, 2002).

Crouch, Harold, 'Democratic Prospects in Indonesia', *Asian Journal of Political Science*, 1/2 (1993), 77–92.

—— *Government and Society in Malaysia* (Ithaca, NY: Cornell University Press, 1996).

—— and James W. Morely, 'The Dynamics of Political Change', in James W. Morley (ed.), *Driven by Growth: Political Change in the Asia-Pacific Region* (Armonk, NY: M. E. Sharpe, 1999).

Dae-Jung, Kim, 'Is Culture Destiny? The Myth of Asia's Anti-Democratic Values', *Foreign Affairs*, 73 (1994), 189–94.

Dahl, Robert A., *Polyarchy: Participation and Opposition* (New Haven, CT: Yale University Press, 1971).

de Nevers, Renée, 'Democratization and Ethnic Conflict', in Michael Brown (ed.), *Ethnic Conflict and International Security* (Princeton, NJ: Princeton University Press, 1993).

DeVotta, Neil, *Blowback: Linguistic Nationalism, Institutional Decay, and Ethnic Conflict in Sri Lanka* (Stanford, CA: Stanford University Press, 2004).

Diamond, Larry, 'Introduction', in Larry Diamond, Juan Linz, and Seymour Martin Lipset (eds.), *Democracy in Developing Countries: Asia* (Boulder, CO: Lynne Rienner Publishers, 1989).

—— 'Three Paradoxes of Democracy', *Journal of Democracy*, 1/3 (1990), 48–60.

—— 'Toward Democratic Consolidation', in Larry Diamond and Marc F. Plattner (eds.), *The Global Resurgence of Democracy* (Baltimore, MD and London: Johns Hopkins University Press, 1996).

—— 'Introduction: In Search of Consolidation', in Larry Diamond, Marc F. Plattner, Yun-han Chu, and Hung-mao Tien (eds.), *Consolidating the Third Wave Democracies: Themes and Perspectives* (Baltimore, MD and London: Johns Hopkins University Press, 1997).

Diamond, Larry, *Developing Democracy: Towards Consolidation* (Baltimore, MD: Johns Hopkins University Press, 1999).

—— and Mark F. Plattner (eds.), *The Global Resurgence of Democracy* (Baltimore, MD: Johns Hopkins University Press, 1996).

—— —— (eds.), *Democracy in East Asia* (Baltimore, MD and London: Johns Hopkins University Press, 1998).

—— Juan Linz, and Seymour Martin Lipset (eds.), *Democracy in Developing Countries: Asia* (Boulder, CO: Lynne Rienner Publishers, 1989).

—— —— —— 'Introduction: What Makes for Democracy?', in Larry Diamond, Juan Linz, and Seymour Martin Lipset (eds.), *Politics in Developing Countries: Comparing Experiences with Democracy* (Boulder, CO: Lynne Rienner Publishers, 1995).

—— —— —— (eds.), *Politics in Developing Countries: Comparing Experiences with Democracy* (Boulder, CO: Lynne Rienner Publishers, 1995).

Dixon, Paul, 'Consociationalism and the Northern Ireland Peace Process: A Glass Half Full or Half Empty?', *Nationalism and Ethnic Politics*, 3/3 (1997), 20–36.

Dorney, Sean, *Papua New Guinea: People, Politics and History Since 1975*, rev. edn (Sydney: ABC Books, 2000).

Downs, Anthony, *An Economic Theory of Democracy* (New York: Harper and Row, 1957).

Drakakis-Smith, David, *Pacific Asia* (London and New York: Routledge, 1992).

Duverger, Maurice, *Political Parties: Their Organization and Activity in the Modern State* (New York: Wiley, 1954).

Easterly, William, *The Elusive Quest for Growth: Economists' Adventures and Misadventures in the Tropics* (Cambridge, MA and London: MIT Press, 2001).

—— and Ross Levine, 'Africa's Growth Tragedy: Policies and Ethnic Divisions', *Quarterly Journal of Economics*, 112/4 (1997), 1203–50.

Eaton, Kent, *Politicians and Economic Reform in New Democracies: Argentina and the Philippines in the 1990s* (University Park, PA: The State University of Pennsylvania Press, 2002).

Ellis, Andrew, 'The Politics of Electoral Systems in Transition: The 1999 Elections in Indonesia and Beyond', *Representation*, 37 (2000), 241–8.

Emmerson, Donald K., 'A Year of Voting Dangerously?', *Journal of Democracy*, 15/1 (2004), 94–108.

Eriksson, Mikael, Peter Wallensteen, and Margareta Sollenberg, 'Armed Conflict, 1989–2002', *Journal of Peace Research*, 40 (2003), 593–607.

Esman, Milton, *Ethnic Politics* (Ithaca, NY: Cornell University Press, 1994).

Farrell, David, *Electoral Systems: A Comparative Introduction* (Hampshire and New York: Palgrave, 2001).

Fearon, James D., 'Ethnic and Cultural Diversity by Country', *Journal of Economic Growth*, 8 (2003), 195–222.

Fedderke, Johannes, and Robert Klitgaard, 'Economic Growth and Social Indicators: An Exploratory Analysis', *Economic Development and Cultural Change*, 46/3 (1998), 455–89.

Feith, Herbert, *The Decline of Constitutional Democracy in Indonesia* (Ithaca, NY: Cornell University Press, 1962).

Fiji Constitution Review Commission, *The Fiji Islands: Towards a United Future* (Suva: Parliament of Fiji, 1996).

Fishman, Joshua, 'Some Contrasts Between Linguistically Homogeneous and Linguistically Heterogeneous Polities', in J. Fishman, C. Ferguson, and J. Das Gupta (eds.), *Language Problems of Developing Nations* (New York: Wiley, 1968).

Forester, Geoff, and R. J. May (eds.), *The Fall of Soeharto* (Bathurst, NSW: Crawford House Publishing, 1998).

Fraenkel, Jon, 'The Alternative Vote System in Fiji: Electoral Engineering or Ballot-Rigging?', *Commonwealth and Comparative Politics*, 39/1 (2001), 1–31.

—— 'Electoral Engineering in Papua New Guinea: Lessons from Fiji and Elsewhere', *Pacific Economic Bulletin*, 19/1 (2004), 122–33.

—— and Bernard Grofman, 'A Neo-Downsian Model of the Alternative Vote as a Mechanism for Mitigating Ethnic Conflict in Plural Societies', *Public Choice*, 121 (2004), 487–506.

Freedom House, *Freedom in the World: The Annual Survey of Political Rights and Civil Liberties 1998–1999* (New York: Freedom House, 1999).

Friedman, Edward (ed.), *The Politics of Democratization: Generalizing East Asian Experiences* (Boulder, CO: Westview Press, 1994).

Furnivall, J. S., *Colonial Policy and Practice: A Comparative Study of Burma and Netherlands India* (Cambridge: Cambridge University Press, 1948).

Gallup, J., 'Cambodia's Electoral System: A Window of Opportunity for Reform', in Aurel Croissant, Gabriele Bruns, and Marei John (eds.), *Electoral Politics in Southeast and East Asia* (Singapore: Friedrich Ebert Stiftung, 2002).

Ganesan, N., 'Democracy in Singapore', *Asian Journal of Political Science*, 4/2 (1996), 63–79.

Geertz, Clifford, *The Religions of Java* (New York: Free Press, 1960).

—— (ed.), *Old Societies and New States: the Quest for Modernity in Asia and Africa* (New York: Free Press, 1967).

Ghai, Yash (ed.), *Autonomy and Ethnicity: Negotiating Competing Claims in Multi-ethnic States* (Cambridge: Cambridge University Press, 2000).

Griffin, James, 'Papua New Guinea', in R. Brissenden and J. Griffin (eds.), *Modern Asia: Problems and Politics* (Milton: Jacaranda Press, 1974).

Grimes, Barbara (ed.), *Ethnologue: Languages of the World* (Dallas, TX: SIL International, 2002).

Gunther, Richard, and Larry Diamond, 'Types and Functions of Parties', in Larry Diamond and Richard Gunther (eds.), *Political Parties and Democracy* (Baltimore, MD and London: Johns Hopkins University Press, 2001).

Gurr, Ted Robert, 'Peoples Against States: Ethnopolitical Conflict and the Changing World System', *International Studies Quarterly*, 38/3 (1994), 349–53.

—— 'Ethnic Warfare on the Wane', *Foreign Affairs*, 79/3 (2000), 52–64.

—— *Peoples Versus States: Minorities at Risk in the New Century* (Washington, DC: United States Institute of Peace Press, 2000).

Hadenius, Axel, *Democracy and Development* (Cambridge: Cambridge University Press, 1992).

Haggard, Stephan, *Pathways From the Periphery: the Politics of Growth in the Newly Industrializing Countries* (Ithaca, NY: Cornell University Press, 1990).

—— 'Democratic Institutions, Economic Policy, and Development', in Christopher Clague (ed.), *Institutions and Economic Development* (Baltimore, MD and London: Johns Hopkins University Press, 1997).

—— 'The Politics of the Asian Financial Crisis', in Laurence Whitehead (ed.), *Emerging Market Democracies: East Asia and Latin America* (Baltimore, MD and London: Johns Hopkins University Press, 2000).

—— and Steven B. Webb, *Voting for Reform: Democracy, Political Liberalization and Economic Adjustment* (New York: Oxford University Press, 1992).

—— and Robert Kaufman, *The Political Economy of Democratic Transitions* (Princeton, NJ: Princeton University Press, 1995).

Hale, Henry, 'Explaining Ethnicity', *Comparative Political Studies*, 37/4 (2004), 458–85.

Hardgrave, Robert L., 'India: The Dilemmas of Diversity', in Larry Diamond and Marc F. Plattner (eds.), *Nationalism, Ethnic Conflict and Democracy* (Baltimore, MD: Johns Hopkins University Press, 1994).

Harris, Peter, and Ben Reilly (eds.), *Democracy and Deep-Rooted Conflict: Options for Negotiators* (Stockholm: International Institute for Democracy and Electoral Assistance, 1998).

Hartmann, Christof, Graham Hassall, and Soliman M. Santos Jr, 'Philippines', in Dieter Nohlen, Florian Grotz, and Christof Hartmann (eds.), *Elections in Asia and the Pacific: A Data Handbook*, 2 vols. (Oxford: Oxford University Press, 2001).

Hegre, Håvard, Tanja Ellingsen, Scott Gates, and Nils Petter Gleditsch, 'Towards a Democratic Civil Peace? Democracy, Political Change and Civil War, 1816–1992', *American Political Science Review*, 95/1 (2001), 33–48.

Henders, Susan J. (ed.), *Democratization and Identity: Regimes and Ethnicity in East and Southeast Asia* (Lanham, MD: Lexington Books, 2004).

Hewison, Kevin (ed.), *Political Change in Thailand: Democracy and Participation* (London: Routledge, 1997).

—— Richard Robison, and Garry Rodan (eds.), *Southeast Asia in the 1990s: Authoritarianism, Democracy and Capitalism* (Sydney: Allen and Unwin, 1993).

Hicken, Allen, 'From Province to Parliament: Party Aggregation in Developing Democracies', Paper presented to the annual meeting of the American Political Science Association, Philadelphia, 2003.

—— 'Thailand', in Andrew Reynolds, Ben Reilly, and Andrew Ellis, *Electoral System Design: The New International IDEA Handbook* (Stockholm: International Institute for Democracy and Electoral Assistance, 2005).

—— 'Parties and Elections', in Erik Kuhonta, Dan Slater, and Tuong Vu (eds.), *Southeast Asia in Political Science: Theory, Region, and Method* (Stanford: Stanford University Press), forthcoming.

—— *Building Party Systems: Elections, Parties and Coordination in Developing Democracies* (forthcoming).

—— and Yuko Kasuya, 'A Guide to the Constitutional Structures and Electoral Systems of East, South and Southeast Asia', *Electoral Studies*, 22 (2003), 121–51.

Horowitz, Donald L., *Ethnic Groups in Conflict* (Berkeley, CA: University of California Press, 1985).

—— 'Comparing Democratic Systems', *Journal of Democracy*, 1/1 (1990), 73–9.

—— *A Democratic South Africa? Constitutional Engineering in a Divided Society* (Berkeley, CA: University of California Press, 1991).

—— 'Making Moderation Pay: The Comparative Politics of Ethnic Conflict Management', in J. V. Montville (ed.), *Conflict and Peacemaking in Multiethnic Societies* (New York: Lexington Books, 1991).

—— 'Self-determination: Politics, Philosophy, and Law', *Nomos*, 39 (1997), 421–63.

—— 'Constitutional Design: Proposals Versus Process' in Andrew Reynolds (ed.), *The Architecture of Democracy: Constitutional Design, Conflict Management, and Democracy* (Oxford: Oxford University Press, 2002).

—— 'The Alternative Vote and Interethnic Moderation: A Reply to Fraenkel and Grofman', *Public Choice*, 121 (2004), 507–16.

Hsieh, John Fuh-sheng, 'The SNTV System and Its Political Implications', in Hung-Mao Tien (ed.), *Taiwan's Electoral Politics and Democratic Transition: Riding the Third Wave* (Armonk, NY: M.E. Sharpe, 1996).

—— 'Electoral Politics in New Democracies in the Asia-Pacific Region', *Representation*, 34/3&4 (1997), 157–65.

—— 'Continuity and Change in Taiwan's Electoral Politics', in John Fuh-Sheng Hsieh and David Newman (eds.), *How Asia Votes* (New York: Chatham House, 2002).

Hsieh, John Fuh-sheng, and David Newman (eds.), *How Asia Votes* (New York: Chatham House, 2002).

Huntington, Samuel P., *Political Order in Changing Societies* (New Haven, CT: Yale University Press, 1968).

—— *The Third Wave: Democratization in the Late Twentieth Century* (Norman, OK: University of Oklahoma Press, 1991).

Hutchcroft, Paul D., and Joel Rocamora, 'Strong Demands and Weak Institutions: The Origins and Evolution of the Democratic Deficit in the Philippines', *Journal of East Asian Studies*, 3 (2003), 259–92.

Im, Hyug Baeg, 'Faltering Democratic Consolidation in South Korea: Democracy at the End of the "Three Kims" Era', *Democratization*, 11/5 (2004), 179–98.

Johnson, Chalmers, *MITI and the Japanese Miracle: The Growth of Industrial Policy* (Stanford, CA: Stanford University Press, 1982).

Jones, Mark P., 'A Guide to the Electoral Systems of the Americas', *Electoral Studies*, 14/1 (1985), 5–21.

—— 'A Guide to the Electoral Systems of the Americas: An Update', *Electoral Studies*, 16/1 (1997), 13–15.

Karatnycky, Adrian, 'The 1998 Freedom House Survey: The Decline of Illiberal Democracy', *Journal of Democracy*, 10/1 (1999), 112–25.

Kohli, Atul, 'Centralization and Powerlessness: India's Democracy in a Comparative Perspective', in Joel S. Migdal, Atul Kohli, and Vivian Shue (eds.), *State Power and Social Forces: Domination and Transformation in the Third World* (Cambridge: Cambridge University Press, 1994).

Kim, Byung-Kook, 'Party Politics in South Korea's Democracy: The Crisis of Success', in Larry Diamond and Byung-Kook Kim (eds.), *Consolidating Democracy in South Korea* (Boulder and London: Lynne Rienner Publishers, 2000).

Kim, Yung-Myung '"Asian-style democracy": A critique from East Asia', *Asian Survey*, 37/12 (1997), 1119–34.

King, Dwight Y., *Half-Hearted Reform: Electoral Institutions and the Struggle for Democracy in Indonesia* (Westport, CT and London: Praeger, 2003).

Kitschelt, Herbert, Zdenka Mansfeldova, Radek Markowski, and Gábor Tóka, *Post-Communist Party Systems: Competition, Representation and Inter-Party Cooperation* (New York: Cambridge University Press, 1999).

Krauss, Ellis S., and Robert Pekkanen, 'Explaining Party Adaptation to Electoral Reform: The Discreet Charm of the LDP?', *Journal of Japanese Studies*, 30/1 (2004), 1–34.

Laakso, Markku, and Rein Taagepera, 'Effective Number of Parties: A Measure with Application to Western Europe', *Comparative Political Studies*, 12 (1979), 3–27.

Landé, Carl, *Leaders, Factions and Parties: The Structure of Philippine Politics* (New Haven, CT: Yale University Southeast Asia Monograph No. 6, 1965).

Lane, Jan-Erik, and Svante Ersson, *Comparative Political Economy* (London: Pinter Publishers, 1990)

—— ——, *Comparative Politics: An Introduction and a New Approach* (Cambridge: Polity Press, 1994).

Laothamatas, Anek, 'A Tale of Two Democracies: Conflicting Perceptions of Elections and Democracy in Thailand', in Robert H. Taylor (ed.), *The Politics of Elections in Southeast Asia* (Cambridge: Woodrow Wilson Center and Cambridge University Press, 1996).

—— (ed.), *Democratization in Southeast and East Asia* (Singapore: Institute of Southeast Asian Studies, 1997).

Laver, Michael, and Norman Schofield, *Multiparty Government: The Politics of Coalition in Europe* (Oxford: Oxford University Press, 1991).

LeDuc, Lawrence, Richard G. Niemi, and Pippa Norris (eds.), *Comparing Democracies 2: New Challenges in the Study of Elections and Voting* (Thousand Oaks, CA: Sage, 2002).

Lee, Junhan, 'Primary Causes of Asian Democratization', *Asian Survey*, 42/6 (2002), 821–37.

Levine, Stephen, 'Culture and Conflict in Fiji, Papua New Guinea, Vanuatu, and the Federated States of Micronesia', in Michael E. Brown and Šumit Ganguly (eds.), *Government Policies and Ethnic Relations in the Asia-Pacific* (Cambridge, MA and London: MIT Press, 1997).

Liddle, R. William, 'Coercion, Co-optation, and the Management of Ethnic Relations in Indonesia', in Michael E. Brown and Šumit Ganguly (eds.), *Government Policies and Ethnic Relations in the Asia-Pacific* (Cambridge, MA and London: MIT Press, 1997).

Lijphart, Arend, *The Politics of Accommodation: Pluralism and Democracy in the Netherlands* (Berkeley, CA: University of California Press, 1968).

—— *Democracy in Plural Societies: A Comparative Exploration* (New Haven, CT: Yale University Press, 1977).

—— *Democracies: Patterns of Majoritarian and Consensus Government in Twenty-One Countries* (New Haven, CT and London: Yale University Press, 1984).

—— *Power Sharing in South Africa* (Berkeley, CA: Policy Papers in International Affairs No. 24, Institute of International Studies, University of California, 1985).

—— 'Electoral Systems, Party Systems and Conflict Management in Segmented Societies', in R. A. Schreirer (ed.), *Critical Choices for South Africa: An Agenda for the 1990s* (Cape Town: Oxford University Press, 1990).

Lijphart, Arend, 'Foreword: "Cameral Change" and Institutional Conservatism', in Lawrence D. Longley and David M. Olson (eds.), *Two Into One: The Politics and Processes of National Legislative Cameral Change* (Boulder, CO: Westview Press, 1991).

—— 'The Alternative Vote: A Realistic Alternative for South Africa?', *Politikon*, 18/2 (1991), 91–101.

—— *Electoral Systems and Party Systems: A Study of Twenty-Seven Democracies, 1945–1990* (New York: Oxford University Press, 1994).

—— 'Prospects for Power-Sharing in the New South Africa', in Andrew Reynolds (ed.), *Election '94 South Africa: the Campaigns, Results and Future Prospects* (Claremont: David Phillip Publishers, 1994).

—— 'Electoral Systems', in Seymour Martin Lipset (ed.), *The Encyclopedia of Democracy* (Washington, DC: Congressional Quarterly Press, 1995).

—— 'Multiethnic Democracy', in Seymour Martin Lipset (ed.), *The Encyclopedia of Democracy* (Washington, DC: Congressional Quarterly Press, 1995).

—— 'Self-determination Versus Pre-determination of Ethnic Minorities in Power-sharing Systems', in Will Kymlicka (ed.), *The Rights of Minority Cultures* (Oxford: Oxford University Press, 1995).

—— 'The Puzzle of Indian Democracy: A Consociational Interpretation', *American Political Science Review*, 90/2 (1996), 258–68.

—— *Patterns of Democracy: Government Forms and Performance in Thirty-Six Countries* (New Haven, CT and London: Yale University Press, 1999).

—— 'Constitutional Design for Divided Societies', *Journal of Democracy*, 15/2 (2004), 96–109.

—— and Bernard Grofman (eds.), *Choosing an Electoral System: Issues and Alternatives* (New York: Praeger, 1984).

Lin, Jih-Wen, 'Party Realignment and the Demise of SNTV in East Asia', unpublished paper, Institute of Political Science, Academia Sinica, Taiwan (2005).

Linz, Juan, 'The Perils of Presidentialism', *Journal of Democracy*, 1/1 (1990), 51–69.

—— 'Presidential or Parliamentary Democracy: Does It Make a Difference?', in Juan Linz and Arturo Valenzuela (eds.), *The Failure of Presidential Democracy* (Baltimore, MD: Johns Hopkins University Press, 1994).

—— and Alfred Stepan (eds.), *The Breakdown of Democratic Regimes*, 3 vols. (Baltimore, MD: Johns Hopkins University Press, 1978).

—— and Arturo Valenzuela (eds.), *The Failure of Presidential Democracy*, 2 vols. (Baltimore, MD: Johns Hopkins University Press, 1994).

—— and Alfred Stepan, *Problems of Democratic Transition and Consolidation: Southern Europe, South America, and Post-Communist Europe* (Baltimore, MD: Johns Hopkins University Press, 1996).

References

Lipset, Seymour Martin, *Political Man: The Social Basis of Politics* (New York: Doubleday, 1960).

—— 'The Indispensability of Political Parties', *Journal of Democracy* 11/1 (2000), 48–55.

Lipset, Seymour Martin, and Stein Rokkan, 'Cleavage Structures, Party Systems, and Voter Alignments: An Introduction', in Seymour Martin Lipset and Stein Rokkan (eds.), *Party Systems and Voter Alignments: Cross-National Perspectives* (New York: Free Press, 1967).

Londregan, John B., and Keith T. Poole, 'Poverty, the Coup Trap, and the Seizure of Executive Power', *World Politics*, 42 (1990), 151–83.

Lustick, Ian, 'Lijphart, Lakatos, and Consociationalism', *World Politics*, 50 (1997), 81–117.

MacIntyre, Andrew, *The Power of Institutions: Political Architecture and Governance* (Ithaca, NY: Cornell University Press, 2003).

Mainwaring, Scott, 'Presidentialism, Multipartism, and Democracy: The Difficult Combination', *Comparative Political Studies*, 26/2 (1993), 198–228.

—— and Timothy Scully, 'Introduction', in Scott Mainwaring and Timothy Scully (eds.), *Building Democratic Institutions: Party Systems in Latin America* (Stanford, CA: Stanford University Press, 1995).

—— and Timothy Scully (eds.), *Building Democratic Institutions: Party Systems in Latin America* (Stanford, CA: Stanford University Press, 1995).

—— and Matthew S. Shugart (eds.), *Presidentialism and Democracy in Latin America* (Cambridge: Cambridge University Press, 1997).

Maisrikrod, Surin, 'Political Reform and the New Thai Electoral System', in John Fuh-Sheng Hsieh and David Newman (eds.), *How Asia Votes* (New York: Chatham House, 2002).

Mansfield, Edward, and Jack Snyder, 'Democratization and War', *Foreign Affairs*, 74/3 (1995), 79–97.

March, James, and Johan P. Olsen, 'The New Institutionalism: Organizational Factors in Political Life', *American Political Science Review*, 78 (1984), 734–49.

Marsh, Ian, Jean Blondel, and Takashi Inoguchi (eds.), *Democracy, Governance and Economic Performance: East and Southeast Asia* (Tokyo: United Nations University Press, 1999).

Massicote, Louis, and André Blais, 'Mixed Electoral Systems: A Conceptual and Empirical Survey', *Electoral Studies*, 18/3 (1999), 341–66.

Mauro, Paolo, 'Corruption and Growth', *Quarterly Journal of Economics*, 110/3 (1995), 681–712.

Mauzy, Diane K., 'Electoral Innovation and One-Party Dominance in Singapore', in John Fuh-Sheng Hsieh and David Newman (eds.), *How Asia Votes* (New York: Chatham House, 2002)

May, R. J., 'Ethnicity and Public Policy in the Philippines', in Michael E. Brown and Šumit Ganguly (eds.), *Government Policies and Ethnic*

Relations in the Asia-Pacific (Cambridge, MA and London: MIT Press, 1997).

—— 'Elections in the Philippines, May 2001', *Electoral Studies*, 21/4 (2002), 673–80.

McCargo, Duncan, 'Democracy Under Stress in Thaksin's Thailand', *Journal of Democracy*, 13/4 (2002), 112–26.

—— 'Introduction: Understanding Political Reform in Thailand', in Duncan McCargo (ed.), *Reforming Thai Politics* (Copenhagen: Nordic Institute of Asian Studies, 2002).

McGarry, John, and Brendan O'Leary, 'Introduction: The Macro-Political Regulation of Ethnic Conflict', in John McGarry and Brendan O'Leary (eds.), *The Politics of Ethnic Conflict Regulation: Case Studies of Protracted Ethnic Conflicts* (London and New York: Routledge, 1993).

McGibbon, Rodd, 'Secessionist Challenges in Aceh and Papua: Is Special Autonomy the Solution?', *Policy Studies*, 10 (Washington, DC: East-West Center, 2004).

McKean, Margaret, and Ethan Scheiner, 'Japan's New Electoral System: la Plus ca Change . . .', *Electoral Studies*, 19/4 (2000), 447–77.

McRae, Kenneth (ed.), *Consociational Democracy: Political Accommodation in Segmented Societies* (Toronto: McLelland and Stewart, 1974).

Migdal, Joel S., *Strong Societies and Weak States: State–Society Relations and State Capacities in the Third World* (Princeton, NJ: Princeton University Press, 1988).

Mill, John Stuart, *Considerations on Representative Government* (New York: Liberal Arts Press, 1958 [1861]).

Milne, R. S., '"The Pacific Way"—Consociational Politics in Fiji', *Pacific Affairs*, 48/3 (1975), 413–31.

Montinola, Gabriella R., 'Parties and Accountability in the Philippines', *Journal of Democracy*, 10/1 (1999), 126–40.

—— 'The Philippines in 1998: Opportunities Amid Crisis', *Asian Survey*, 39/1 (1999), 64–71.

Morley, James W. (ed.), *Driven by Growth: Political Change in the Asia-Pacific Region* (Armonk, NY: M.E. Sharpe, 1999).

Mozaffar, Shaheen, 'Electoral Systems and Their Political Effects in Africa: A Preliminary Analysis', *Representation*, 34/3&4 (1997), 148–56.

—— James R. Scarritt, and Glen Galaich, 'Electoral Institutions, Ethnopolitical Cleavages and Party Systems in Africa's Emerging Democracies', *American Political Science Review*, 97/3 (2003), 379–90.

Mukherjee, Bumba, 'Political Parties and the Size of Government in Multiparty Legislatures: Examining Cross-Country and Panel Data Evidence', *Comparative Political Studies*, 36/6 (2003), 699–728.

Murray, David, 'Thailand's Recent Electoral Reforms', *Electoral Studies*, 17/4 (1998), 525–35.

Nettle, Daniel, 'Linguistic Fragmentation and the Wealth of Nations: The Fishman-Pool Hypothesis Reexamined', *Economic Development and Cultural Change*, 49/2 (2000), 335–48.

Niou, E., and P. Paolino, 'The Rise of the Opposition Party in Taiwan: Explaining Chen Shui bian's Victory in the 2000 Presidential Election', *Electoral Studies*, 22/4 (2003), 721–40.

Nohlen, Dieter, Florian Grotz, and Christof Hartmann (eds.), *Elections in Asia and the Pacific: A Data Handbook*, 2 vols. (Oxford: Oxford University Press, 2001).

Nordlinger, Eric A., *Conflict Regulation in Divided Societies* (Cambridge, MA: Center for International Affairs, Harvard University, 1972).

Norris, Pippa, *Electoral Engineering: Voting Rules and Political Behavior* (New York: Cambridge University Press, 2004).

North, Douglas, *Institutions, Institutional Change and Economic Performance* (Cambridge: Cambridge University Press, 1990).

O'Donnell, Guillermo, Philippe Schmitter, and Laurence Whitehead, *Transitions From Authoritarian Rule*, 4 vols. (Baltimore, MD: Johns Hopkins University Press, 1986).

Ockey, James, 'Change and Continuity in the Thai Political Party System', *Asian Survey*, 43/4 (2003), 663–80.

Okole, Henry, 'Papua New Guinea's Brand of Westminster: Democratic Traditions Overlaying Melanesian Cultures', in Haig Patapan, John Wanna, and Patrick Weller (eds.), *Westminster Legacies: Democracy and Responsible Government in Asia and the Pacific* (Kensington: University of New South Wales Press, 2005).

Olsen, Mancur, *The Logic of Collective Action: Public Goods and the Theory of Groups* (Cambridge, MA: Harvard University Press, 1971).

Ordeshook, Peter, and Olga Shvetsova, 'Ethnic Heterogeneity, District Magnitude and the Number of Parties', *American Journal of Political Science*, 38 (1994), 100–23.

Organization for Security and Cooperation in Europe, *Copenhagen Document of the Conference on the Human Dimension* (1990).

Organization for Security and Cooperation in Europe, *Helsinki Document* (1992).

Özbudun, Ergun, 'Institutionalizing Competitive Elections in Developing Countries', in Myron Weiner and Ergun Özbudun (eds.), *Competitive Elections in Developing Countries* (Durham, NC: Duke University Press, 1987).

Payne, J. Mark, Daniel Zovatto, Fernando Carrillo Flórez, and Andrés Allamand Zavala, *Democracies in Development: Politics and Reform in Latin America* (Washington, DC: Inter-American Development Bank, 2002).

Pei, Minxin, 'The Fall and Rise of Democracy in East Asia', in Larry Diamond and Marc F. Plattner (eds.), *Democracy in East Asia* (Baltimore, MD and London: Johns Hopkins University Press, 1998).

Pinkney, Robert, *Democracy in the Third World*, 2nd edn. (Boulder, CO and London: Lynne Rienner, 2003).

Posner, Daniel N., 'Measuring Ethnic Fractionalization in Africa', *American Journal of Political Science*, 48/4 (2004), 849–63.

—— *Institutions and Ethnic Politics in Africa* (New York: Cambridge University Press, 2005).

Powell, G. Bingham, *Contemporary Democracies: Participation, Stability, and Violence* (Cambridge, MA: Harvard University Press, 1982).

—— *Elections as Instruments of Democracy: Majoritarian and Proportional Visions* (New Haven, CT and London: Yale University Press, 2000).

Przeworski, Adam, 'Democracy as the Contingent Outcome of Conflicts', in Jon Elster and Rune Slagstad (eds.), *Constitutionalism and Democracy* (Cambridge: Cambridge University Press, 1988).

—— *Democracy and the Market: Political and Economic Reforms in Eastern Europe and Latin America* (Cambridge: Cambridge University Press, 1991).

Putnam, Robert, *Making Democracy Work: Civic Traditions in Modern Italy* (Princeton, NJ: Princeton University Press, 1993).

Rabushka, Alvin, and Kenneth Shepsle, *Politics in Plural Societies: A Theory of Democratic Instability* (Colombus, OH: Merrill, 1972).

Rae, Douglas W., *The Political Consequences of Electoral Laws* (New Haven, CT: Yale University Press, 1967).

—— and Michael Taylor, *The Analysis of Political Cleavages* (New Haven, CT: Yale University Press, 1970).

Reed, Steven R., 'Democracy and the Personal Vote: A Cautionary Tale from Japan', *Electoral Studies*, 13/1 (1994), 17–28.

—— 'Evaluating Political Reform in Japan: A Mid-Term Report', *Japanese Journal of Political Science*, 3/2 (2002), 243–63.

Reilly, Benjamin, 'Democracy, Ethnic Fragmentation, and Internal Conflict: Confused Theories, Faulty Data, and the "Crucial Case" of Papua New Guinea', *International Security*, 25/3 (2000), 162–85.

—— 'The Africanisation of the South Pacific', *Australian Journal of International Affairs*, 54/3 (2000), 261–8.

—— *Democracy in Divided Societies: Electoral Engineering for Conflict Management* (Cambridge: Cambridge University Press, 2001).

—— 'Evaluating the Effect of the Electoral System in Post-Coup Fiji', *Pacific Economic Bulletin*, 16/1 (2001), 142–9.

—— 'Political Engineering and Party Politics in Papua New Guinea', *Party Politics*, 8/6 (2002), 701–18.

—— 'Social Choice in the South Seas: Electoral Innovation and the Borda Count in the Pacific Island Countries', *International Political Science Review*, 23/4 (2002), 355–72.

—— 'Political Parties and Political Engineering in the Asia-Pacific Region', *Asia Pacific Issues: Analysis from the East-West Center*, 71 (December 2003), 1–8.

Reilly, Benjamin, 'Ethnicity, Democracy and Development in Papua New Guinea', *Pacific Economic Bulletin*, 19/1 (2004), 46–54.

—— 'Elections in Post-Conflict Societies', in Edward Newman and Roland Rich (eds.), *The UN Role in Promoting Democracy: Between Ideals and Reality* (Tokyo: United Nations University Press, 2004).

—— 'State Functioning and State Failure in the South Pacific', *Australian Journal of International Affairs*, 58/4 (2004), 479–93.

—— 'The Global Spread of Preferential Voting: Australian Institutional Imperialism?', *Australian Journal of Political Science*, 39/2 (2004), 253–66.

—— 'Does the Choice of Electoral System Promote Democracy? The Gap Between Theory and Practice', in Philip G. Roeder and Donald Rothchild (eds.), *Sustainable Peace: Power and Democracy after Civil Wars* (Ithaca, NY and London: Cornell University Press, 2005).

—— and Andrew Reynolds, *Electoral Systems and Conflict in Divided Societies* (Washington, DC: National Research Council, 1999).

Reynolds, Andrew, 'Constitutional Engineering in Southern Africa', *Journal of Democracy*, 6/2 (1995), 86–100.

—— *Electoral Systems and Democratization in Southern Africa* (Oxford: Oxford University Press, 1999).

—— (ed.), *The Architecture of Democracy: Constitutional Design, Conflict Management and Democracy* (Oxford: Oxford University Press, 2002).

—— Ben Reilly, and Andrew Ellis, *Electoral System Design: The New International IDEA Handbook* (Stockholm: International Institute for Democracy and Electoral Assistance, 2005).

Rich, Roland, 'Designing Democracy Along the Pacific Rim', *Democracy at Large*, 2/1 (2006), 1–2.

Riker, William, *The Theory of Political Coalitions* (New Haven, CT: Yale University Press, 1962).

Robinson, Mark, and Gordon White (eds.), *The Democratic Developmental State* (Oxford: Oxford University Press, 1998).

Rodan, Gary, 'Elections without Representation: The Singapore Experience Under the PAP', in Robert H. Taylor (ed.), *The Politics of Elections in Southeast Asia* (Cambridge: Woodrow Wilson Center and Cambridge University Press, 1996).

—— (ed.), *Political Oppositions in Industrialising Asia* (London: Routledge, 1996).

Rodrik, Dani, 'Where Did All the Growth Go? External Shocks, Social Conflict, and Growth Collapses', *Journal of Economic Growth*, 4/4 (1999), 385–412.

Roeder, Philip G., 'Power Dividing as an Alternative to Ethnic Power Sharing', in Philip G. Roeder and Donald Rothchild (eds.), *Sustainable Peace: Power and Democracy after Civil Wars* (Ithaca, NY and London: Cornell University Press, 2005).

Roeder, Philip G., and Donald Rothchild (eds.), *Sustainable Peace: Power and Democracy after Civil Wars* (Ithaca, NY and London: Cornell University Press, 2005).

Rood, Steven, 'Elections as Complicated and Important Events in the Philippines', in John Fuh-sheng Hsieh and David Newman (eds.), *How Asia Votes* (New York: Chatham House, 2002).

Ross, Michael L., *Timber Booms and Institutional Breakdown in Southeast Asia* (New York: Cambridge University Press, 2001).

Rüland, Jürgen, 'Constitutional Debates in the Philippines: From Presidentialism to Parliamentarism?', *Asian Survey*, 43/3 (2003), 461–84.

Russett, Bruce, *Grasping the Democratic Peace* (Princeton, NJ: Princeton University Press, 1993).

Rustow, Dankwart A., 'Transitions to Democracy: Towards a Dynamic Model', *Comparative Politics*, 2/2 (1970), 337–63.

Sakamoto, Takayuki, 'Explaining Electoral Reform: Japan Versus Italy and New Zealand', *Party Politics*, 5/4 (1999), 419–38.

Sartori, Giovanni, 'Political Development and Political Engineering', *Public Policy*, 17 (1968), 261–98.

—— *Parties and Party Systems: A Framework for Analysis* (New York: Cambridge University Press, 1976).

—— *Comparative Constitutional Engineering: An Inquiry Into Structures, Incentives and Outcomes* (London: Macmillan, 1994).

Schedler, Andreas, Larry Diamond, and Marc F. Plattner (eds.), *The Self-Restraining State: Power and Accountability in New Democracies* (Boulder, CO and London: Lynne Rienner Publishers, 1999).

Schumpeter, Joseph A., *Capitalism, Socialism and Democracy* (New York: Harper, 1947).

Sherlock, Stephen, *Struggling to Change: The Indonesian Parliament in an Era of Reformasi* (Canberra: Centre for Democratic Institutions, 2003).

—— *Consolidation and Change: The Indonesian Parliament After the 2004 Elections* (Canberra: Centre for Democratic Institutions, 2004).

Shoesmith, Dennis, 'Timor-Leste: Divided Leadership in a Semi-Presidential System', *Asian Survey*, 43/2 (2003), 231–52.

Shugart, Matthew S., 'Presidentialism, Parliamentarism, and the Provision of Collective Goods in Less-Developed Countries', *Constitutional Political Economy*, 10 (1999), 53–88.

—— and John M. Carey, *Presidents and Assemblies: Constitutional Design and Electoral Dynamics* (Cambridge: Cambridge University Press, 1992).

—— and Martin P. Wattenberg, 'Introduction: the Electoral Reform of the 21st Century?', in Matthew S. Shugart and Martin P. Wattenberg (eds.), *Mixed-Member Electoral Systems: The Best of Both Worlds?* (New York: Oxford University Press, 2001).

—— —— 'Mixed-Member Electoral Systems: A Definition and Typology', in Matthew S. Shugart and Martin P. Wattenberg (eds.),

Mixed-Member Electoral Systems: the Best of Both Worlds? (New York: Oxford University Press, 2001).

—— —— 'Conclusion: Are Mixed-Member Systems the Best of Both Worlds?', in Matthew S. Shugart and Martin P. Wattenberg (eds.), *Mixed-Member Electoral Systems: The Best of Both Worlds?* (New York: Oxford University Press, 2001).

Shugart, Matthew S., and Martin P. Wattenberg (eds.), *Mixed-Member Electoral Systems: The Best of Both Worlds?* (New York: Oxford University Press, 2001).

Sisk, Timothy D., *Democratization in South Africa: The Elusive Social Contract* (Princeton, NJ: Princeton University Press, 1995).

—— *Power Sharing and International Mediation in Ethnic Conflicts* (Washington, DC: United States Institute of Peace Press, 1996).

Slater, Dan, 'Indonesia's Accountability Trap: Party Cartels and Presidential Power After Democratic Transition', *Indonesia*, 78 (October 2004), 61–92.

Smith, Anthony D., *The Ethnic Origins of Nations* (Oxford: Blackwell, 1986).

Smith, Graham (ed.), *Federalism: The Multiethnic Challenge* (London and New York: Longman, 1995).

Snyder, Jack, *From Voting to Violence: Democratization and Nationalist Conflict* (New York and London: W.W. Norton, 2000).

Soares, Dionisio da Costa Babo, Michael Maley, James J. Fox, and Anthony J. Regan, *Elections and Constitution Making in East Timor* (Canberra: State, Society and Governance in Melanesia Project, 2003).

Sollenberg, Margareta, Peter Wallensteen, and Andrés Jato, 'Major Armed Conflicts', in Stockholm International Peace Research Institute, *SIPRI Yearbook 1999: Armaments, Disarmament and International Security* (Oxford: Oxford University Press, 1999).

Standish, Bill, 'Limited Preferential Voting: Some Early Lessons', Paper presented at conference on Overcoming Constraints in Papua New Guinea, Lowy Institute for International Policy, Sydney, 18 January 2005.

Stepan, Alfred, and Cindy Skach, 'Constitutional Frameworks and Democratic Consolidation: Parliamentarism Versus Presidentialism', *World Politics*, 46/1 (1993), 1–22.

Suryadinata, Leo, *Elections and Politics in Indonesia* (Singapore: Institute of Southeast Asian Studies, 2002).

Taagepera, Rein, and Matthew S. Shugart, *Seats and Votes: the Effects and Determinants of Electoral Systems* (New Haven, CT and London: Yale University Press, 1989).

Tan, Paige Johnson, 'Anti-Party Reaction in Indonesia: Causes and Implications', *Contemporary Southeast Asia*, 24/3 (2002), 484–508.

Taylor, Charles L. and Michael C. Hudson, *World Handbook of Political and Social Indicators* (New Haven, CT: Yale University Press, 1972).

—— and David A. Jodice, *World Handbook of Political and Social Indicators* (New Haven, CT: Yale University Press, 1983).

Taylor, Michael, and V. M. Herman, 'Party Systems and Government Stability', *American Political Science Review*, 65/1 (1971), 28–37.

Taylor, Robert H. (ed.), *The Politics of Elections in Southeast Asia* (Cambridge: Woodrow Wilson Center and Cambridge University Press, 1996).

Teehankee, Julio, 'Electoral Politics in the Philippines', in Aurel Croissant, Gabriele Bruns, and Marei John (eds.), *Electoral Politics in Southeast and East Asia* (Singapore: Friedrich Ebert Stiftung, 2002).

The Foundation on Inter-Ethnic Relations, *The Lund Recommendations on the Effective Participation of National Minorities in Public Life & Explanatory Note* (1999).

Tollison, Robert D., 'Rent Seeking', in Dennis Mueller (ed.), *Perspectives on Public Choice: A Handbook* (New York: Cambridge University Press, 1997).

Tsebelis, George, 'Elite Interaction and Constitution Building in Consociational Democracies', *Journal of Theoretical Politics*, 2/1 (1990), 5–29.

Turner, Mark (ed.), *Central–Local Relations in Asia-Pacific: Convergence or Divergence?* (Hampshire and New York: Palgrave, 1999).

United Nations Development Programme, *Human Development Report 2004* (New York: United Nations Development Programme, 2004).

—— *Indonesia Human Development Report 2001* (Jakarta: BPS-Statistics Indonesia, Bappenas and UNDP, 2001).

van Klinken, Gerry, 'Ethnicity in Indonesia', in Colin Mackerras (ed.), *Ethnicity in Asia* (London and New York: RoutledgeCurzon, 2003).

Vanhanen, Tatu, *Prospects of Democracy: A Study of 172 Countries* (London and New York: Routledge, 1997).

Varshney, Ashutosh, *Ethnic Conflict and Civil Life: Hindus and Muslims in India* (New Haven, CT and London: Yale University Press, 2002).

Vatikiotis, Michael R., *Political Change in Southeast Asia: Trimming the Banyan Tree* (London: Routledge, 1996).

Velasco, R., 'Philippine Democracy: Promise and Performance', in Anek Laothamatas (ed.), *Democratization in Southeast and East Asia* (Singapore: Institute of Southeast Asian Studies, 1997).

Walker, Scott, and Kyung-Tae Kang, 'The Presidential Election in South Korea, December 2002', *Electoral Studies*, 23/4 (2004), 840–5.

Weaver, R. Kent, and Bert A. Rockman (eds.), *Do Institutions Matter? Government Capabilities in the United States and Abroad* (Washington, DC: The Brookings Institution, 1993).

Webb, Paul, 'Conclusion: Political Parties and Democratic Control in Advanced Industrial Societies', in Paul Webb, David Farrell, and Ian

Holliday (eds.), *Political Parties in Advanced Industrial Democracies* (Oxford: Oxford University Press, 2002).

White, Gordon, 'Constructing a Democratic Developmental State', in Mark Robinson and Gordon White (eds.), *The Democratic Developmental State* (Oxford: Oxford University Press, 1998).

Whitehead, Laurence, *Democratization: Theory and Experience* (Oxford: Oxford University Press, 2002).

Wilkinson, Steven I., 'India, Consociational Theory, and Ethnic Violence', *Asian Survey*, 40/5 (2000), 767–91.

—— *Votes and Violence: Electoral Competition and Ethnic Riots in India* (New York: Cambridge University Press, 2004).

Willey, Joseph, 'Institutional Arrangements and the Success of New Parties in Old Democracies', in Richard Hofferbert (ed.), *Parties and Democracy* (Oxford and Malden, MA: Blackwell, 1998).

Woo-Cumings, Meredith (ed.), *The Developmental State* (Ithaca, NY: Cornell University Press, 1999).

Wurfel, David, 'Democracy, Nationalism and Ethnic Identity: The Philippines and East Timor Compared', in Susan J. Henders (ed.), *Democratization and Identity: Regimes and Ethnicity in East and Southeast Asia* (Lanham, MD: Lexington Books, 2004).

Young, Crawford, *The Politics of Cultural Pluralism* (Madison, WI: University of Wisconsin Press, 1976).

Zakaria, Fareed, 'Culture is Destiny: A Conversation with Lee Kwan Yew', *Foreign Affairs*, 73/2 (1994), 109–26.

Index

Note: page numbers in *italic* refer to figures and tables.